MW00329146

AN INSIDE LOOK AT

SONOMA
COUNTY

This book was produced by
Copyright Studio, Paris, France, in collaboration with
Color Print Graphix, Antwerp, Belgium, and
Atomium Books, Wilmington, Delaware.

Original concept and project coordination
Jean-Paul Paireault

Project coordination in California
Mona Abadir, Lightwater Concepts Inc., Sausalito, California

First published in the United States by
      Atomium Books Inc.
      Suite 300
      1013 Centre Road
      Wilmington, DE 19805

Copyright © Atomium Books Inc., 1991
All rights reserved. No part of this book may be reproduced,
stored in a retrieval system, or transmitted, in any form or by
any means, electronic, mechanical, photocopying, recording,
or otherwise, without the prior permission of the publishers.

Printed in Belgium by Color Print Graphix.

First U.S. Edition
ISBN 1-56182-027-X
2 4 6 8 10 9 7 5 3 1

Beyond The Grapes

AN INSIDE LOOK AT
SONOMA
COUNTY

RICHARD PAUL HINKLE
DAN BERGER
Photography
JEAN-PAUL PAIREAULT

atomium books

TABLE OF CONTENTS

INTRODUCTION

Sonoma County was the real birthplace of wine in the Golden State. Today Sonoma remains a true wine artist's community, despite its sprawlingness and the amazing diversity of its climes. And despite the early beginnings, Sonoma has never lost its perspective on what it is.

In some ways, the fabrics that make up this county's clothes are dissimilar from those in the NapaValley in the same ways that France's Bordeaux and Burgundy districts are unalike. The two most famous wine-growing regions of France are sharply divided along social lines. The Bordelais look down their long, aristocratic (and moneyed) noses at the Burgundians, whom they see as plebians. "Gardeners!" they scoff, partly in reference to Burgundy's myriad tiny vineyard plots, divided up among so many owners that the land is counted not so much in acres as in numbers of vines. The Bordelais also use that derisive term because most Burgundian winegrowers *are* short-sleeved, dirt-under-nail farmers, craftsmen whose name on the bottle usually is the name of the man with purple toes, not some absentee owner-by-inheritance. The Bordelais bristle, too, that boorish Burgundians drink their wine from water tumblers.

The Burgundians, for their part, see the Medocians as imperial, remote, storied people with manicured lawns, coiffed women, and absurd formality. To the Burgundian "gardeners," the Bordelais, however, are ivory-tower owners in name only whose concern is focused on one more step up the social ladder.

A kind of parallel exists between Napa and Sonoma. Napans are seen as landed gentry who spend their waking hours not making wine, but promoting it. Sonomans see themselves as adherents to the work ethic, denim denizens of the dirt, the tractor, and the must pump — folks for whom the phrase "black tie" means a bandanna to keep sun off the back of the neck.

The broad brushstroke of these generalizations, here and abroad, is obviously such a simplification as to be almost a caricature. Yet there are fair-sized grains of truth here. There is no real "feud" between Bordeaux and Burgundy, though a visitor to a Medoc bistro may get a strange look when he asks for Chassagne. And there is no real "feud" between Napa and Sonoma, though there is a constant wariness over what's happening "over there." A lot of attention is paid to "the other side of the mountain."

In truth, many Sonoma wineries honestly respect the work Napa has done with its image, which seems to be wrapped in Cabernet more than any other wine. That image has gained worldwide acceptance for a wide range of wines, and that has benefited Sonoma. Moreover, a lot of Napa wineries buy Sonoma grapes. In fact, one of the proudest Napa families, that of Louis Martini, counts its best vineyards in Sonoma, not Napa. And Beringer has invested heavily in Sonoma soil with its Knight's Valley vineyards as well as its ownership of Chateau Souverain and the old Italian Swiss Colony facility. From Sonoma fruit comes Franciscan's successful Estancia wines, as well as some of the best Chardonnays from Phelps, most of Silver Oak's Cabernet, Chateau Montelena Chardonnay . . .

Even the world's largest winery has a significant presence here. The brothers Ernest and Julio Gallo could have opted to make their first foray into fine wine by buying land in Napa. Instead they chose Sonoma. They long have considered Sonoma fruit the equal of any in the world. Today the Modesto-based firm owns more than 2,000 acres here, and has reduced its use of Napa fruit.

The tenor of this county is Italian more than any other culture. The names of the second wave of wine development, in the years after 1900, ring with the sound of Tuscany, Piedmont, and Sicily — names like Sebastiani, Foppiano, Pedroncelli, Sbarboro, Rossi, Martini & Prati, Trentadue, Seghesio, Rochioli, and a dozen more. These were the real developers of Sonoma's image and wine, though before them came the first wave, beginning with the Spanish.

Spaniards first discovered Sonoma as early as 1602, and Spanish influence soon dominated because of the importance of the Franciscan missions. General Mariano Guadalupe Vallejo, assigned by the government to rule the northern province of Mexico, oversaw the construction of the mission at Sonoma, the final link in the mission chain, in 1823, two years after Mexico won its independence from Spain.

Another ethnic influence in the county meanwhile came from Russia, though not in wine terms. Russians were the first to actively settle here, in the 1800s, which accounts for the name of the snaking Russian River that cools a broad swath of the northern portion of the county's vineyards. The Russians came not for grapes and wine, but for trapping. Seals and otters provided the initial lure. In 1812, Ivan Kuskov and his company of Russians bought some land from the Kashaya Pomo Indians and built Fort Ross, which still stands along the rugged Sonoma coast north of Bodega Bay.

Winegrowing was important in the early days. The Catholic Church required wine for the celebration of Mass, and thus winemaking became mandatory at each of the 21 Franciscan missions, including the first, founded at San Diego in 1769. But Father Junipero Serra, not exactly a wine connoisseur, was content with the hardy Mission variety, an undistinguished grape that was planted at probably every mission in the system, including Sonoma. It was with the Mission grape that Vallejo first made wine, a decent red wine by all accounts, but far from classic. He was soon persuaded to switch by the man whom many consider the father of California's wine industry, Agoston Haraszthy, an

ersatz "count" who had fled his native Hungary under a political cloud (or so he said). Although Frenchman Jean-Louis Vignes had begun a winery in what is now downtown Los Angeles in the late 1830s — considered the first commercial winery in the state — the best quality wines in the early years were made in Sonoma by Haraszthy.

Haraszthy is a fascinating and colorful character in California lore whose vitae includes such spectacular failures as a wine and grapegrowing venture in Wisconsin, and another in San Diego (where as the town's first sheriff he obtained a contract to build a jailhouse, which subsequently collapsed). Those failures didn't dissuade Haraszthy, who then moved north to Mission Dolores south of San Francisco, where yet another wine investment soured — and where he was accused of embezzlement from the San Francisco Mint, which he managed. (He was never convicted.)

Haraszthy finally moved to Sonoma County in 1857, having convinced himself that it held more promise than Wisconsin and San Diego for winemaking. Six years later, his sons, Arpad and Attila, married the twin daughters of Vallejo, Jovita and Natalie. Meanwhile, Haraszthy became an influential winegrower, founding the Buena Vista Winery and later traveling to Europe to collect many thousands of cuttings for grapevine transplantation in the New World. Legend says that among the grapevines

Haraszthy brought back was the "California original," Zinfandel, though a number of authorities now feel the grape was already in the United States when Haraszthy made his voyage across the sea. (Indeed, there are those who feel that the Yugoslavian grape Plavac or the southern Italian grape Primitivo is the real Zinfandel, but the question still remains open to debate among scholars and wine lovers.)

Haraszthy's wines soon bettered the mediocre efforts of Vallejo and Vignes, and finally, after numerous failures, Haraszthy was at last considered a success. Without financial help from the state, Haraszthy aided the development of winegrowing by distributing some of the grapestock he brought over, and he promoted Sonoma so successfully that the influx of new French and German winegrowers soon pushed the price of land from $6 an acre to $150!

By the time of the 1875 harvest, Sonoma County was the largest producer of wine in the state, having made more than three million gallons in a year — 40 percent of the state's production. Los Angeles ranked second with just over one million gallons; Napa ran fourth. Despite this success, Haraszthy soon left for Nicaragua and another investment scheme, and was never heard from again. It is believed that he died after falling off a tree trunk while trying to cross a crocodile-infested stream.

Back in Sonoma, varietal wines were yet to be seen. Most of those made by Haraszthy and Vallejo were generics. Wine historian William Heintz suggests that Captain James H. Drummond made the first varietal, a Cabernet Sauvignon, in 1882. Drummond had retired from the British Army in India in 1878 and settled on an estate at Glen Ellen in the Sonoma Valley, 20 miles north of Haraszthy's digs. He imported grape cuttings from Château Lafite and Château Margaux, so the story goes, at the outrageous price of 25 cents each. The wine he made was called Dunfillan, paying homage to his native Scotland. The labels featured the insignia of his 34th Cumberland regiment. After his death, his stepson, Frederic T. Bioletti, carried on his work. Bioletti became the most respected viticultural professor of his day, and a man who ranked with A.R. Morrow and Kanaye Nagasawa as the best tasters of their time.

Two women stood out as early Sonoma County winegrowers. Eliza Hood's Los Guilicos Ranch covered 1,400 acres at the foot of Mount Hood, and Kate Warfield farmed Ten Oaks Vineyards at Agua Caliente in the Sonoma Valley. When Ten Oaks was awarded a First Premium award at the California State Fair in 1885, Warfield's miffed male counterparts demanded a second test. The second tasting only confirmed the results.

German immigrant Emanuel Goldstein built a magnificent stone winery in 1886 at the peak of a ridge in the Mayacamas Mountains straddling Napa and Sonoma counties. Goldstein called his winery Mount Peak and he made wine from some 200 acres of vineyards. Today the vineyard, renamed Monte Rosso, is the Louis M. Martini Winery's premier ranch, splendidly draped across several peaks just below Bismark Knob.

Author Jack London created wine as well as words here on the Glen Ellen acreage that was for years managed by Milo Shepard, a shirttail relative of the writer. London was better known for his efforts at raising hogs at his "piggery," and for other agricultural enterprises than for his wines. Grapes from the Jack London Ranch today go to Kenwood Vineyards for some of that winery's most concentrated wines.

Though the county's development as a vine-growing paradise began essentially in the south, near the town of Sonoma, the northern portions of the county were developed, too. J.N. Bailhache planted 50 acres of vines in Healdsburg in 1881, and that year Andrea Sbarboro bought the Truett Ranch for a company of 100 individuals. The joint venture was given the name Italian-Swiss Colony and before long the place was a haven for immigrants to San Francisco who knew more about grapes and olives than big-city life. The village in which the winery was located was named Asti, for the Piedmontese town where Barolo, Barbaresco, Barbera, and especially Asti Spumante reign. Later, in the 1930s, under the wise leadership of Pietro C. Rossi, Italian Swiss Colony became the largest winery in the country, boasting more than 1,300 acres of grapes and more than eight million gallons of wine storage.

To the west, 12 miles east of the fledgling city of Santa Rosa, three Korbel brothers began making wines when their initial interest, logging, was played out. There were perhaps a dozen other significant winery developments in Sonoma, but none as controversial as the Fountaingrove Winery, about which little is written.

In 1875, Thomas Lake Harris founded Fountaingrove on the northern edge of Santa Rosa as a commune — perhaps it's best to call it a cult — that was an outgrowth of The Brotherhood of the New Life, originally founded in Brocton, New York. Among Harris's colleagues here were Jacob Moore, the developer of the Diamond grape (still grown along the East Coast); Dr. John Hyde, an expert on Missouri Riesling; and Kanaye Nagasawa, a young Japanese nobleman who would become the most respected winemaker and taster of his time.

The wines of Fountaingrove were widely marketed; some were even sent to Europe through a network established by Lady Maria Oliphant, who had endowed the Brotherhood. However, controversy over the cult arose after reports that Harris separated spouses; meanwhile his own sexual conduct was attacked as profligate because he reportedly permitted favorites to live in luxury while the remainder were forced to live in near slavery conditions.

Eventually, Oliphant's son sued the Brotherhood to recover his mother's invested funds; then Harris's young daughter commited suicide. At last the Brotherhood collapsed. Harris left, returning to New York, and that elevated Nagasawa into the limelight. Nagasawa's winemaking skills soon were widely recognized, and he became friendly with Bioletti as well as famed naturalist Luther Burbank, who lived nearby.

Fountaingrove sank into disuse during Prohibition and the name now is known to locals more for a development of luxury homes on the east side of Highway 101 than for any of the wines.

Prohibition shuttered most Sonoma wineries, though in the northern reaches of the state, where field blends of hearty red wine grapes grew, the industry (such as it was) survived by selling grapes to home winemakers. The true rebirth of the county as a fine winegrowing region didn't begin until the mid-1970s, perhaps a decade after Napa's began. Sonoma's reawakening was marked by the influx of some wealthy men with big dreams.

The rise of wineries such as Chateau St. Jean (1974), De Loach (1975), Jordan (1976), Matanzas Creek (1977), and a dozen others helped give the county an image that superb wines could be made here, certainly the equal of those on the other side of the hill. One of the most important developments in the history of the industry, however, was to come in the mid-1980s when former East Coast wholesaler Bruno Benziger, who had founded Glen Ellen Vineyards and Winery ostensibly as a retirement venture, persuaded Americans that Chardonnay need not be expensive. His Proprietor's Reserve line of wines, priced at $5 a bottle or less, opened up the industry, bringing in new drinkers and sparking a tremendous push in overall sales.

This county with 150 wineries has now become home to some of the most engaging artistes in the wine world, cottage industry leaders ranging in personal style from the philosophical Patrick Campbell (Laurel Glen) to the outrageous Jim Bundschu (Gundlach-Bundschu), from the gentlemanly Crawford Cooley (Hacienda) to the crusty Ed Gauer (Gauer Estate), from the effusive Barry Lawrence (Eagle Ridge) to the almost reclusive Andy and Debra Cutter (Duxoup), from the sublime Fred Fisher (Fisher Vineyards) to the irrepressible David Coleman (Adler Fels).

Though Napa and Sonoma are physically closer to one another — just over a hill, a 20-minute drive — than some people realize, the places are worlds apart in terms of relationships. Napans tend to be friendly to one another, yet they remain a bit wary and jealous and perhaps even a trace bitter of one another. (One Napa wine owner speaks derisively of the famed Opus One of the Mondavi/Rothschild joint venture as "Oh Pius One.") Growers and winemakers are constantly bickering.

Sonoma winemakers, though still business foes, see each other with a less jaundiced eye. Winery owners routinely lend neighbors equipment when theirs breaks in the middle of the harvest; growers call neighbors when their frost alarms go off, to suggest turning on the protecting sprinkler system. Wineries and growers get along with more understanding of each other, and each other's problems, than do the Napa winemakers' and growers' groups.

This charming, relaxed county is much larger than many people realize, ranging from the Carneros off San Pablo Bay, where on a clear day you can see San Francisco, to the wild forests of the Russian River basin, to the rolling hills of the Alexander and Knight's valleys, to the searing heat of Cloverdale in the north. Moreover, because there is less worldwide acclaim than in Napa, prices for land here are a cut below those of its more famous neighbor, and thus prices for the wines have long been a bargain.

But that may be changing. People are beginning to see the value in owning a hunk of this rising star, No. 2 though it may be. Since 1984, four major corporations have shelled out in excess of $40 million each to buy wineries. And the buyers are not in this game for fun. They envision big profits. The buyers are biggies: Suntory (Chateau St. Jean), Klein Foods (Rodney Strong), Hiram Walker (Clos du Bois), and Chevron (Gauer Estate).

Moreover, the huge investments here by the Gallos and the Jordans were joined in the early days of the 1990s by names that someday may become far better known than they are today: Kunde, Nunn's Canyon, Peter Michael, and others seeking a way of life that appears to be worth the effort it takes.

As a Los Angeles-to-Santa Rosa commuter plane hit the tarmac one January day, soon after a brief shower had glistened the air, the flight attendant said on the loudspeaker, "Ladies and gentleman, I'd like to be the first to welcome you to paradise, uh, Santa Rosa." No one on board was sure if the gaff was intentional or merely perceptive. In either case, the conclusion is the same.

ADLER FELS

David Coleman founded Adler Fels winery almost as a product of his own audaciousness. The result is a Tudor-styled winery hand built by David and his wife, Ayn Ryan, on a ridge overlooking the Valley of the Moon.

But this project seemed for a long time as if it wasn't to be. First, there was the financing, which developed slowly. Then there was the bureaucracy that had affable David scratching his graying head.

Adler Fels was named for a local landmark (it's German for "Eagle Rock"). It was founded in 1980 after Coleman decided to make wine. Coleman had been a graphics designer who had designed labels for some 60 wineries. His creative labels featured dramatic designs and colors as well as gold foils and non-traditional

Adler Fels is located on a ridge at the northernmost tip of the Sonoma Valley, just at the southern edge of the city of Santa Rosa, off a serpentine road that winds into the hills and then quits amid the trees and brush.

die-cut borders that revolutionized label design.

One of Coleman's first projects was the design for Chateau St. Jean's now-famous label: a major departure from the plain, rectangular labels of the past.

The success of his label clients as wineries prompted Coleman to think about creating his own winery. During visits to Chateau St. Jean,

he discussed the idea with Ayn, who was working there at the time. Her uncles owned St. Jean and she is from an Armenian family that has made wine for five generations.

Coleman and Ryan discussed opening a winery of their own with Lila Merzoian, Ayn's mother and the sister of the principals in the Chateau St. Jean winery. With that connection, Merzoian felt comfortable providing an initial loan for Adler Fels, and took an active role in the winery as cook and culinary director.

The hobby winery that David and Ayn started was supposed to remain small, but David is an eager fellow. The winery never stopped growing, even though financing barely kept pace. David and Ayn knew that if Adler Fels were to expand, they'd have to build the winery.

Launching a construction project high atop a hill didn't bother either of them. David is adventuresome — he flies his own plane and is an inventor. Coleman designed a device called a Variable Capacity Tank that adjusts to the amount of wine in it. He says it eliminates the need for additional processing that partially empty tanks require. Today these tanks are widely used in the industry. Even with both David and Ayn working at the building project, things proceeded slowly, cash being the biggest worry. David, however, had developed quite a nose for Sauvignon Blanc and from the beginning was turning out some of the area's best Sauvignon Blancs. National fame for this wine, especially his 1982, helped bring Adler Fels' cash flow to a level where the construction could continue.

During construction, Coleman and county officials disputed some of the permit filings and the county threatened to close down the facility. After negotiations and compromises on both sides, Coleman finally gained the permits he needed to make the building legal.

Although their wines soon became cult items in some circles, the Colemans decided to make no more than 15,000 cases of wine per year, and to focus on small lots of vineyard-designated wines. *DB*

Owner/winemaker David Coleman and his wife, Ayn Ryan, built the Adler Fels winery with their own hands. The property turns out some of the best Sauvignon Blanc in the county plus a range of wines that includes a sparkling-wine blend of Riesling and Gewurztraminer.

ALDERBROOK VINEYARDS

One way to start a winery is to buy vineyard land first and then hire people to grow grapes, make wine, and market it. But finding the right people isn't easy, so usually what happens is that vineyard owners merely sell their grapes to other wineries.

Alderbrook Vineyards found a different way to structure itself. It was founded to make use of the fruit of an existing vineyard and to develop a brand with a specific goal. The vineyard here was owned by Mark Rafanelli, at the south end of Healdsburg in the cool Dry Creek Valley. The goal was to make only white wines, to make them with the grace and the delicacy characteristic of Dry Creek, and to incur only a tiny debt.

Rafanelli, the first cousin of David Rafanelli, owner of the A. Rafanelli Winery nearby, wanted to ensure that the grapes from his vineyard would be made into wine annually by a brand in which he was a partner. John Grace, Rafanelli's vineyard manager, wanted to remain and coordinate sales. And Phil Staley, a dentist in Hayward, simply wanted to make wine.

Alderbrook's partners built a single-story tasting room in the southern Dry Creek area, just south of Healdsburg. The porch wraps around the rambling ranch-style building whose windows are open to the vineyards.

The three formed a partnership in 1981 to operate the winery they called Alderbrook. The plan was for grapes from Rafanelli's vineyard to be sold to the joint venture to make fine wine. Grace would manage the vines and Staley would make the wine in a building (which includes an attractive tasting room) owned by Rafanelli. The tasting room is a separate business entity from the wine brand.

If all this sounds complicated, it's not. Grace is the one full-time person who's on the property all the time, and he's there "more than

On cool days, an inviting congregating point for visitors to the northern reaches of Sonoma County is the Alderbrook winery's tasting-room fireplace, ringed with white alder paneling.

six days a week," he says. Grace says the venture has worked out well for the partners. He is paid for the work he does managing the vineyards. In addition, he's a partner in the Alderbrook brand. Staley makes the wine and is on the property five days a week. Rafanelli is responsible for maintaining the buildings.

The vineyard has 38 acres of Chardonnay and 17 acres of Sauvignon Blanc. Those varieties make two of the three dry wines the partners produce. The third wine is a superb dry Semillon produced from the marvelous fruit of Jack Long's vineyard up the road, near Dry Creek Vineyard. Alderbrook also makes small amounts of Muscat Canelli and Gewurztraminer for winery sales.

The tasting room, completed in the mid-1980s, was designed to look like an open New England barn, with a lot of bleached pine.

When Alderbrook first opened its doors, plans called for the winery to grow slowly. In the first decade, the partners hoped the winery would produce about 10,000 or 15,000 cases of wine. But success came rapidly, and by 1990 production was in excess of 30,000 cases, the wine was distributed in 25 states, and plans were afoot to make even more wine.

The wine itself is clean, fresh, and soft with a roundness from aging in a variety of French oak barrels. And the low-key label used on the bottle — a muted gray with gold lettering — has become a symbol of quality. *DB*

ALEXANDER VALLEY VINEYARDS

Alexander Valley Vineyards lies at the heart of the Alexander Valley, which stretches north along the Russian River from Chalk Hill to Cloverdale.

The valley's first American settler was Cyrus "Aleck" Alexander. Pennsylvania-born, young Alexander sought his fortune in mining in Illinois before trapping his way across the continent, first in the Rocky Mountains, later in Santa Fe and Wyoming. In San Diego to hunt sea lions and otters, he joined up with trader and ship-owner Captain Henry D. Fitch.

In 1841 Fitch secured the 48,000-acre Sotoyome grant that Alexander had scouted from the Mexican government. Aleck was to settle and manage the grant and, in return, receive 9,000 acres of it for himself after six years. He planted an orchard, sowed wheat, and killed bears and coyotes to put meat on the table.

Later, he built a tannery; planted grapes, apples, and peaches; and erected a mill and a brick kiln. A religious man, he built a small church in the 1850s. In 1868 he added a school-house, which still stands. Alexander ran the ranch until the day he died: December 27, 1872.

In late 1962 Harry Wetzel, chairman and CEO of Garrett Corporation (aircraft equipment

This lovely Victorian house required a great deal of work. "The roof collapsed in 1973," remembers Hank Wetzel. "We had to jack it up, dig a basement, pour a foundation, and move walls. We remilled the original lumber, and saved the original door frames, molding, gingerbread, and fireplaces."

manufacturers), and his wife, Maggie, purchased a piece of Alexander Valley from the heirs of Alexander's granddaughter. They began planting wine grapes the following year. The property included a run-down Victorian house with a boarded-up front porch.

"The weeds were five feet high, and steers kept poking their heads through the windows," recalls Hank Wetzel (Harry and Maggie's son, or more properly Harry H. Wetzel III). "We kids slept in sleeping bags on cots the first year, but we also found a lot of things worth restoring: Aleck's first home, an adobe built in 1842; the schoolhouse; the Victorian building, built

The graves of pioneer Cyrus Alexander and his wife, Rufena, stand in the shade of ancient valley oaks on a low rise above the valley that bears his name. Cyrus died in 1872; Rufena lived on until 1908.

in 1848; and the gardens, with rock walls and ponds."

The restoration was an ongoing process. A well had to be dug, a septic system installed. The old schoolhouse was turned into a guest house. When the roof collapsed on the Victorian structure in 1973, the whole house had to be redone from the foundation up. Two years later, work began on a winery.

Hank, now winemaker and general manager, was still in prep school when his parents bought the Alexander Valley property. He tended the vines during summer vacations. Figuring that fermenting wine might be easier than hoeing weeds, he set out for the University of California's Davis campus to study winemaking. During his senior year, the family sat down to draw up a winery plan.

By September 1975 the winery was up and running, in time for a smooth first crush. "As wine master, I try to stress the character of each grape variety, while keeping the acid balance high enough so that the wines are fresh," says Hank, whose wife, Linda, handles all bookkeeping responsibilities. Marketing and sales at Alexander Valley Vineyards are handled by a former college co-ed football player who loves nothing more than a "night out with the boys, playing poker." Meet Hank's sister, Katie Wetzel Murphy, whose husband, Denny, is the son of noted winegrower Tim Murphy. *RPH.*

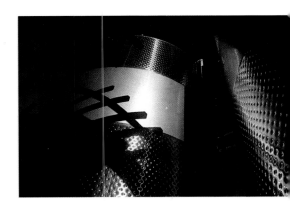

Dimpled "jackets" on these stainless-steel tanks circulate a coolant that allows Hank, Alexander Valley's winemaker, to control precisely the temperature of his white wines as they undergo fermentation. Cooler fermentations allow for greater fruitiness in the wines.

ARROWOOD VINEYARDS & WINERY

For decades after Prohibition ended, California's wine industry remained mired in mediocrity. With few exceptions, most of the wine made was undistinguished.

When the industry finally began to wake from its stupor in the early 1970s to produce wines of world-class quality, one man was at the vanguard of Chardonnay production: Richard Arrowood.

It's true that Stony Hill, Mayacamas, and others had made successful Chardonnays before him, but Arrowood was one of the key designers of the new winemaking that brought California worldwide acclaim for its top white wines.

Arrowood Vineyards and Winery hadn't been conceived yet. That would come later, the culmination of a dream. Arrowood first gained acclaim as a winemaker at Chateau St.

The Arrowoods deliberately chose a low-key design for their winery — that of a simple country barn. They save the superlatives and sophistication for their wines.

Jean, where he made a rich style of Chardonnay, widely praised. He also made an amazing string of dessert wines, notably late-harvest Rieslings and Gewurztraminers.

Arrowood, a graduate of Fresno State University's School of Viticulture and Enology, got his start in the industry when he began making wine at Sonoma-Cutrer Vineyards with winemaker Rod Strong. (An associate at the vine-

yards back then was Forest Tancer, who later would become one of the state's most talented winemakers, at Iron Horse Vineyards.)

In 1973, Arrowood was the first employee hired by Chateau St. Jean, then being formed. And in 1975 Arrowood leaped into the headlines when he produced a series of wines that changed California Chardonnay production permanently.

The concept was simple — as breakthroughs often are: Arrowood knew that different vineyards, with different soils and microclimates, yield different grape characteristics. To explore this belief, he kept the fruit from different vineyards separate, but kept most other winemaking variables equal. Thus, any differences in the wines could be traced back to the grapes. In 1975 he made seven different Chardonnays, each with a different vineyard name.

The wines differed upon release, and they changed in different ways as they aged. Over the years the various vineyards showed their pluses and minuses, and over time some of the vineyard designations were kept, others discarded. The most successful designations, wines from the Robert Young and Belle Terre ranches, both in Alexander Valley, became world famous and remained constant in the line.

However, the success of his breakthrough sowed the seeds of Arrowood's discontent. Having to make wines in the same style year after year to satisfy the loyal Chateau St. Jean buyer, Arrowood wasn't permitted to experiment with different styles.

During the early 1980s, St. Jean faced financial problems, and in 1984 the winery was bought by Suntory of Japan. At that point, Arrowood was already weary of making large amounts of wine in one style. He wanted to make wine in small quantities once again, and to experiment more than he had.

Moreover, Arrowood wasn't happy under corporate ownership. "We had a difference of opinion in management style," says Arrowood

Dick and Alis Arrowood founded their winery in 1986, but it came as the culmination of a dream, for Arrowood had been at the forefront of the reawakening of California's wine industry in the 1970s, and one of those responsible for putting the state on the world map as a maker of top-quality Chardonnays.

of his decision to leave what he calls "The Chateau." "I wanted to build my own winery, which would give me the ability to have my own brand and not get lost in the corporate shuffle. I enjoy making wine and especially the smaller lots of wine, and in larger companies sometimes that is lost."

In 1986, Arrowood bought property for a winery. It was deep in Sonoma Valley, south of Chateau St. Jean and just east of Glen Ellen. The small parcel of land sloped up into brush-covered foothills that come alive with wildflowers in spring. The design Dick and Alis Arrowood chose for their winery was a simple country barn, faced with wood paneling and painted white. The modest structure was erected behind a bank of oaks on a knoll overlooking Sonoma Valley, to maintain a low-key image. Thus the winery isn't readily visible to the passing cars 200 yards away on Highway 12.

Construction of the winery, completed in 1987, gave the Arrowoods the place to begin another chapter in the Arrowood saga. For a time, Dick remained winemaster and executive vice president at Chateau St. Jean, but in 1990 he decided to leave the Chateau for good to focus all his energies on the family business.

Over the years Arrowood had worked with many grape growers and got to know them

Dick and Alis Arrowood built their modest winery behind a bank of local trees to hide it a bit from view of cars on Highway 12 and to shelter the porch from the sounds of traffic.

well, so when he began making Chardonnay under his own name, he chose to buy from some of the best — the Alary Ranch and Preston Ranch in Russian River Valley, and Jimtown Ranch and Russ Green Ranch in Alexander Valley.

The first Arrowood wines showed major differences from those he had made at St. Jean. Instead of the buttery richness that dominated so many of his earlier Chardonnays, Arrowood Vineyards and Winery's Chardonnay emphasized the delicate tropical-and-citrus notes in the fruit, and had excellent acidity. One reason for this was Arrowood's growing realization that leaving the grape skins in contact with the

Chardonnay juice before fermentation — so-called skin contact — robbed the wine of some of its freshness.

Moreover, from the release of the first Cabernet, in 1985, Arrowood made red wine that was a major step forward over "The Chateau's." Arrowood's Cabernets were finely crafted with lean fruit and without excessive tannins; Chateau St. Jean's red wines had more depth, but more coarseness, too.

The focus at Arrowood Vineyards and Winery would be on just three varieties, including Merlot. The late-harvest Rieslings he won fame for earlier were not made here.

Arrowood limited his production to no more than 15,000 cases a year — a far cry from Chateau St. Jean, which was making about 250,000 cases a year when Arrowood left.

Arrowood put some of the finest equipment inside his 10,000-square-feet winery. Most of his fruit is selected from prime growers whom Arrowood got to know well over the two decades he had been Chateau St. Jean's winemaker. His first wines — Chardonnay, Cabernet, and Merlot — gained wide acceptance, justifying Arrowood's move into his own winery. Later releases were even better than the first wines. *DB*

Arrowood put some of the finest equipment available into his winery and limits production to no more then 15,000 cases a year, focusing on just three varieties — Chardonnay, Cabernet, and Merlot.

Arrowood's small vineyard, planted adjacent to the winery, provides only a tiny amount of Arrowood's production demands. The remainder of the wine is made from grapes from select growers around the county — growers Arrowood respected during his time at Chateau St. Jean.

BANDIERA WINERY

Ballooning over the wine country has become an exciting tourist attraction, especially in the northern part of Sonoma County, where Bandiera is located. On any Saturday it's not uncommon to see a balloon floating almost silently over the vines.

In Bordeaux and Burgundy, quality wine is often linked to specific vineyards. The wine of Château Latour comes from grapes grown in sight of the winery where they are fermented.

It is assumed, therefore, that a wine with a label designation of simply "Bordeaux" — meaning the grapes could have been grown anywhere in the district — is a lesser wine. Consumers know that the communal appellation of Bordeaux rarely signifies a wine of much quality.

One of the concepts that differentiates California from France is this disparity in image. For example, the appellation "Napa Valley" is considered among the most prestigious in the state and indicates a wine of high quality, even though the valley has more than 32,000 acres of grapes.

John B. Merritt found a way to marry the best elements of the French and American systems to make the Bandiera label one of the most value-oriented brands in the business. He did it by offering great value at a time when others were increasing prices based on the "how-much-will-the-market-bear" method.

Bandiera Winery was founded in 1937 by Emil Bandiera and operated by the Bandiera family until 1980, when it was acquired by a group of investors. Where the winery is located, in the northernmost section of Sonoma County, in hot Cloverdale, has little to do with the wines it makes today.

Under the new owners, Bandiera underwent a complete renovation in 1980. In 1982, Merritt, who had been a co-founder and winemaker at Gundlach-Bundschu Winery from 1970 to 1981, joined Bandiera and improved the quality of the wines. The winery's fortunes changed again in 1984 when it signed a national marketing agreement with the Seagram Classics Wine Co. The idea was to produce quality wines at reasonable prices and to make them from the best regions of the state, using production techniques that permitted the wines to be made less expensively than "estate-bottled" wine.

Grapes would be purchased based on quality and price. Little consideration was given for grapes from a specific sub-region. Quality, more than regional designation, was the major factor. The grapes come largely from Chiles Valley, a sub-region of the Napa Valley that is not very well known. Merritt also buys grapes from the Carneros in southern Sonoma Valley.

Merritt makes the wines in a style that makes them enjoyable with food. Ageworthiness wasn't a major factor; he was aiming for early drinkability, a market niche that so many wineries ignored in the early 1980s.

Another marketing strategy was to design for each wine a label illustrating the various California wild flowers. The designs were so attractive that they appealed to people who knew little or nothing about wine, and thus Bandiera wines were often impulse purchases by people who later became brand loyalists.

By the late 1980s, Bandiera had prestigious Carneros Chardonnays and Napa Valley Cabernets, each of which sold for less than $6 a bottle.

"If this winery had been built in the Napa Valley instead of here, it would have cost six times as much and so would the wines," says Merritt. "We keep a copy of 'The Emperor's New Clothes' in our office." *DB*

Even though
Bandiera maintains
down-to-earth
prices, winemaker
John Merritt flies
high with his wines.

The old hand-crank
press that once was
a staple of wineries
around the world
has since been
replaced at almost all
California wineries
by mechanical
presses that extract
the juice without
bitterness
or astringency.

BELLEROSE VINEYARD

Owner Charles Richard poses in front of his vineyard, where he tills the soil with a pair of Belgian draft horses, Rowdy and Chucky. "Working the land with horses is much slower than doing the job with a tractor," says Richard, "but that very slowness allows me to really see and feel the rhythms of the land, of Nature."

The early hook for Bellerose was "roses and rosés." The flower bushes still follow the fence lines, but rosé wines are past tense for Charles and Nancy Richard.

"We made rosé wine from Merlot, with a touch of Johannisberg Riesling, in our first year, 1980, adding a little Cabernet Sauvignon to the blend in the second year," explains Charles. "I was trying to create a California version of Tavel, and some people thought we had succeeded, but it turned out to be a distraction from our major purpose here."

That "major purpose" is the production of wines in the Bordeaux manner, wines that make full use of the various Bordeaux grape varieties working in concert with one another in differing proportions, depending upon the vintage: Cabernets Sauvignon and Franc, Merlot, Malbec, and Petit Verdot for the red, called Cuvee Bellerose; Sauvignon Blanc and Semillon harmonizing for the white.

"Concert" and "harmonizing" are not idly chosen terms. Charles' initial goal in life was to become a concert guitarist and music professor, and he earned a master's degree in music from the University of San Francisco. "Being a virtuoso is not a thing you can force," he says wistfully. "Andrés Segovia, the great classical guitarist, said of his protégé, John Williams, 'God has laid a finger upon his brow.' Well, God didn't lay his finger quite so heavily upon my brow!"

Though Richard has given up playing the guitar, he has not given up his sense of rhythm. "I hear the rhythms here," he says with a peaceful, serene look in his eyes. "Here, we follow the cycles of the seasons. We have to harvest, then we prepare and replenish the soils. After

"Working the land
with horses. . .
allows you to feel
the bumps and
smells, the texture
and appearance of
the land," says
Charles Richards.

that comes pruning, caring for the vines in anticipation of the next part of the rhythm. Working with horses, as I do, those rhythms become that much more evident to me."

Horses. Belgian draft horses. Rowdy and Chucky — big fellows both, and sturdy as a pair of mountains. "I always say Rowdy's name first," Charles muses. "He's my right-wheel horse. He's older, larger, and steadier. He's more mature than Chucky, who's younger and a little more exuberant.

"Working the land with horses is much slower than doing the job with a tractor, but that very slowness allows me to really see and feel the rhythms of the land, of Nature. It puts you back on Nature's pace. The nature of horsedrawn implements allows you to feel the bumps and smells, the texture and appearance of the land."

Richard the artist relies heavily on experience, appearance, taste, and feel for decisions on fruit maturity and handling wines in the cellar — but is quick to fall back on technology for confirmation. "For me to rely on intuition alone would be a lot like a musician who can play only by ear. There's a whole world of music that he can never partake of — he'll miss certain nuances that the composer wrote into

his music, hints at interpretation. "Interpretation. That's our job as winemakers, to interpret what we're given with each vintage. If we have the insight into the 'score' that scientific analysis provides, we have that much greater a chance to interpret well." *RPH*

Oak barrels are
being washed out
in front of the
handsome wooden
winery at Bellerose,
adorned by roses.
Roses are planted at
the end of each row
of vines at Bellerose
in accordance with
old French practice.
Roses predict
mildew problems,
being more sensitive
to mildew than
grapevines.

BELVEDERE WINERY

Peter Friedman, the original partner with Rodney Strong in Sonoma Vineyards, always felt there were two concepts the American wine consumer could understand: wines that offered great value and vineyard-designated wines of consistent quality.

After he left Sonoma Vineyards following a corporate restructuring, Friedman mentioned his beliefs to a tennis-playing friend, William Hambrecht, a San Francisco financier and partner in the high-tech investment banking firm Hambrecht & Quist. Hambrecht, a wine lover and the man who brought Chalone Inc. public with a stock offering, also had a great interest in grape growing and winemaking.

Hambrecht liked Friedman's idea and with his impetus, Belvedere Winery was founded in 1979. The winery was named for the Marin County community where Hambrecht lived, and was located on Westside Road in Healdsburg. The business objectives were twofold:

First, Belvedere would produce world-class wines from grapes grown in top vineyards whose designations, already used by other wineries, had established an image for quality. This "Grapemaker Series" of wines included Chardonnay and Pinot Noir from Charles and

The Belvedere winery was set up to market not only the Discovery wines but also those in the Grapemaker series. By the late 1980s, the latter wines had been changed and the Belvedere brand name was enlarged on the label.

Helen Bacigalupi's Russian River vineyard; Cabernet Sauvignon and Merlot from Robert Young in Alexander Valley; York Creek Cabernet from the vineyard high atop the Napa Valley; and wines from Rene di Rosa's Winery Lake Vineyard in the Carneros.

Second, Belvedere also would blend wines from stock bought in the bulk market and sell them reasonably. These wines were called the "Discovery Series." A phrase on the label said they were "Discovered and Bottled by Belvedere Winery."

The Discovery wines took off. It was a time of increasing volumes in the wine trade,

Belvedere's western-style tasting room, which features a hothouse window, is in the same attractive building that houses a conferece room. The winery is attached on a lower level.

and Belvedere scoured the state to find wines to blend. Prices rarely exceeded $5 a bottle.

Don Frazer made the wines in the Grapemaker line, with Paul Draper of Ridge Vineyards as consultant. There was one hidden drawback in the premium line: all the Grapemaker wines had different label designs, so there was no real consumer identification with Belvedere as the producer of the wines. In 1984, after the 1981 Belvedere Winery Lake Pinot Noir won the sweepstakes award at the San Francisco Fair wine competition, Rene di Rosa got calls for the wine because the only name listed on the award was "Winery Lake," not Belvedere!

Then changes hit both wine lines. First, the Discovery line outgrew the Westside Road winery's capacity, so the blended-wine crew moved to a new facility in Healdsburg. Then Frazer left to become winemaker at nearby de Lorimier Winery. Erich Russell, owner of tiny Rabbit Ridge Winery, replaced him.

By 1989, competition and lack of image had caused a slump in sales of the Grapemaker wines. And the Discovery line was hit by shortages in the bulk-wine market, which drove prices up and forced Belvedere to buy large quantities of locally grown grapes.

Then the Grapemaker series was dropped in favor of a Belvedere Winery label blending the best of all the single-vineyard wines. *DB*

The tasteful tasting room at Belvedere Winery, located off Westside Road south of Healdsburg in the Russian River area, has flowers growing under the beams.

BUENA VISTA WINERY

The old Sherry House at the original Buena Vista Cellars, as drawn by former wine-country artist Sebastian Titus in the 1970s. The tree-studded old cellars are a favorite stop for visitors and the site of Buena Vista's famed Vintage 2000 industry meetings.

The view toward the future has to look pretty good for Buena Vista, and if you know your Spanish, you'll recognize the play on words. For *buena vista* means, literally, "good view." One could opt for a more poetic translation — perhaps "beautiful vision" — and add more than mere nuance, for Buena Vista's vision for the future is both sound and attractive.

"My family has been in this business six generations," notes Buena Vista's youthful president, Marcus Moller-Racke. He says it quietly, almost matter-of-factly. But there is an undercurrent of passion in his voice, because for the Moller-Racke family wine is more than a business. "My family has never invested money in anything but the wine business. Yes, it's our business, but more than that it's our future!"

That future seems assured when you match the thirtyish Moller-Racke's words with his achievements. There are at least six accomplishments in his short tenure as president of Buena Vista that prove his vision and foresight.

First, he quickly advanced Jill Davis to the position of head winemaker. Not the sort of thing you might expect from a young, Teutonic male. But Moller-Racke sees ability before gender, and Davis, who trained at Beringer after her schooling at U.C. Davis, has staked a clear claim as one of California's very best winemakers.

Second, Moller-Racke was not too proud to take a page out of his predecessor's book and turn it into a full-fledged chapter with his own personal stamp. I refer to the startling success of "Spiceling," a proprietary wine that melded the spiciness of Gewurztraminer and the apricot fruitiness of White Riesling.

Third, and maybe most important, Marcus has boldly expanded the winery's Carneros vineyard plantings to 900 acres, which means that over 90 percent of Buena Vista's wines are now estate bottled. "Our clear goal is to become entirely estate bottled," explains Moller-Racke. "The supply of quality grapes has already become a key issue in the production of fine premium wines. If we are to improve our quality we have to be assured of a consistent source of excellent fruit so as to control our own destiny."

Fourth, Moller-Racke and Buena Vista have become major voices and proponents of the Carneros Quality Alliance, the finest regional organization thus far created in California. Where most regional groups have previously been restricted to wineries and have been organized only for promoting and marketing the appellation, the Carneros Quality Alliance has gone far beyond those self-serving goals.

This organization has not only included grape growers, but goes out of its way to acknowledge the important, even primary, role they play in the quality of wine. The Quality Alliance set up an extensive research project to determine whether there are any flavor factors that set Carneros Pinot Noirs apart from those grown in other parts of California. The study did indeed identify a distinct, common strawberry component. There is even talk of a possible joint tasting room/restaurant in the future.

No winemaker worth his Cabernet will rely solely on agricultural, scientific, technological, and artistic skills. There is a keen, almost dramatic sense of the mystical and religious in winegrowing. Always has been, always will be. Count on it.

Fifth, under Moller-Racke Buena Vista has aggressively added to its marketing portfolio here and abroad. In January 1988 Buena Vista's parent firm, A. Racke (headquartered in Bingen-am-Rhein, Germany, and owned by the Moller-Racke family), acquired the house of Thorin, a Burgundian fixture since the 9th century. Prior to that, Buena Vista had acquired distribution rights to Bricout Champagnes.

In April 1989 Moller-Racke announced a joint venture with Sonoma County Pinot Noir star Robert Stemmler. "We were very pleased to add Stemmler to our family of wines," he crowed at the time. "Bob is known for producing superb wine, but his winery capacity was limiting what he could do. With us, he'll have the benefit of working with winemaker Jill Davis, and perhaps with our vineyards."

Sixth, Marcus Moller-Racke has stepped up alongside Robert Mondavi as an industry leader who recognizes the need to make plans and set long-term goals to ensure the industry's survival in a country fed contradictory messages about wine's social and nutritional value.

"We have committed ourselves to doing anything and everything possible to stabilize our industry," Marcus avers. "I grew up with wine, surrounded by wine. Wine was in every church. It was in songs and poetry,

The sun sets behind the 2,586-foot-high east peak of Mount Tamalpais (center), in Marin County. The vinelands of the Carneros descend gently toward the San Francisco Bay (here called San Pablo Bay), which sits between the vines and the Coast Range.

pointing to the positive aspects of life. The world is going at such a fast pace today that there is a powerful need to balance things out. When you sit down with friends and have a glass of wine, it relaxes you. So we have to make sure that good wines remain here, in the long term."

Key to that, says Moller-Racke with certainty, is education that shows wine as an everyday, meal-time beverage for American consumers, one that promotes moderation. "This is totally critical. The American public, today, is faced with contradictory images. In one, the media shows celebrities meeting, enjoying a glass of wine, and generally having

The fountain shoots a thin stream of water upward in front of the old cellar at the original Buena Vista Winery, on the east side of Sonoma. Here, a tasting room with picnic tables offers samples of Buena Vista wines. The main production cellar, however, is several miles southeast, in the middle of the Carneros district.

a good time. This shows wine as a common beverage, as something good. But then, there's also the image of alcohol as something dangerous, especially when it's abused, or when you drive under the influence, or when you are too young to drink."

Buena Vista has tried to make wine a bit easier for consumers to get a handle on with innovative back labels. In 1988 Buena Vista introduced a new format of back label, designed to get more usable information across to buyers.

"For a lot of wineries, the back label is used for such stuff as 'How wonderful the sun looks going down behind our vineyard.' We decided to react directly to the questions we get every day in our tasting room. 'Is it sweet?' 'Do I serve it as a cocktail? With dinner?' And, 'Please don't tell me that it goes with everything!'

"So we tried to put everything into simple terms, terms that could be commonly understood. So residual sugar is not expressed in grams per liter, but rather in 'dry,' 'medium,' or 'sweet.' And the trade tells me, yes, these back labels do give some help to confused consumers." Which, in the end, may help Americans enjoy the simple pleasures of wine. *RPH*

One of the original oak ovals, perhaps even old enough to have been used by founder Count Agostin Haraszthy (pronounced "Harris'-thee"). A self-guided tour of the old cellar is still offered and gives some insight into how things were done in the real old days.

DAVIS BYNUM WINERY

Lindley Bynum certainly couldn't have known, when he wrote the thin treatise *California Wines and How to Enjoy Them* in the 1960s, that this book would prompt his son, Davis, to quit his job and leap into the wine business with both La Feet.

"Chateau La Feet," that is, that being Davis's sobriquet for the blended wine whose success enabled him to found his own winery near the winding Russian River.

Lindley Bynum had been a historian and wine judge who instilled in his son a sense of the joys of wine. In 1965 Davis, then a reporter for the *San Francisco Chronicle*, resigned his job to open a small winery in the rear of a store in Albany, just down the road from the University of California at Berkeley. Bynum bought bulk wine, which he blended and sold. Some of it was called Barefoot Bynum — Davis nicknamed it the Chateau La Feet of California.

That wine became successful and in 1973 Bynum ran out of space in Albany, so he relocated to Sonoma County, to a small hillside location. There he and his wife, Dorothy, renovated a 1950s hop kiln on the 82-acre River Bend ranch that became the permanent home for the Bynum winery. The winery was near

"Spartan" and "compact" are the words that come to most minds when touring the small, cramped, not-well-lighted barrel storage room at Davis Bynum. Ambience aside, under winemaker Gary Farrell, the Bynum winery produces an array of excellent wines.

what later became Hop Kiln Winery, another property used in years past to dry hops for beer.

Most of the wines Bynum now makes and markets are from nearby vineyards. This cool region makes white wines of delicacy; in the reds, the soil here favors deeply scented Pinot Noirs over Cabernet.

Bynum's fortunes changed dramatically in 1978 when he hired Gary Farrell as his winemaker. Farrell, a quiet, bearded man, is perfectly suited for making wine from these grapes. His greatest successes with the Bynum wines are with Gewurztraminer and Pinot Noir. The former wine is diminishing in production in

The Davis Bynum Winery on Westside Road is one of the most picturesque in Sonoma County — a cluster of unpretentious, older buildings linked by walkways filled with flowers.

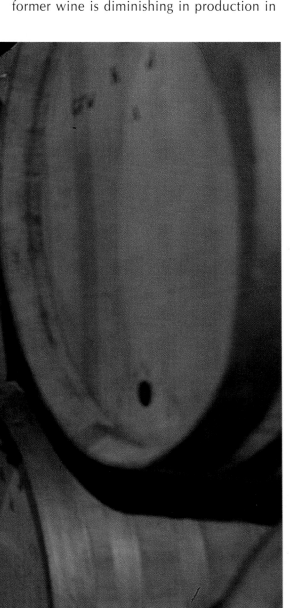

California, partially because of the public's inability to pronounce it. But Bynum's off-dry Gewurztraminer was marvelously complex and matched beautifully with a wide variety of foods, notably Thai and other oriental cuisine.

The Pinot Noir, a notoriously knotty problem for many winemakers, has been conquered by Farrell. He makes it in a lighter style than some, but only in color, not in flavor. The wines are silky and deeply complex, full of the berrylike spice one expects from Burgundy. The flavors of Bynum Pinot Noirs, going back to the 1978 — Farrell's first here — are deeply complex and rewarding.

Bynum's Chardonnays and Cabernets likewise are leaner, less oafish than a lot of the wines made by those seeking more flavor impact. The idea here is that the grapes, rather than the oak or the procedure used to turn them into wine, should be the spokesman for the winery. And Farrell does a wonderful job of controlling those grapes that come into the winery without the perfect flavor profile. He is a master at attaining finesse.

Today, Dorothy Bynum's oil painting artistry adorns some of the reserve wines that Bynum makes. Marketing of the Bynum wines is handled by Hampton Bynum, the third generation of Bynums interested in the wine business. *DB*

The vineyards here in the western edge of the county are often planted on sloped, hillside land that drains well and gives extra character to the grapes. However, the smaller crops yield less wine.

CARMENET VINEYARD

Vines meet the sky, high atop the western slope of the Mayacamas Mountains. At Carmenet the vines are planted in iron-rich, reddish clay soils, which are excellent for the red Bordeaux varieties grown at this hilltop site.

Robert Frost was once asked how one went about writing a poem. "Well, first, something has to happen to you," the poet said curtly. When he noted that his message hadn't quite gotten across, he continued, "Then you put some words on a piece of paper and ride them like a horse until you have a poem."

One of the best at riding ideas into reality is Dick Graff, chairman of Chalone, Inc. California's most intriguing consortium of wineries — Chalone, Edna Valley, Carmenet, and Acacia — blossomed out of Dick's fertile, musically trained mind. It took some riding, but the experience and the idea that formed the foundation for this quartet were sound from the outset.

"When we reopened inactive Chalone in 1966, I worked backwards in determining our winemaking style," muses Graff, whose curly hair and mustache frame twinkling, almost devilish, eyes. "I knew which of the great wines I admired, particularly in Burgundy, so I decided to go and visit the producers and find out how they were making those marvelous wines. What I found out was this: they were using the same procedures that they had used for hundreds of years, the advances of technology notwithstanding."

When the model was wrestled, ridden, and worked to perfection at Chalone's isolated Pinnacles hideaway — high in the hills above Monterey's Salinas Valley — Graff and Chalone president Phil Woodward took the concept south to the foggy truck farms of Edna Valley, setting up a partnership with Jack Niven (owner of Paragon Vineyard) to reproduce the Burgundian atmosphere.

Carmenet became the third jewel in Chalone's crown with the 1984 acquisition of a

Caves are perfect for the aging of wine in barrels, keeping temperature down and humidity up — which means less loss to ullage (evaporation). These caves are man-made, tunneled into the side of a hill just above the main amphitheater of vineyard.

nascent Sonoma Valley winegrowing estate in the iron-rich hills above Agua Caliente, next door to Louis Martini's famed Monte Rosso Vineyard. These warm hillside slopes are perfect for the Bordelais model that Carmenet has come to be. (Carmenet is an ancient French term for the grape varieties used in red Bordeaux wines.)

Winemaker Jeff Baker, a husky fellow with a gruff exterior, grew up in a farming family — his dad grew oranges in Ventura County — but went through Stanford University with an eye toward medicine. But the desire to "live with my body, to live out of doors" was too great, so he spent two quarters at Berkeley studying soil science and plant nutrition before setting out in search of the grape.

In 1973 he got his master's degree at Davis and went to Mayacamas for three years. "My goal had been to work in a small, premium, mountain winery," Jeff recalls. "Working with Bob Travers at Mayacamas, I learned the role eccentricity plays in winemaking. The 'rules' we had learned in school were for safety.

"We don't do any 'safe' winemaking here. We're looking for exceptional quality, so we take some risks. But they're risks backed up by paying attention to the technology we know, to make sure that our risks don't turn out sour. That's what attracted me to the Chalone group in the first place — their willingness to fail once in a while, in return for moving the state of the art of winemaking along to a higher level." *RPH*

The muscular Jeff Baker, winemaker and general manager, inspects Carmenet's White in the main cave. The Carmenet White is a blend of Sauvignon Blanc and Semillon. "We like the dry, Graves style of Sauvignon Blanc, so we barrel ferment," notes Chalone Chairman Dick Graff.

CHALK HILL WINERY

In the early 1970s, Fred Furth was a successful antitrust lawyer. He had just settled a class-action suit worth $82 million (his cut: $4.2 million). But he was getting fat in places other than his bank account.

"I was putting on almost five pounds a year," says the now-trim founder of Chalk Hill Winery. "The doc told me I needed to get out and do something, maybe find a place in the country. So I rented an airplane and flew around Sonoma County and Napa Valley. I noticed that there was only one road into Napa Valley, Highway 29. Out here, east of Windsor, the area was open, almost wild.

"We bought our first parcel, 240 acres, in 1972. We planted our first 40 acres of grapes in 1974 and sold our first crop in 1977. Boy, was that a lesson! We delivered our grapes in September, were told how much we'd be paid in December, received half-payment in February, and then final payment in June. How can you do business that way? Right then, I began to design our winery."

Along the way, the six-feet-three Furth discovered an affinity for designing and building things. A 60,000-case winery, with model kitchen. Vineyards now approaching 300 acres. A complete office and conference cen-

Chalk Hill's winery is set in a natural amphitheater, almost like a stage, with terraced rows of vines opposite as the audience. Some of the terraced slopes are so steep that employees pray for snow in the wintertime — hoping for a little free skiing.

ter. A slate-roofed stone manse that reminds one of Europe. An equestrian center (Fred's wife and daughter are skilled horsewomen). Pool, tennis court, volleyball court, baseball diamond. A self-contained 1,100-acre estate.

"We are very nearly that," explains Furth with a laugh that hides none of his pride. "I believe in developing sound infrastructures. We have our own water and sewage systems; we've properly buried power and phone lines; we have nearly 30 miles of roads and a maintenance shop that services 40 vehicles and all our winery equipment. The only outside services we buy are telephone and electricity.

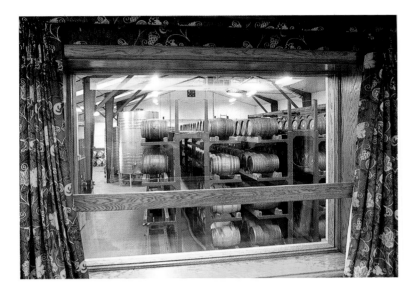

A gaily curtained window looks into the barrel cellar, where Chalk Hill Cabernets and Merlots quietly gather age. As red wines rest in barrel, a slow oxidation softens tannins and expands fruit flavors.

Maybe we need to buy some generators and put in our own phones!"

If he's kidding about the last, he's quite serious about the estate concept. "Our slogan is 'Chalk Hill — A Way of Life,' but it's more than mere slogan for us," he says. "I believe in trying to live an integrated life. We grow our own grapes. We employ 100 people here for the winery, the equestrian center, our construction, the ranch, and our maintenance shop."

Though he sold his San Francisco home and moved self and family to the estate, he still gives half his time to his San Francisco law firm (which has corporate clients like Kellogg, Columbia Pictures, and Santa Fe Railroad).

Vineyardist Mark Lingenfelder is a twelfth-generation caretaker of vines, and winemaker David Ramey is as experienced with Sonoma County fruit as anybody, having distinguished himself at Simi and Matanzas Creek before joining Chalk Hill in 1990.

"Sonoma County has cool weather, which produces dynamite grapes," says Ramey, who also made wine in France (Château Pétrus) and Australia (Lindeman's) before settling here. "Chalk Hill has great grapes and a first-class, professional team that possesses a keen desire to excel." The results are clearly shown by the wines — tart Sauvignon Blancs, vivacious Chardonnays and Cabernet Sauvignons — made with the Chalk Hill stamp. *RPH*

Chalk Hill's exhibition kitchen is fully equipped both for cooking classes and to handle the catering of winery events. The matching of wine and food has become an effective means of moving Americans from something they know (food) to something they don't (wine).

CHATEAU DE BAUN

Folks in the wine business tend to take it all a bit too seriously at times. Business is bad, we have to sell harder; Americans don't drink wine, we have to cram "civilization" down their throats; it rained during crush, wine's going to have to cost more. Dreary.

Enter Ken DeBaun. Take a strange new grape variety that nobody ever heard of, and build a new winery based entirely upon that huge unknown. Is this guy serious?

What would *you* think of an entrepreneur whose office is furnished in redwood, early Western, complete with a humongous, shaggy

buffalo head ("Oscar"), a collection of percussion pistols and rifles, a huge redwood burl desk, and oversized redwood burl chairs covered with sheepskin?

DeBaun is an engineer, out of the Stevens Institute of Technology, Hoboken, New Jersey. Though he had long enjoyed wine, his entry into the business of growing grapes and producing the product came about almost by accident. "Well, I acquired this 20-acre Gewurztraminer vineyard, out west of Santa Rosa, in a property-tax swap," he chuckles. "I sold the grapes, but even though the wines won medals I found that the wineries didn't always honor

Glittering by night, Chateau de Baun's visitors' center was constructed in the "French Chateau" style. Stone walls give a "cool" cellar feel, but huge windows let in light enough to make "warm" the more operative adjective.

their grape-buying contracts. So I figured I'd better take control of the product through the whole process.

"I've never been a traditionalist. Everybody makes Cabernet and Chardonnay. I had heard of this new grape variety that Harold Olmo had developed at Davis, so I called him, even though he had been retired a couple of years, and asked him if I could taste some of the wines the students had made from Symphony.

"One of the bottles had been opened several times over the eight years since the wine had been made, but there was still that distinc-

A full acre of formal garden — "Jardin Symphonie" — surrounds the handsome chateau. Umbrella-shaded tables extend from a spacious rear patio out into a walnut orchard, which has picnic facilities of its own.

tive aroma from the Muscat side and the longevity from the Grenache side."

Symphony is a unique variety, developed over four decades. It is a cross between the nearly red variety, Grenache Gris, and the highly aromatic white grape, Muscat of Alexandria. And what DeBaun, along with winemaker Jamie Meves (formerly Pat Paulsen's winemaker), has done with the variety is equally innovative. For they have, with a single variety, created wines to take you through a meal from soup to nuts. There are sparkling wines, both dry and sweet, and table wines that run a complete scale of sweetness levels.

Amid the spotless precision of DeBaun's industrial-park winery lie hints of humor. A pair of computer-driven Vaslin presses bear the names Gilbert and, sure, Sullivan. Stainless-steel fermenting tanks are not numbered, but bear names of composers: Mozart, Schubert, Vivaldi, Boccherini, and even Copland and Williams, to preserve the theme of tying Old World to New.

To have assessed, ahead of time, what Ken DeBaun wanted to do with this unknown and unusual grape variety, well, you'd have had to say, "No way." But, judging from the evidence of what's been accomplished in a few short years, based entirely on the quality and consistency of the wines, it's been a successful composition. (Background music up.) *RPH*

The interior of the chateau, which has no winemaking facilities at present, is spacious. The central, oval tasting area is an efficient use of space, and the grounds are very popular for weddings.

CHATEAU ST. JEAN

B ob and Ed Merzoian owned a successful table-grape business in the San Joaquin Valley when they chose to delve into the other kind of grape business — wine.

To establish a premium property meant putting it where the grapes grew best, and the spot they chose was cool Sonoma Valley.

The concept of the winery, developed with partner W. Kenneth Sheffield, was to be super-premium, with great attention paid to top-end varietal wines, mainly Chardonnay. To achieve top quality, they hired a young local kid who had earned an enology degree at Fresno State.

Richard Arrowood was then working at Sonoma-Cutrer Vineyards with winemaker Rodney Strong. It was there that Arrowood first began to learn about the various vineyards and appellations of Sonoma County, and

One of the small hills on nearby Sugarloaf Ridge, just up the hill from the winery, has a curvature to it that, by coincidence, is not unlike the curve in the top of the Chateau St. Jean wine label.

where he began to learn about Chardonnay growing in Alexander Valley, as well as other regions.

Chateau St. Jean vineyards and winery was founded in 1973. By then Arrowood knew about some of the county's different regions and how grapes from them make different wines. To be able to watch how each of these styles changed with bottle age, he made

Chardonnays from different vineyards, keeping the grapes separate. It was a bold decision as well as being logistically difficult. The fruit from each vineyard had to be vinified and aged in barrels separately. Then master blends had to be made, respecting vineyard integrity.

Chateau St. Jean put out Chardonnays designated Wildwood, Beltane, Gauer Ranch, Belle Terre, and Robert Young, among others. Some designations survived, including the latter two, which are now mainstays of the line. Others were cut. Sometimes the price of the grapes was too high. Some vineyards produced fruit of erratic quality. Arrowood even rejected fruit from some growers because he found it difficult to work with them. Fruit from Mendocino County that had been excellent was dropped from the program after the winery decided to use only Sonoma County fruit.

Soon the public could see the ways in which Chardonnay grew in various regions, and could get an idea about the style of wine a particular vineyard yielded from one year to the next. Eventually prices for these Chardonnays — none of them bargain basement — reflected the public's demand for them. The Robert Young wine was the most famous in the first few years, and by the early 1980s was on strict allocation, demand was so great. And it became the priciest.

Meanwhile, Arrowood also was making a name for himself with a series of unctuous, wonderfully scented and balanced Rieslings and Gewurztraminers made in dessert style. The richest and sweetest of these wines, often called Individual Dried Bunch Selected Late Harvest, were equivalent in weight and general character to German dessert wines called Trockenbeerenauslese, abbreviated TBA. However, where the German TBAs sold for $50 and $100 a half bottle, St. Jean's wines were selling for a fraction of that. Connoisseurs found them to be superb wines and great values.

The Japanese wine
and spirits firm
Suntory, which
bought Chateau
St. Jean in 1984, has
spent millions
upgrading the
property and
helping to extend
its image.

The rest of the St. Jean line was an impressive array of table wines including Fume Blanc, Pinot Blanc, off-dry Johannisberg Riesling, and Gewurztraminer. Some of the wines had vineyard designations; the Fume Blancs called Pat Paulsen, La Petite Etoile, and Forrest Crimmins gained fame for their concentration of flavors. Arrowood also made Cabernet Sauvignon, Merlot, and Zinfandel, some with vineyard designations. One of them, Laurel Glen, later became the brand of a winery owned by Patrick Campbell.

After a time, most of the red wine program was discontinued.

In the late 1970s, the company decided to delve into sparkling wine. So St. Jean built a facility at Graton, to the west. They hired Pete Downs to make the wines, and by 1980 the winery was producing a number of sparkling wines, including many under contract for other wineries.

By the early 1980s, all seemed to be running smoothly. Chateau St. Jean had a name that rang quality bells for many consumers, the winery had gained a national reputation, and sales were brisk. But that's not always enough to keep a winery healthy. It takes a tremendous amount of money to keep a winery afloat in its first decade, and even after the winery reaches a point where the cash flow is strong,

The winery at Chateau St. Jean was designed to feel like a Spanish courtyard, with columns and archways surrounding a patio. The tasting room, however, is in a renovated home on the property that was built in 1920 by the Goff family, the original owners of the Kenwood ranch.

the debts accrued in the first years still must be paid back. And this is where St. Jean ran into troubles.

It started with a decline in the table-grape industry in the San Joaquin Valley, still the Merzoians' main business. As the Merzoians faced financial hardship in that business, the fiscal fortunes of St. Jean came under attack, too. Before long, both entities faced financial deadlines that couldn't be met simultaneously.

In late 1984, Suntory International, the giant Japanese wine and spirits company, paid a reported $40 million for Chateau St. Jean. It was the largest winery deal in California history to that point.

Situated along Highway 12 at the northern edge of Kenwood in Sonoma Valley, Chateau St. Jean is a visitor's delight. Not only does the tasting room offer fascinating wines, but it is surrounded by a profusion of flowers, and towering trees shade the courtyard from the searing sun in summer.

Suntory helped St. Jean move ahead and keep its place in the fine wine headlines. It spent many millions upgrading St. Jean, adding new facilities and new oak barrels in which to age the wines and reinstating the red wine program. The infusion of cash helped Arrowood extend the image of the property he had helped create.

However, although Japanese ownership of the winery may have solved its financial problems, the corporate style of the new owners irritated some of the old-time employees, and a number of them left the company soon after the sale. Among them were a national sales manager, Vineyard Manager Barney Fernandez (later a force at Ferrari-Carano up-county), and President Allan Hemphill, later to run the Gauer Estate property.

Arrowood remained winemaker, but in the meantime, with Suntory's accord, he made plans for his own winery. In 1990 he left the chateau to devote full time to his own project.

St. Jean remains a force in fine winemaking under the direction of Arrowood's longtime assistant and successor, Don Van Staaveren, and the company has added a dimension to its fine wine image by importing some exceptional wines from overseas, including a line of Italian wines. *DB*

Though Chateau St. Jean has made a string of vineyard-designated Chardonnays using grapes from different Sonoma County areas, the vineyards planted on the home ranch have also made excellent and widely praised Chardonnays.

CHATEAU SOUVERAIN

The story of Chateau Souverain and its previous incarnations illustrates how difficult it is to enter and prosper in the wine business.

The story of Souverain really starts with J. Leland Stewart, a wine pioneer not in the Sonoma County area, but in the Napa Valley. Stewart founded Souverain Cellars in 1943 to make premium varietal wines on a ridge east of the center of the Napa Valley, and he was successful, making a string of excellent wines and blazing some new trails for various grape varieties.

In 1970, however, Lee Stewart decided to retire, and sold his winery to a group of Napa Valley investors. They, in turn, sold the winery, located off Deer Park Road above St. Helena, to pilot Tom Burgess and his wife,

In Chateau Souverain's tastefully decorated restaurant, chef Pat Windisch creates some of the most stunning menus in Sonoma County.

Linda, who changed the name to Burgess Cellars. However, the Souverain name then popped up on two new wineries, one constructed on an eastern slope of the Napa Valley (Souverain of Rutherford) and the other here in the northern reaches of Sonoma County, near Geyserville, and not far from some of the finest vineyards of the Alexander Valley. It was initially called Souverain of Alexander Valley.

Before construction of either winery could be completed, however, the baking and food products giant, Pillsbury, bought both wineries from the investor group, intending to operate them for the production of premium wine. But such are the vagaries of the wine business, and so complex — and costly — are its problems, that Pillsbury realized shortly after that it had stubbed its toe. Pillsbury had lost a lot of money — one report said as much as $10 million — on the venture and finally chose to leave the wine business by selling both properties.

The Napa Valley property was sold to a group of investors who already owned the Freemark Abbey winery, and the name of that property was changed to Rutherford Hill Winery. The second property, in Sonoma County, wasn't sold until 1976. It was acquired by a consortium of more than 200 local grape growers under the name North Coast Cellars. These growers, who aimed to make premium wine from their own grapes and others purchased on the open market, changed the name of the facility to Souverain Cellars.

That plan proceeded well under the direction of the brilliant winemaker Bill Bonetti, formerly head of winemaking at the Charles Krug Winery in the Napa Valley. (Coincidentally, his assistant at Charles Krug, Phil Baxter, later became winemaker at Napa Valley's Souverain property. When Bonetti left Souverain, Tom Eddy replaced him and carried on the tradition by making a string of lovely wines.

But marketing is a difficult job and Souverain Cellars never was able to achieve a reputation for super-premium wine. One reason was the fact that the winery had no deep pockets to buy expensive oak barrels for aging, and also had to use the grapes of some of the grower-members of the cooperative, which wasn't always in the best interests of the wine.

Moreover, even special projects that looked like sure money-makers fizzled. In one

Chateau Souverain was designed to look like an old hop kiln, a building once common in these parts for drying hops used in beer making.

not-well-publicized case, Kraft Foods entered the wine business by creating a line of wines called Mont Rouge, some of which would be made at Souverain Cellars. It was a deal that looked like it would greatly benefit Souverain, but before the wines were released, Kraft pulled the plug on the program, and Souverain's sweetheart deal was dead.

After a decade of struggling to find its niche in the wine business, Souverain found itself saddled with a burdensome bank loan, a shrinking market for its products, and an ownership and operating base that had many frictions. Sailing wasn't smooth, and finally the growers' group put the facility on the market.

In a sophisticated business arrangement, Wine World Estates of St. Helena acquired Souverain in 1986. Wine World Estates (a division of Nestlé USA, the company that also owns Beringer Vineyards in the Napa Valley and other wine properties) swung a deal in which Souverain first declared bankruptcy. Then instantly, with approval of the bankruptcy court, Wine World bought the property out of bankruptcy for a price of $9.6 million.

It was a deal all participants could live with, and that began the current life of the property, certainly its most prosperous and prestigious incarnation. Wine World's former president E. Michael Moone changed the

During a major facelift in 1990, the entrance to the winery was remodeled and an elegant wine bar/bistro was added to the restaurant.

name of the facility to Chateau Souverain. (Interestingly, during its brief operation by Pillsbury, Souverain had developed a low-priced brand of wine called Chateau Souverain.)

Immediately, winemaker Tom Peterson was given the benefit of Wine World's vast resources. These included two of the best vineyard management specialists in the industry, Bob Steinhauer and George Buonaccorsi; a renovated winemaking facility; an expanded and upgraded restaurant with a menu designed by talented chef Gary Danko; and a series of contracts with some of the best vineyards in the county.

The Zinfandel growing in the Geyserville area has long made rich, potent wines, notably under the label of Ridge Vineyards in Cupertino, located south of San Francisco. After Wine World purchased Chateau Souverain in 1986, it also began making a rich Zinfandel from the locally grown grapes.

Moreover, Wine World added new French Nevers and American oak barrels. Peterson instituted a regime of keeping separate the fruit received from each vineyard and making blending and bottling decisions on each lot. In some cases, Peterson found lots that were exceptional, and these were bottled as vineyard-designated wines. Other lots ended up in the winery's reserve program.

Peterson experimented to improve all the wines, notably the Sauvignon Blanc and Chardonnay. Both wines took on more depth and richness. Moreover, a Zinfandel from specific vineyards became a hit, with spice and raspberry scents. All the Chateau Souverain wines remained reasonable in price and good values.

Although Danko left the Chateau Souverain restaurant in 1990, his legacy is seen in one of the most elegant and creative menus in the county, and lunch, dinner, and Sunday brunches here are grand experiences.

The restaurant replaced Danko with Patricia Windisch, who had been the chef at Beringer for four years, and the quality of food at the restaurant only improved. *DB*

A vineyard of ancient vines that had produced tiny amounts of dense Zinfandel in the Geyserville area was finally deemed to be so unproductive that the vines were ripped out in 1990 and replaced by new vines intended to produce a more consistent crop.

CHRISTOPHER CREEK WINERY

The little creek running through the property that John and Susan Mitchell bought in 1988 had no name, so they named it after their son, Christopher. "We told the Foppianos we had named it Christopher Creek, and they said that on their property it was called Foppiano Creek," says Susan. Still, the fact that the creek's name changed as it meandered west didn't dampen their enthusiasm, nor change their name for the creek and their winery.

Christopher Creek's history dates to 1974, when Bill and Helen Chaikin bought the property and planted Syrah and Petite Sirah on the sloping hillsides just south of Healdsburg.

These two Rhone varieties have a long history in the northern Russian River Valley. The Foppiano family pioneered Petite Sirah a decade earlier here, and Foppiano Petite Sirah gained a reputation for aging handsomely in the bottle.

Bill Chaikin, who was 59 when he began the project here, called the winery Sotoyome after Rancho Sotoyome, a Mexican land grant in 1840. Soto was a Pomo Indian chief; Sotoyome reportedly means "home of Soto." The Chaikins produced wine more for the love of it than for commercial reasons, so Sotoyome was never widely marketed.

In 1986, the Chaikins decided to retire, and

The Petite Syrah and Syrah that go into Christopher Creek's wines were planted on the sloping hillsides of its vineyards in 1974, when the original owners first founded the winery.

put the property on the market. But the winery was no state-of-the-art facility and Petite Sirah and Syrah had not yet come into favor the way they would four years later. There were no immediate takers for the Sotoyome ranch. Two years later, the property was still on the market, listed for about $600,000 including a lovely home, the small winery, ten acres of vines, and 3,000 cases of wine in inventory.

British-born John Mitchell had worked for one of the world's largest sugar companies, based in England. "For the first 27 years of my life I tried to prevent fermentation," he says. "With sugar, you have to prevent fermentation

Cellarmaster Craig Kimball and his assistant, Mame the "guard dog," are John and Susan Mitchell's only employees at the small Christopher Creek Winery. Kimball is also a handyman who helped design and build the winery's cozy tasting room.

or you have disaster." John had met Susan in the Bay area and they were wed there, settling in Tiburon.

They began to realize they liked wine. "We were tasting wine and enjoying it with dinners regularly," explains Susan. "We said that if life were perfect, we'd live in the middle of a vineyard and make wine. But we never really thought it would happen."

One day on a tour of the wine country, the Mitchells happened by the Sotoyome ranch and were struck by the beauty of the place. They made an offer, it was accepted, and Christopher Creek was born.

"We bought this place because Petite Sirah makes incredibly interesting wines," says Mitchell. He was surprised by the high quality of the first wines he made, the 1988 Syrah and 1988 Petite Sirah. Winemaker for the project from the start was consultant Paul Brasset, the full-time winemaker at White Oak in the Alexander Valley.

To operate the business without bank debt, the Mitchells developed the new property slowly, with their own hands and with the aid of cellarmaster/carpenter Craig Kimball. A tasting room was added, paneled with redwood taken from the old tanks that used to store wine, and a passive air flow system was built into a side wall of the old winery to keep barrels cool. *DB*

The classic curved knife of the harvest, called a serpette, is a razor-sharp instrument used by pickers to cut the grape bunches off the vine. At Christopher Creek, the small, ten-acre vineyard is easy enough to pick in a single day.

CLOS DU BOIS

Clos du Bois was founded by Frank Woods and partners on the premise that wines are grown in the vineyard. While that might be common knowledge today, it wasn't widely known or accepted in 1974, when the first 2,000 cases were made. What Woods knew then, and most everybody knows today, is that viticultural decisions have to be based on their effects on the wines. "What might not be financially feasible for the grape grower is imperative to the winegrower," Woods would say.

Clos du Bois vineyard plantings are in Alexander Valley (nearly 600 acres) and Dry Creek Valley (100 acres), parallel valleys 65 air-miles north of San Francisco. Ocean fogs filter over the rolling hills night and morning, and burn off to days warm enough to mature the grapes without burning out acidity and flavor.

Woods slowly built the brand over the years. In 1981 he hired John Hawley, an honors graduate of U.C. Davis, as winemaker. In 1988 Woods sold the winery for a reported $40 million to the Canadian spirits firm Hiram Walker, whose wine division is run by veteran wine man Terrence Clancy.

Clancy is a piece of work. If his view of wine events often runs contra to accepted

When you are barrel fermenting more than 100,000 cases of Chardonnay, you need thousands of 60-gallon French oak barrels, which is exactly what you see here in the main warehouse, stacked six high on metal frames that a forklift can easily move.

thinking, it's because he has experience and confidence enough to trust his own instincts. Take his background. Formal education: BS in political science (Occidental College), MA in English literature (San Francisco State). Real education: Gallo (sales), Peace Corps (Micronesia), Seagrams and Somerset (president of San Martin when it enjoyed its high point of success).

After a short consulting stint, Clancy was hired in 1980 by Hiram Walker to head their Acquisitions and Expansions division. The following year, he convinced Walker to purchase Callaway Vineyards & Winery in Temecula

A tank or barrel sample of Sauvignon Blanc is ready for the lab, where it will be analyzed chemically and organoleptically — which is to say, tasted to see how it's coming along.

(midway between San Diego and Los Angeles). By focusing on what the region does best, Callaway became known for its non-oak-aged Chardonnay, "Calla-lees."

When Clos Du Bois was acquired, much was made of the fact that Hiram Walker had spent all that money on a label without a winery. Clos du Bois was operating out of leased facilities, and had not yet begun construction on its present winery. "In a sense, that was true," laughs Clancy. "What you buy first is a name. And if that name, that good reputation is supported by good vineyards and a sound staff, then you've got something of value. And we got the 590 acres of Alexander Valley vineyards that made the Clos du Bois name great, and the staff that made it work!

"The job then was to take what we had been given and make wines that were better. And to do a better job at marketing. And to improve our sales. You see, the quality of the product is emulated by the quality of the people . . . and vice versa. The goal, essentially, is not to stand still."

Though Clancy made his mark with Callway by eliminating red wines ("the region is better suited to whites"), he never considered trimming Clos du Bois' list. "The simple reason is that we have people capable of making a number of high quality wines," says Clancy.

"You know the rule: If it works, don't tinker with it.

"We did eliminate the River Oaks label, but only because we're not interested in selling low-end wines. We'll spend a little more time on our Reserve wines, and add a Reserve Merlot." The Merlots have long been quality performers at Clos du Bois, powerful wines that remain beautifully proportioned with anise, black currant, and peppermint fruit.

In volume, the Merlot is second only to the popular Barrel Fermented Chardonnay, a fresh, accessible wine, with buttery texture and inviting clove fruit. Indeed, the Chardonnay accounts for nearly half of the winery's 200,000-case annual production. Three other Chardonnays — all in the $20 price range — are made in much smaller lots. The "Flintwood" Chardonnay is made in a lean, austere style.

The "Calcaire" Chardonnay, named for the calcareous soils of its Alexander Valley origin, is rich with vanillin oakiness, and full of lemon and clove fruit. As if that trio were not enough to confuse, there's also a "Winemaker's Reserve" Chardonnay, made from the best lots from the best Sonoma County locations, aiming for voluptuousness.

Clos du Bois also makes Sauvignon Blanc (oily grass and figs, with solid acidity), Gewurztraminer (floral and fleshy with nutmeg spice and apple fruit), Pinot Noir, and a variety of Cabernets. The Cabernet pattern mirrors that of Chardonnay: one that's accessible, one vineyard-designated (Briarcrest), one a Bordeaux-styled blend (Marlstone), and a Winemaker's Reserve.

If there is any significant change to be found in Hiram Walker's acquisition of Clos du Bois, it would have to be the attitude that filters out from Clancy's office. On his desk is the sign, "A Poor Workman Blames His Tools."

"I don't believe in centralized management," says Clancy firmly. "You hire the best people you can afford, agree on what the goals are, then let

The old downtown winery is nothing more than a rented, sheet-metal structure, which was plenty good enough to produce dozens of award-winning wines. The early '90s saw the erection of a new winery for Clos Du Bois, in the middle of the Alexander Valley.

them do their jobs — keeping in constant contact on a conversational level. We have to be concerned with solving the problem — not with titles, bonuses, and new cars. Curiosity and love is how great things are accomplished. I don't think you can work effectively in the wine business and not be a romanticist."

Romantic that he is, Clancy is also pragmatic enough to keep his finger on the pulse of the marketplace. "The last place a winery president should be is in the winery!" he states emphatically. "I have to be in the marketplace, asking the right questions of the right people. There's no business in America more competitive than wine in terms of units of product versus per capita consumption . . . in which the U.S. is behind Poland! If that doesn't get you going, then nothing will!"

Clancy is always on the go. In 1989 Walker acquired the Whitbread share of the 460-acre Atlas Peak Vineyards (Napa Valley), and the following year took a three-year option to buy William Hill (also Napa Valley). "Hill is a brilliant operation, and Atlas Peak is one of the most exciting vineyards in California history," says Clancy before trundling off to another meeting, another challenge. Which only means that Clos du Bois and its sister wineries are in excellent hands. *RPH*

Gondolas full of vine-ripened Chardonnay grapes line up to be crushed and stemmed, and then fermented in individual, 60-gallon French oak barrels. Clos Du Bois does Chardonnay the hard way, but it pays off in wines that are full of flavor — and fairly priced.

One of the oldest sayings in the wine business is that "It takes a lot of beer to make fine wine." Most of that beer is consumed during the harvest season, when 18-hour days fill the six or eight weeks of crush season.

B. R. COHN WINERY

Bruce Cohn didn't have fine wine in mind when he bought a Sonoma Valley ranch in 1974. "I just wanted to raise my kids in a better atmosphere than the big city," says Cohn. By the time he began looking for a more rural life, Cohn was already the successful manager of the Doobie Brothers rock band. But life on the road, living out of a suitcase, had become anathema to Cohn, and he had seen too much of drug use and other big-city vices to want to remain. The move back to the land was natural for Cohn. He was reared here. "I milked goats in Forestville as a kid, and later in the city I missed the rural life."

Finding the right property wasn't easy. There was a lot of land available in Sonoma County at the time, but little of it appealed to him. One spot that looked promising was a parcel of land up Sonoma Highway in Kenwood, land later to become Chateau St. Jean. But the owner wanted to keep a piece of land for himself in the grapevines, planning to build a home on it one day. "I didn't want to look out my window and see his house," says Bruce.

Down the road, south of Glen Ellen, in the Sonoma Mountain foothills, there was a place that felt right. It had an old home on it, built in 1920, with large rooms and lots of windows

After Bruce Cohn decided to open a winery, he had to give it a name. One of his first thoughts was Olive Hill, because of the great number of mature olive trees that line the driveway to his house. When Cohn decided to name the winery after himself, he paid homage to the trees by adorning his wine label with a drawing of their foliage and fruit.

that looked out onto the sloping hillside. Also, the house was set well back from the road and its noise. The 55-acre ranch sloped southeast and had rich soil that was well-drained, perfect for wine grapes. And there was a huge grove of olive trees for shade. A historic point of interest: the ranch's natural spring had been a stagecoach watering hole on the route from Santa Rosa to Sonoma.

Bruce bought the property in 1974, becoming only the third owner of the land since the Spanish Land Grant era. Because much of his vineyard land faces south and is protected from winds by the western hills, it is

The B.R. Cohn Winery began producing wine even before the winery building itself was completed. Cohn's stainless-steel fermenting tanks sat out on a concrete pad while the old dairy barn on the property was converted into a modern winery.

much warmer than neighbors' vineyards on either side. Also, a higher elevation makes the property virtually free of frost.

"This is kind of a banana belt," says Cohn, who didn't realize at first how warm the property was. In the early years, the fruit from his Cabernet vineyard, planted in 1968, was sold to wineries such as Gundlach-Bundschu, Veedercrest, Sebastiani, Kenwood, and Gallo. Soon the demand for his grapes grew and Bruce toyed with making his own wines. He figured he could convert a dairy barn next to the house into a winery.

His first experiments proved that his Cabernet Sauvignon did, indeed, ripen better than his neighbors', so he added more Cabernet vines, bonded a winery, and called it B.R. Cohn.

The first B.R. Cohn wines were made in 1984, by winemaker Helen Turley. The Chardonnay and Cabernet Sauvignon were well-received. By 1985, however, it was clear that Cohn's top wine would be Cabernet. His version ranked as one of the best Cabernets in the area.

Turley left in 1987 and John Speed replaced her. His first Cabernets were even more impressive than those that came before. Cohn Cabernets are full-bodied, dense, and packed with a delicately roasted character from the French oak barrels in which they age. *DB*

Bruce Cohn has thought of harvesting the olives from the mature olive trees, and making olive oil. However, the trees were not originally grown for produce; they were grown for shade and ambience, "and getting up there on ladders to harvest the olives would be time-consuming and very expensive," he says.

H. COTURRI AND SONS

In one sense, the Coturri boys are traditionalists, making big, hearty wines — natural yeasts, no filtering, no fining — from fully ripe fruit. In another, they are iconoclasts, taking on the federal government over warning labels.

"In 1986, the Bureau of Alcohol, Tobacco, and Firearms said that all wines had to carry a sulfite warning label, beginning in 1987," ruminates slender Tony the winemaker. "But we told them, 'Hey, our wines don't have any sulfites.' They said, 'All wines have sulfites. You can't make wine without sulfites.' We said, 'We do.'"

So, the Coturri boys sent seven samples off to the Treasury Department's lab for anaylsis. "They say you have to have less than 350 milligrams of sulphur dioxide per liter to be excused from the warning label," says Tony with a sly, knowing chuckle. "Five of our samples had none at all, one tested at one milligram, another at two. The last came from our gnarliest mountain vineyard, and we figured it must have been the yeast!"

Harry Coturri, who ran a janitorial service in San Francisco until his retirement, acquired a summer home on the slopes of Sonoma Mountain high above the Sonoma Valley in 1963. A penchant for home winemaking convinced Harry and sons, Phil and Tony — who had moved into the summer home in the late '60s — to turn pro in 1979, along with partner Dan Parun.

Tony, who makes the wines, is a University of San Francisco graduate who taught school for five years, working with learning-disabled kids. Phil, who tends the vines, is the poet of the family. He also manages other vineyards to keep the partners' tiny, 3,000-case operation afloat.

"Hillside farming is, by definition, labor intensive," says the burly Phil, who favors Greatful Dead T-shirts. "In a hillside situation, you have to be able to balance the vine.

You can see the thickness, the density, and the viscosity of Coturri red wines in the glass. They are opaque and have a blackness rarely seen. This comes from being grown in mountain vineyards and from processing techniques that aim for intensity and power.

The wine cellar, filled with oak barrels, is the traditional shot for most wineries, but a lot of winemaking takes place in the vineyard, where every decision has an effect on wine quality.

There's a symmetry to a 'chalice-formed' vine that leads to balanced fruit. And balanced fruit is the first and most important step toward balanced wines."

If the discussion sounds as if it might slip into existentialist theory at any moment, that's hardly surprising. Though Phil Coturri claims to be an old-fashioned traditionalist, his penchant for writing poetry (his English degree from Sonoma State was based on "Beat" poetry) and his philosophical pronouncements add a different dimension altogether.

"I'm also against metal grape stakes. We only use split redwood stakes that we drive in by hand. If I have to look at grape stakes half the year — when the vines are dormant — I'd much rather look at wood than metal. I don't suppose the grapes grow any better with wooden stakes, but I do think they're happier."

The Coturri wines are not meant to be quaffing wines, but rather are healthy beasts that require attention (they need to be decanted) and time (they need air to fully open up).

As Tony Coturri remonstrates, "You don't just open the bottle, pour a glass and toss it down the hatch. That's like cutting off an unopened rosebud and keeping it in a vase until the color starts to show, then throwing it away!" *RPH*

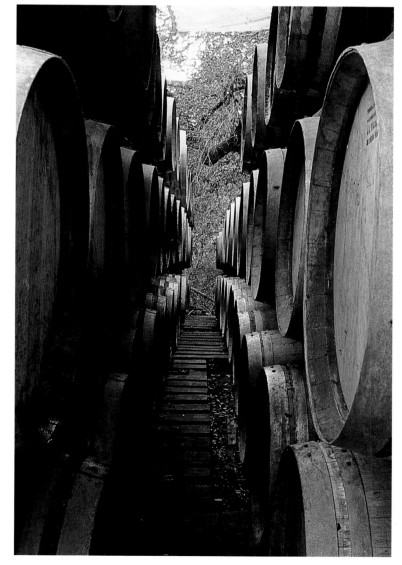

Oak barrels are a must at Coturri, where Zinfandel accounts for more than half the winery's production. Some Cabernet and Pinot Noir are made, and from an old "mixed" vineyard the Coturris make a red blend called Albarrello, the Italian term for low pruned vines.

DEHLINGER WINERY

Dehlinger and many wineries that make great Pinot Noir extract the color and flavor from the skins by using the old-fashioned method of punching down the "cap" of skins that forms at the top of the fermenting tank. They use a long stick with a flat plate at the bottom to submerge the skins many times a day.

When Tom Dehlinger chose the Forestville area of Sonoma County in which to plant his vineyard in 1975, he knew the region had the potential to turn out top-flight Pinot Noirs and Chardonnays. But he didn't know that it would take a decade of trial and error to analyze the challenge properly, let alone meet it.

In this remote region there are few wineries, so there is no "book," no collective experience a winemaker can draw on for answers. Progress is made by experimentation in the vineyard, which takes a long time — a decade just to see what happens after the wine has been in the bottle a while.

In the late 1980s Dehlinger saw that the blending decisions he made in the winery could be refined by identifying the different

quality levels of the grapes in his vineyard. He then decided to use only grapes off his own 50-acre property. This permits him to track the wine, vine by vine.

So he and vineyard manager Marty Hedlund mapped out areas of the vineyard that produced different flavors and aromas. By 1990, the vineyard map had been gerrymandered so much you'd have thought it was drawn by a two-year-old with a broken Etch-a-Sketch.

"Up here we get more intense flavors," explains Dehlinger as he walks to the top of one of the sloping vineyards. Here the soil is redder and thinner than the darker brown, sandy loam lower down in the vineyard. "So we are using different vine-training methods to get more uniform growth."

Four different regions were identified and the vines color-coded. Then all the vines in one area were retrained to grow in a different manner to maximize quality.

"Pinot Noir is the greatest intellectual challenge," says Dehlinger. His style of Pinot Noir has evolved from the early years toward more depth and richness. To keep the oak flavors in check, Dehlinger uses mostly puncheons (130 gallons each, not the common 60-gallon casks).

The Chardonnay here also has changed, from lean and delicate to a richer style. The wine still retains the high acidity so typical of the western Russian River area.

It is this attribute that sets Russian River grapes apart from those of the other growing regions nearby. Dehlinger points out that even in the hottest days of the summer, the nighttime temperatures here are in the 40s, retaining the naturally high acidity.

On the rolling hills here, Dehlinger also makes Cabernet Sauvignon, which is fairly hard when released, but ages beautifully. Pinot Noir is his main focus, however. One of the experiments Dehlinger and assistant winemaker Fred Scherrer have adopted is a modified "whole cluster" method of fermentation, in which the grapes are not crushed as much as they are pulled off the stalks whole and dumped into a fermenter with juice to begin the fermentation. The fruitiness of the wine is thus retained and accented. However, the depth of the wine comes from the flavor development that occurs on the vine rather than through any artificial methods of gaining extract in the winery. *DB*

Tom Dehlinger, a quiet-spoken man, has developed a reputation locally for some of the best wines made in the county, but because of his reticence the wines get little nationwide publicity. Still, the connoisseur set is getting the word that Dehlinger Pinot Noir, in particular, is a prize worth seeking out.

DE LOACH VINEYARDS

De Loach is one of many California wineries that use drain tanks for grapes before fermentation. The grapes are dropped into the tanks and slide down a funnel-shaped cone, where they drain through a screen before being dropped into the grape crusher below.

The Russian River area in western Sonoma County is one of the world's coolest winegrowing regions. Its slowly ripening grapes can produce superb wines.

It is to this region that Cecil and Christine De Loach chose to retire. Their property is picturesque: its ancient, gnarled vines had been planted in 1905 by Italo Barbieri, 22 acres of vineyard that Cecil says were "billed as Zinfandel," though it unquestionably had small amounts of Petite Sirah, Barbera, and Mataro, among other Italianate varieties, growing here and there.

The De Loach family moved to the property in 1971 and son Michael and his wife, Rachel, helped to plant additional acreage. Cecil wanted to sell grapes and enjoy his semiretirement, following a hectic career as a San Francisco fireman.

The plan to swap the city for an agrarian lifestyle in this quiet region northwest of Santa Rosa had one fatal flaw: winemaking can become addictive, as Cecil soon found out.

He admits that when he made a few gallons of homemade Zinfandel in 1975, "it was probably for reasons of ego." But then, objectively (he still thinks), he felt his Zinfandel "tasted better than some of the Zinfandels from the wineries I was selling my grapes to. Also, it seemed like a swell way to make a living."

In 1979, De Loach went commercial. "We went to a bank and got a loan and built a modern winery, and that year we made Gewurztraminer, Pinot Noir, and White Zinfandel," he says.

At the time there were only four White Zinfandels on the market, De Loach recalls, and his, made from high-quality Russian River fruit, turned out to be one of the best in the state. It

The De Loach winery tasting room, with its attractive art-filled foyer and a cupola for a crown, is approached through a sunny courtyard. There, visitors might see the winery's cats, Pinot and Winkie, sunning themselves. And they'll not be able to miss Pookie, the big white dog who greets visitors warmly and doesn't mind nibbling lunch scraps.

has remained so. De Loach reached production of 27,000 cases a year of White Zinfandel; production stopped when he knew he'd have to compromise quality.

In 1981, Randy Ullom was named associate winemaker and he slowly made changes in the wines. The Gewurztraminer became nearly dry; the Chardonnay became broader, richer, almost sweet in the finish; the Pinot Noir increased in elegance; the Sauvignon Blanc and Fume Blanc (similar wines) improved to the point where, in the latter 1980s, De Loach was winning plaudits for them to equal those for his Chardonnay. In 1990 Ullom was promoted to winemaker and Cecil became wine master.

De Loach's top wines are released with the designation OFS. De Loach says it stands for Our Finest Selection, though staff members smile and say there is a hidden meaning for the letters. The best wine in the line is probably the exciting Zinfandel, made from the old "Italian field blend" of Zinfandel with tiny amounts of the other grapes tossed in for spice and complexity.

Total production at De Loach leveled off at 100,000 cases in the early 1990s. The De Loaches now own 278 acres of land, including a ranch in Healdsburg.

One of the secrets to De Loach's excellent wines is the coolness of the region. Morning and evening fog blankets the low-lying vineyards most months of the year, and keeps the grapes on the vine longer than just about any growing region in the United States. *DB*

Cecil De Loach relies on grapes from the cool west Russian River growing region for his estate-bottled wines, but as production has grown to 80,000 cases, he has looked to his property in Healdsburg for additional tonnage.

DE LORIMIER WINERY

Al de Lorimier moved his family to the remote Alexander Valley to provide a more rural setting than the streets of San Francisco, where he was a world-famed surgeon. Eventually, the prunes growing on the 64-acre property were converted to grapes.

Al de Lorimier and his family lived in the fog belt in San Francisco, and the kids never really knew what summer was all about.

"We wanted to have a place where we could go swimming in the summer," says Sally de Lorimier. Her father was a world-renowned pediatric surgeon at University of California Medical Center in San Francisco, and "he was a workaholic, so we needed a place where he could go to relax, but where he could putter around, and farming seemed like a good thing."

It was 1974, before the Alexander Valley was known for fine wine. The de Lorimiers bought a ten-acre prune orchard off Highway 128. A few vines were planted on the parcel, but de Lorimier's only interest in grapes was the end product: he liked wine with his meals.

De Lorimier began to chat with neighbor Henry Dick, who said his prunes hadn't been planted correctly. Dick advised de Lorimier to plant Chardonnay. It wasn't an idle remark: Dick's Belle Terre Ranch has since become world famous as the source of Chardonnay for Chateau St. Jean's award-winning wines.

"Dad liked the Bordeaux style of wine and he didn't see many of them being made around here," says Sally. So, in 1985, the de Lorimier Winery was built. Today, de Lorimier is at the forefront of the so-called Meritage wines, blends of traditional Bordeaux varieties, both white and red.

Vineyard manager Alex Vyborny added an array of Chardonnay clones to the de Lorimiers' 64 acres here. Though de Lorimier Chardonnay is made entirely from grapes of that variety, the winery blends the various clonal selections into a wine called Prism. Winemaker Dennis Hill set

The first vintage of de Lorimier's proprietarily named wines was 1986, and some 5,000 cases were produced. The names included Spectrum (a Sauvignon Blanc/Semillon blend), Lace (a dessert-styled Sauvignon Blanc), and Prism (made entirely from Chardonnay).

the style. When he left to join Mill Creek Winery, former Belvedere winemaker Don Frazer made the Chardonnay even more complex.

Meanwhile, the rest of the wines focused on the blending of the Bordeaux varieties. These estate-bottled wines differ from vintage to vintage. To give the wines distinctiveness, Hill and Frazer crafted each wine not to maintain rigidly a house style, but to maximize the quality that the grapes yielded from year to year, taking advantage of the range of soils found on the de Lorimier ranch.

The prototype white-Bordeaux blend is a Graves-style wine called Spectrum, a blend of Sauvignon Blanc and Semillon, aged in oak barrels to achieve rich flavors offsetting the crispness of the varieties. The classic herbal spice of the varieties is evident.

Mosaic, on the other hand, is a Cabernet-Sauvignon-based wine that has Merlot and Cabernet Franc added for complexity. The Cabernet Sauvignon can vary in the final blend between 50 and 90 percent. Because the final blend is not assembled until right before bottling, "these wines usually take a while before the flavors settle out," says Sally. Because of that, the winery waits a full four years before releasing the red wine. The winery also makes a late-harvest Sauvignon Blanc called Lace.

The winery is a true family project. Al's wife, Sandy, has responsibility for administration and accounting. Daughter Sally handles sales and marketing. DB

After an initial purchase of ten acres, de Lorimier added 54 more acres and planted Merlot and Cabernet France to blend into the Cabernet Sauvignon for his Mosaic, a red wine patterned after the great wines of Bordeaux.

DOMAINE MICHEL

Even though the winery is located technically in Healdsburg, a relatively warm region, Domaine Michel is on the western flank of a ridge in the northern reaches of the area, where fog blankets the rolling slopes until well into the morning. Thus the grapes ripen slower here than at neighboring ranches.

The idea was a good one. Jean-Jacques Michel would, like his friend Tom Jordan, acquire premium vineyard land and build a winery in California's north coast region, where the grapes ripened sufficiently to make great wine.

Michel, a Swiss entrepreneur who lived in Geneva, bought 100 acres on the western slopes of Sonoma County north of Healdsburg, east-facing land in the Dry Creek area. He dubbed the place Domaine Michel. At about the time Jordan was releasing its first Cabernet Sauvignon in 1979, Michel began planting the vineyard here. More acreage was planted in 1980, and then a winery design, emulating a Mediterranean villa, was conceived. The large courtyard featured a long reflecting pool. It was a building offering hospitality and gra-

cious living, in which winery personnel could host retailers, wholesalers, and members of the press.

When the winery was finished in early 1986, some $10 million had been spent on the project, and the structure at the heart of it was a replica of an authentic mission. Hand-made tiles lined the floors; hand-carved beams led up to a bell cloister. The handsome

residential quarters designed in a European fashion were for Michel on his frequent stays in the villa.

To ensure that Domaine Michel would be a superior property, nothing was left to chance. Michel was joined by his long-time business associate and friend, Ridge Bullock (who has since become a partner and president of the winery). They hired as general manager Michael Rowan, who had guided the fortunes of Jordan before, and lured Phil Baxter away from his longtime position as wine-maker at Rutherford Hill Winery in the Napa Valley to take over winemaking chores. Michel designed a wine label that was subtly elegant, featuring pastel and metallic colors and a balance as the symbol of the winery. (Michel is an attorney as well as an investment banker.)

To make certain Domaine Michel's products were viewed in only the best light, Michel sold anything less than top-notch under a different label. For example, the first Cabernet Sauvignon — the 1983, which had been crushed and fermented at Jordan — was not released as a Domaine Michel wine, but rather as a "second label" wine, La Marjolaine. It was very good wine, but not good enough to be a Domaine Michel wine. A marketing plan was drawn up, housed in an inch-thick book with contingency plans for every eventuality. Nothing was left to chance.

In 1986, with the building completed and wine in the tanks from the 1983 harvest and beyond, all was in readiness for the introduction of California's latest chic wine property. And Domaine Michel made an impressive debut. Valets were hired to park cars. Candles ringed the large reflecting pool and floated in the water; tables were set around the inside overhang of the villa; and a sumptuous, Spanish-style feast was served to some 250 guests. Among them were members of San Francisco's and Geneva's high society, the latter flown in for the event by Jean-Jacques. Also in attendance were Andre and Dorothy Tchelistcheff,

The attractive villa built as the part-time home of the founder, Jean-Jacques Michel, features a large courtyard. Under the eaves of the roof covering the inner courtyard, guests are sheltered from the cooling winds.

The bell cloister atop Domaine Michel's main building overlooks the winery's rolling hillside vineyards. Slower-then-anticipated sales gave consumers a bonus: wines that have a bit more bottle age than competing wines.

he the dean of California winemakers and consultant to Domaine Michel, as well as a dozen other wine dignitaries, including Margrit and Robert Mondavi.

Surely this would be another jewel in California's wine crown as the state made its mark among the great winemaking countries of the world.

Yet curiously, in the months following the party, it became clear that something was missing. It was public image, or rather a lack of it. To be sure, the opening-night party had made the newspapers, but the stories were on the society page and nothing was written about the wine.

One noticeable example of this failure to capture the public's fancy was in the winery's invisibility. As visitors to the Dry Creek area crossed over Lambert Bridge and approached West Dry Creek Road, they encountered a sign listing the wineries on either side. Domaine Michel was not on that sign. Nor was there any indication, at the entrance to Wine Creek Road, that the winery was at the end of the mile-long street. Instead, the only sign read, "No outlet." Domaine Michel's permit precluded public tastings and only allowed tours by appointment.

With no public image, and with the number of wineries in the state growing to more

The entrance to the barrel cellar at Domaine Michel is a sight seen rarely èxcept in the finest chateaux in the world. The twin oak doors lead to a cool room filled with upright oak tanks, with the small barrels in recesses. The highly shined floor is exceptional in wineries because they're so hard to keep clean.

than 800 (from 300 when Domaine Michel was being planned), Domaine Michel became just another California winery with nice wines to sell. The jet-set debut had quickly been forgotten.

Before long, Baxter left, returning to the Napa Valley. (He ended up at Round Hill.) Fred Payne from Girard Winery was hired to replace him, and a new era began in 1989.

By 1990 the wines were better than ever, but sales had slowed and the winery was at least 18 months behind in releasing its wines to the market. Of course, this gave the consumer the added benefit of seeing the wines with more bottle age, but it was clear that the

Winemaker Fred Payne joined Domaine Michel in 1989 and changed the style of winemaking slightly. He uses fruit from this rolling hillside vineyard to make a lean and delicate Chardonnay that ages nicely, and Cabernet from an adjoining plot to make a wine not unlike Jordan's, but with a bit more concentration.

winery was still lagging in public image.

The wines, however, were lovely — notably the Chardonnays, which offered wonderful complexity and richness. The 1986 Chardonnay, for example, had aged beautifully and was a grand example of cool-climate wine growing, with a delicate spice character interplaying with citrus and a faint onionskin element. Payne points out that "this is a very cool area, considering it's Healdsburg. We get cooling winds in the afternoons. Also, the vineyards are planted on good soil, with good drainage."

The Cabernet Sauvignons also show the cooler influence, with a lovely herbal note, but the overriding elements in the wines from the 1988 vintage forward were chocolate, sandalwood, and spice characters wrapped around a black-cherry fruit base.

At the start, Michel said he was dedicated to creating a California winery of "Premier Cru" status, and from his 50 acres of vineyard land, he clearly has the potential for greatness.

Evidence of that is in a Reserve Cabernet that Payne began assembling after the harvest of 1988. The wine, aged in French oak barrels, is what Payne hopes will spark the long-delayed birth of Domaine Michel as a great California producer. *DB*

The vines at Domaine Michel are located in an area west of Healdsburg, in the Dry Creek area, which is normally thought of as a warmer region. But the vines here are planted in a little microclimate that is cooler than many of the neighboring vineyards.

DOMAINE ST. GEORGE WINERY

Driving up Grant Avenue you pass plum trees, vineyards, and an old, ramshackle prune drier before the road narrows and rises. A set of iron gates announces Domaine St. George Winery, formerly known as Cambiaso.

The winery was founded by Giovanni and Maria Cambiaso, at the Repeal of Prohibition in 1934, on land that had been homesteaded in 1852. Indeed, the family home, now winery offices, is said to have been built then. Giovanni learned his winemaking in Italy, then came to California in 1910. He bought the Healdsburg property in 1922, cleared the land

of countless rocks, and planted 34 acres to vines in 1928, initially selling fruit to home winemakers. Until Repeal.

Eventually, son Joe and daughters Rita and Theresa operated Cambiaso. Then, in 1973, the winery was sold for nearly a million dollars to the Four Seas Investment Corporation, whose major investor, Thailand's Supasit Mahaguna, was a certified wine nut — to the point of trying to grow grapes in his humid homeland.

Mahaguna's nephew, Somchai Likit-prakong, came to Sonoma to assume overall management responsibilities. Together with winemaker Bob Fredson — whose family has

Gnarled old vines, most planted in the late 1920s, cling to the thin, rocky soil on the hilltop site of Domaine St. George, which was originally founded in 1934 by Giovanni and Maria Cambiaso, as the Cambiaso Winery.

been growing grapes and making wine for generations in Sonoma County — he has turned the tiny, rustic Cambiaso into Domaine St. George, a major player in the category of "fighting varietals" — inexpensive wines that are still varietally labeled.

When Likitprakong came to Cambiaso with his business degree from the New York Institute of Technology, he was faced with a redwood-framed, corrugated-tin winery with old equipment and musty redwood tanks. As the winery's administrator, Likitprakong put $2 million into upgrading it.

Since then, a forest of oak barrels and

Huge stainless-steel fermenting tanks have gradually replaced old redwood upright tanks as Domaine St. George shifts from hearty old Italian-styled wines to more modern offerings, like the unusual Blush Chardonnay.

uprights has been put in place to ferment and age wines and the winery name has been changed to create a wholly new image. Dennis Canning, then president of Cannon Wines, which markets Domaine St. George, came up with the 1986 name change — the idea was to have something vaguely French-sounding and a coat of arms for the label — and the notion to price the wines aggressively. As a result, Domaine St. George has undergone tremendous growth, going from less than 15,000 cases in 1985 to nearly 350,000 cases in 1990.

Domaine St. George made big waves in 1990 with Blush Chardonnay, introduced with full-page ads in *The Wine Spectator.* "People are looking for other things than Chard, Cab, and White Zin," suggests general manager Bill Harper.

Harper gives full credit to winemaker Bob Fredson, who once had a crow named Jethro that would perch on his shoulder while he drove a vineyard tractor. "Bob knows the vineyards and the growers. He's a good, down-to-earth guy who knows how to merge winemaking theory with winemaking reality. And when the crunch comes, like during a rainy harvest, he knows which vineyards can hang a little longer and which have to come in right now. Because he grew up with it, he has a feel for it that's instinctive. I never had that as a winemaker, so I know how valuable it is." *RPH*

Winemaker Bob Fredson comes from a family that has been growing grapes and making wine in Sonoma County for many generations. He's a down-to-earth man who knows how to merge winemaking theory with winemaking reality, and has helped to make Domaine St. George a major player in the category of "fighting varietals."

DRY CREEK VINEYARD

Some time in the mid-1950s, during one of the numerous wine tastings that David Stare threw for friends and fellow students back on the east coast, it became obvious to Stare that he was an engineering student for reasons not entirely clear to him. That's because he loved wine a lot more than engineering.

And this was no ordinary engineering student. He was a bright light at one of the top engineering schools in the world, Massachusetts Institute of Technology; yet there he was -- more interested in growing grapes and making wine. He even went so far as to try his hand at it with grapes grown in Maryland, at Philip Wagner's Boordy Vineyards. The results were better used as salad dressing than for sipping, he acknowledges today.

Nonplussed, through the 1960s Stare con-

tinued his quest to make fine wine, going so far as to spend time in 1967 making friends with German winemakers while on a business trip in Germany for an American company. That contact merely reinforced his desire to make great wine.

In 1972, Stare moved to California. He bought land and founded Dry Creek Vineyard in an area called, not surprisingly, the Dry Creek Valley. Dry Creek actually has some water in it, and the location Stare chose had been the site of a 40-year-old vineyard. But it was an area that didn't have many wineries in it.

Reflecting on his time in the industry, Stare says, "When I started the winery, in the early to mid-1970s, it was an era when most people entering the wine business had a little bit of money and they were wine freaks. Since the

The Dry Creek tasting room used to be out behind the winery. It was moved to the front in a major re-design in the late 1980s, and today offers visitors a broad lawn on which to picnic during the warmer months.

Dry Creek was started on a shoestring in the early 1970s. Today it's a thriving winery whose national marketing director has watched every step of its development: the founder's daughter, Kim Stare Wallace.

early 1980s, most people entering the wine business had made a ton of money doing something else and were getting in for the lifestyle. Well, I see nothing wrong with that, but I'm proud of the fact that I started the winery on a shoestring and we've been successful.

The growing region is a modest-sized appellation, from the warm Alexander Valley to the north, racing down the western Sonoma County slopes to the cooler Russian River Valley in the southwest. It is cooler by far than the Alexander Valley, but plenty warm enough to grow certain varieties that ripen only irregularly in the Russian River Valley.

Stare chose to locate here in part because of his appreciation of the cool-climate white wines of the Loire Valley, notably Sauvignon Blanc and Chenin Blanc. And true to his aims, his first wines were received by the public with excitement. Today those same varieties represent prototype winemaking for others to learn from.

The first attempt with Sauvignon Blanc -- which Stare called Fume Blanc, following Robert Mondavi's lead and honoring the Loire wines called Blanc Fumé -- turned out spectacularly. And in subsequent years, the wine

showed it could be called the prototype of California's "grassy" style of Sauvignon Blanc.

Stare's Fume Blanc isn't for novices. Generally, first-time wine lovers coming upon a Dry Creek Fume Blanc are a bit confused by its green-leading aromas, aromas that hint at

David Stare, a former engineer, has a passion for sailing, which answers one of the questions most often asked: why are there boats on the Dry Creek labels? He is also a fan of railroad travel, and once took his entire staff 300 miles south by train for dinner.

poblano chili peppers, tarragon, lime, and cilantro.

Stare says the aged versions of his Fume Blanc can smell and taste like an Italian deli; I prefer to call some of the aromas more chili pepper, hay and fresh asparagus in scent, with a creaminess unlike wines of the Loire. The wine, aged in small French oak barrels for a short time, is a good example of how California can out-do the French.

The other classic wine that Stare produces is an California original, a Zinfandel with enough depth and richness to have inspired a lot of imitators. The style isn't particularly brilliant. It simply takes superior, ripe, Dry Creek Valley grapes, which exude a certain jammy quality about them, and ages the resulting wine in barrels for a year to soften the edges. The raspberry jam aroma of this wine often is completed with a faint anise, dill and toast quality. It is a wine of immense joy when matched with barbecued food.

In addition to Fume Blanc, Zinfandel, and Dry Chenin Blanc, Dry Creek makes an amply flavored Cabernet Sauvignon, but it has discarded from its line Petite Sirah, on old favorite. (If you should see an old bottle lurking in the dusty recesses of a wineshop, however, it might not be a bad buy; the wines aged well.)

Dry Creek also makes a line of estate-bottled reserve wines from Chardonnay as well as a Meritage wine blended in the Bordeaux manner from Cabernet Sauvignon and Merlot. Starting with the 1990 harvest, Dry Creek will also make a white Meritage wine from Sauvignon Blanc and Semillon grapes, aged in barrels for complexity.

Dry Creek's early fame grew, in part because few in Sonoma County were doing what Davids Stare was doing. Soon annual production grew to more than 100,000 cases. Today more than a third of the wine made here is estate-bottled, off the 100 acres of grapes surrounding the winery. A portion of the Chardonnay fruit used by Stare for his two Chardonnays comes from the famed Robert Young Vineyard in Alexander Valley, a connection that goes back to Stare's first vintage. The balance of the wine Stare makes is from grapes of local growers -- including one of the best in the appellation, Lou Preston up the road.

For Dry Creek's first few years, Stare was the winemaker Then, as marketing became a critical task, he hired specialists to handle the winemaking chores. Through the 1980s, Larry Levin handled the job with brilliance, making subtle changes to improve the other wines in the line.

For example, at one time Dry Creek made a stunning Dry Chenin Blanc produced largely from fruit bought from the Clarksburg area of the state, near the Stockton Delta. Yet excellent quality fruit from local vineyards could also make a great Chenin Blanc, Levin thought; so he slowly reduced his dependence on Clarksburg fruit and eventually switched completely to Dry Creek fruit. The wine improved annually and today is

Dry Creek chose this dramatic angular-cut label to adorn its Meritage red wine, a premium blended wine made from the traditional Bordeaux varieties that include Cabernet Sauvignon, Merlot, and Cabernet Franc.

PRODUCED & BOTTLED BY DRY CREEK VINEYARD, INC. HEALDSBURG, SONOMA COUNTY, CA USA • ALC 13.4% BY VOL

1986

meritage

DRY CREEK VINEYARD™

D R Y C R E E K V A L L E Y

RED TABLE WINE

Meritage is the name that has been chosen by top premium California wineries to designate their best wines made from traditional Bordeaux varieties. Our 1986 Meritage is a blend of 57% Cabernet Sauvignon, 30% Cabernet Franc and 13% Merlot. It is rich and full flavored, and although it is enjoyable now, you will be richly rewarded by aging it for up to 15 years. Our Meritage represents our best winemaking efforts. CONTAINS SULFITES.

another Dry Creek prototype.

Dave Stare, a humorous fellow, is a local political force and a teacher of wine marketing at Santa Rosa Junior College in addition to his Dry Creek activities. As the winery has grown, he has added key personnel who report to Gary Emmerich, the operations manager, who has been on board since the mid-1970s. And Stare has remained loyal to his staff over the years, through lean times and fat.

By the late 1980s, however, sales had become a major headache. After much discussion, Stare was able to lure his daughter, Kim Stare Wallace, back to the winery where she had grown up and puttered as a pre-teenager.

But the transition from the business world back to the winery was not an easy task for Kim. She had left after high school with plans for a career in the garment industry, and was by then working for a sportswear company.

"I had absolutely no desire to go to work for dad," admits Wallace. "But the company I had been with went out of business, and I began to talk to dad about going to work at the winery." She also admits that she didn't have a particularly fond memory of her earlier days at the winery, when she was a student at Healdsburg High School, working summers and weekends on the bottling line.

"One of the major things about coming

Perhaps no Sauvignon Blanc in California has a more defined image than the Fume Blanc from Dry Creek Vineyards. In recent years the wine has moved away from the its original, more grassy style, but it still retains the herbal and minty elements that its fans love, and the wine ages handsomely for a decade or more.

back here was, what was dad going to pay me? We argued and argued about it," she laughs, pointing out that while she was in the garment industry she was well-paid. Stare finally agreed to a schedule for his daughter that increased Kim's pay annually based on performance. Today Wallace is the national marketing director for a growing and respected winery. *DB*

Dry Creek Vineyard is a far lusher sight than its name suggests. The propery Stare bought to found the winery had actually been the site of a 40-year-old vineyard -- and Dry Creek actually has some water in it.

EAGLE RIDGE WINERY

Only one winery in the United States — and probably in the world — proudly markets a wine with microwave instructions on the back label. Only one winery has the audacity to advertise on the sign of an X-rated drive-in theater. Only one winery would have the courage to take out an ad that said, "Visit . . . and see the smallest dog in Sonoma County, Chichi."

"She's a chihuahua, and she weighs only two and a half pounds," says Barry Lawrence, the unconventional fellow whose winery, Eagle Ridge, is in Penngrove, "one half-inch north of Petaluma," as one of his ads proclaims.

Eagle Ridge Winery is the labor of love that Lawrence founded in 1982 on a hill overlooking the Petaluma Valley. The place has a striking view of the Sonoma Mountains in the background. Lawrence advertises it as "the largest winery in Penngrove" — ignoring the fact that it is the only winery in Penngrove — "but not the first." The first was founded in the 1870s by John Formschlag, a local vintner who lasted through the beginning of Prohibition.

Lawrence got into the business after taking a course at the German Wine Academy in 1978. He returned from the trip and thought about starting a winery, then realized that his

Located at the top of a small rise, Eagle Ridge specializes in white wines, including the rare Ehrenfelser, as well as a deeply concentrated Zinfandel made from grapes off 130-year-old vines growing in Amador County.

family already owned a property that might work. Hillview Ranch, an old dairy, had been operated by his grandfather, Louis Joerger, "the only person ever to blow up a Pacific Gas & Electric Co. dam," says Lawrence. "He was fighting for riparian rights." Lawrence's father, William, eventually took over, and ran the dairy until he retired in 1969.

Barry began to lay the plans in 1981 to open a winery at the site. The winery building, Sonoma County Historic Landmark No. 133, was built in the 1880s as the first commercial creamery in the North Bay counties of Sonoma and Marin. The old dairy was located on

Eagle Ridge Winery, the pet project of Barry Lawrence, is located in the family's former dairy in Penngrove, just east of Highway 101, making it one of the closest wineries for travelers driving north from San Francisco.

Goodwin Avenue. Lawrence unofficially renamed the road Goodwine; the county never formally adopted the name change, but Eagle Ridge correspondence and advertisements carry that name. The telephone number here is 664-WINE; the fax number is 795-VINE.

Promotion is Lawrence's love. When the late Sonomarin drive-in theater, which had shown only adult movies, was in its last months of operation, Lawrence rented out the tall billboard in front — facing Highway 101 — and put out an advertisement for his winery.

Lawrence's microwave-ready wine is called Sierra Jubilee. It's a red wine made from Zinfandel, Muscat, "and a blend of five secret spices," and it's made to be served hot.

"I discovered it while hunting in the mountains," says Lawrence, who also is a flight instructor. "I met a mountain man in Amador County who had this recipe for spiced red wine." One thing led to another and eventually Lawrence bought the recipe. "I used to tell people it cures insomnia and baldness," says Lawrence, winking.

He also claims to be the first winery in the United States to have planted the Ehrenfelser grape, a German cross between Riesling and Sylvaner. From a vineyard planted to Ehrenfelser in 1985, he and winemaker Kevin McGuire craft a stylish off-dry wine. *DB*

Sonoma County officials took a dim view of Lawrence's attempt to change the name of the street on which his winery is located from Goodwin to Goodwine, but he uses the name on his stationery and on his mailbox.

GARY FARRELL

Gary Farrell's first vintage as winemaker at Davis Bynum, in 1978, made an impact on the Pinot Noirs of the western Russian River. His 1978 David Bynum Pinot Noir won numerous medals and set the tone for the young man's future reputation.

One of the joys of watching wine develop in the bottle is the parallel joy of watching people's growing understanding of the region in which that wine's grapes were grown.

For example, in the early, developmental years of the Carneros region of the Napa and Sonoma valleys, winemakers experimented with a wide array of grape types, seeking the optimum combinations of grape growing varieties with regional soils and climates. Soon it became clear, from tasting young and old wines, that Chardonnay and Pinot Noir did better than Cabernet Sauvignon in cool regions.

A prime example is the Russian River Valley, along with its foremost proponent, Gary Farrell. The young man with the Midas touch

may know the Russian River's soil and climate better than anyone.

Farrell has been winemaker for Davis Bynum since 1978. His experience making Bynum wines from Russian River fruit led to development of his own superb wines: Gary created his own brand in 1982.

Russian River is not as well known as some of the other appellations in California, partly because it is so cool. Its greatness is rarely apparent when wines are released to market because of their naturally high acidity. But when they take on bottle bouquet, they can be sublime.

Farrell's greatest wines to date have been Pinot Noirs, which are ranked among California's best. Beginning with his first wines, Farrell has achieved great complexity of fruit, even though the wines may occasionally be lighter in tone and not quite as "rich" as some people prefer.

Rather than make wines of high alcohol and extract that offer fat, chocolaty tastes in their youth, Farrell prefers to make his wines' balance hinge on acidity, ensuring they will age well. The wines may be consumed young, though they are a bit lean when released. They reward unceasingly as they age.

Farrell and others (Williams Seylem, Stemmler, Rochioli, Belvedere, Iron Horse, Laurier, Dehlinger) have proven the Russian River is a great area for Pinot Noir. But only Farrell has made the same statement for a number of other varieties.

And here's where the 9,000-acre Russian River appellation confounds. Farrell, defying most of the odds, has made not only exceptional Chardonnay from grapes grown here (no surprise since the regions is one of the coolest in the state), but also marvelous Zinfandel, Sauvignon Blanc, and Cabernet Sauvignon, all varieties supposedly needing a warmer clime than this one.

Farrell carefully selects grapes from subregions where they ripen well. An unassuming fellow, Gary credits the growers, pointing out that all he does is ask for mature fruit. Yet his track record belies his modesty.

Russian River remains largely misunderstood, but Farrell is one of those capable of changing the region's reputation and stamping it as a multi-variety growing area. That's quite a trick for a fellow who doesn't even own a winery — Farrell makes all his wines at the Bynum facility. *DB*

Fall leaves and a bottle of Gary Farrell Pinot Noir — the perfect match. Farrell, one of the top producers of Pinot Noir in California, has an innate sense of style with the variety. His Russian River Pinot Noirs are always exciting and in great demand.

FERRARI-CARANO WINERY

A 1962 honors law graduate of the University of San Francisco, Don Carano is one of those fellows for whom a successful law practice, with clients like MGM Grand, was not enough. Reno's exciting Eldorado Hotel and Casino, expanded several times during Carano's ownership — it now offers 800 rooms, eight restaurants and 60,000 square feet of gaming — wasn't enough. Nor, it appears, was the satisfaction of growing quality grapes for Sonoma County wineries.

So, Don decided that he needed a winery to most satisfactorily transmogrify his fruit into wine. "Growing grapes was interesting, for a time," says Don, "but the real thrill is seeing the work you've done in the vineyard translated into the bottle . . . in the manner in which you envision it."

At first, looking simply for a weekend retreat in 1978, Don and Rhonda Carano bought 60 acres of vineyard in the Alexander Valley, complete with a historic ranch house that had been built in 1903. Then, in 1981, taking full advantage of information available from U.C. Davis experts, they added four more vineyard sites and made a little wine under the Carano label.

Four years later, the winery began to take physical shape at the western end of Dry Creek Valley. As the '80s ended, four additional vineyard sites had been added, including one in the cool Carneros, former sheep country, at the southern end of the county.

"We started by securing good vineyard sites, both hillside and valley, in varying microclimates," explains Carano. "By placing each grape variety in different settings — in different soils, in different climate zones — we're giving our winemaker, George Bursick, a variety of fruit to work with so as to assure a consistency of style and quality from vintage to vintage. And when we get a wine that doesn't fit our style, or our quality standards, well, we'll bulk it out or sell it under our Carano Cellars label."

Which is exactly what the Caranos did

A northern Italian theme runs through all the Caranos' enterprises, including the Ferrari-Carano Vineyards and Winery, which grew out of their desire in 1978 to have a weekend retreat.

Stainless-steel fermenters, framed by flowers, only hint at the blend of art and technology brought to bear at Ferrari-Carano Winery. The winery sits at the head of Dry Creek Valley, just a stone's throw from Lake Sonoma, a much-used recreational area.

with their 1985 Cabernet Sauvignon, a wine from what many call the best vintage of the decade. "It was a very nice, very elegant Cabernet," admits Carano, "but it wasn't within the style framework that our subsequent vintages were going to set. It was our first red release, and we didn't want to confuse people by putting out a wine markedly different from what our subsequent Cabernets have proven to be — they are bigger, more flavorful wines, which only makes sense, since they've been made from our newer, hillside plantings."

Carano named the winery for his maternal grandmother, Amelia Ferrari. "In 1978, when I first dreamed about winemaking in Sonoma County, I envisioned a winery that, through the use of the finest techniques available, would produce deep, concentrated wines that have complex aromas and flavors, yet be accessible and drinkable upon release," says Carano. "We have never been in a hurry here. We are committed to producing wines of elegance and complexity, and to not releasing them until they are ready. As a hotel owner, I realize the importance of releasing wines that have that special combination of drinkability and ageability."

Like her husband, Rhonda Carano was born and raised in Reno and is second-generation Italian-American. A northern Italian

A member of the winemaking team stands by the receiving hopper as a load of Merlot is moved by a helical screw into the crusher, where the berries are knocked off the stems and broken open to release their sugar-rich juice for fermentation.

theme — Don and Rhonda's ancestors emigrated from towns just 30 kilometers apart — runs through all their enterprises, from the wonderful northern Italian cuisine of La Strada Restaurant at their Eldorado Hotel/Casino, to the European gardens and gourmet kitchen at Ferrari-Carano Vineyards and Winery.

"I learned a lot about cooking from my mother and grandmother," begins the slender, waif-like Rhonda, who is director of advertising and public relations at the hotel and loves nothing better than slipping into the kitchen, shirt sleeves rolled up, and whipping up a palate-pleasing pasta dish.

"Here at the winery, we've got a third of an acre devoted to culinary, medicinal, ornamental, and potpourri herbs and vegetables of all kinds. We have olive, citrus, and other fruit trees planted. And lots of flowers. Flowers make people feel at home."

(There's also a *bocce* ball court and a large putting green, complete with sand traps — Don and Rhonda have taken up golf with a passion — that has three places, at different distances and different levels, to pitch from.)

Before joining Ferrari-Carano, prior to ground-breaking in April 1985, winemaker George Bursick supervised the design of the

Winemaker George Bursick (left) and owners Rhonda and Don Carano work through Chardonnay blends to determine which wines will make up the Ferrari-Carano Alexander Valley Chardonnay and which will be put aside for the winery's Reserve Chardonnay.

award-winning McDowell Valley Vineyards' unique winery and oversaw their winemaking for seven years. "I did my thesis on sensory evaluation, concentrating on the interaction and perception of wine aroma and body," he says with a laugh. "Which means that I ought to know something about tasting wine!"

He knows enough that his goal is to create varietal wines that speak definitively of their individual heritages. "We have a term here, *diversigusti*, from the Italian, which means diversified flavors," explains Bursick, a jazz drummer who plays with a group of wine professionals. "Which means that we produce

Winemaker George Bursick (left) and owners Rhonda and Don Carano work through Chardonnay blends to determine which wines will make up the Ferrari-Carano Alexander Valley Chardonnay and which will be put aside for the winery's Reserve Chardonnay.

multidimensional wines by using several clones of the same varietals planted in many different vineyard locations. These lots of wines are vinified and aged separately until they are blended just prior to bottling."

In charge of Ferrari-Carano's expanding vineyard portfolio — approaching 600 acres — is Barney Fernandez, arguably the finest viticulturist in the county. A founding partner at Gundlach-Bundschu, Fernandez had helped develop several vineyards before being hired as vineyard manager and grower liaison by the then-new Chateau St. Jean in 1974.

After contributing heavily to an unparalleled string of vinous success stories at St. Jean for a dozen years, Fernandez came to Ferrari-Carano to accept a new challenge.

"In 1988 and 1989 we expanded our vineyard holdings, acquiring five new properties in Alexander, Knights, and Dry Creek Valleys, as well as in the Carneros district, in the southernmost part of Sonoma County," notes Fernandez who, with his bushy mustache, black hair, and the right hat, could easily mimic the bandido in *Treasure of the Sierra Madre* who utters the immortal line, "Badges? I don't got to show you no stinking badges!" His wife, Gigi Bundschu Fernandez, still works with her brother, Jim, at Gundlach-Bundschu. *RPH*

Here winemaker George Bursick is pulling a sample of Merlot from French oak barrels. Much softer and less tannic than Cabernet, Merlot thus needs less time in oak than Cabernet, and so has to be checked constantly.

GLORIA FERRER CHAMPAGNE CAVES

The family portrait: Pedro Ferrer, his wife Begonia, Gloria Ferrer, her husband José. José Ferrer, as president of Spain's giant Freixenet, had the idea to come to California and name the winery for his wife. Pedro and Begonia live in Sonoma with their two little boys.

"We feel that we are the first Spanish firm to build an American winery, and this is for the second time," recounts young Pedro Ferrer, director of Gloria Ferrer's parent company, Freixenet U.S.A. "My grandfather bought property in New Jersey in the '30s and began to make wine. But the Spanish Civil War broke out, and it became impossible to continue. My father, José, had long wanted to come back."

The $11 million showplace he's talking about — named for his mother and opened in July 1986 — is tucked into a hillside in the westernmost corner of the Carneros district, the bay-cooled region perfectly suited to sparkling-wine grapes.

Built under the supervision of founding winemaker Eileen Crane (she later left to build Taittinger's Domaine Carneros), the winery itself is extraordinary, both in its Catalonian design and in that much of the production area is beneath the surface of the earth. Indeed, the buff-brown stucco walls seem to rise out of the earth to meet the red-tiled roofline. A terrace off the tasting room looks out over vine-carpeted Carneros and the runways of Sonoma Valley Airport, where stunt planes dart and dance.

Bob Iantosca, Gloria Ferrer's winemaker since July 1987, had originally set out to become a sculptor and jewelry maker, studying fine arts at the University of Arizona. "It's hard to explain, except to say that I wanted some-

thing more alive than metal, more responsive than wood," says Iantosca, whose wife Julia is winemaker at William Wheeler.

Like all sound winemakers, Iantosca spends as much time in the vineyards as he does in the winery. "We've got nearly 200 acres planted on the slope in front of the winery," says the wiry Iantosca. "We've had to change our trellising system, because of the strong, afternoon winds, and put up a fence to keep deer out."

Winemaking is, for Iantosca, a melding of many different abilities. "It's like you have to be a botanist, a farmer, a chemist, a carpenter, a mechanic, and an accountant. Of course, you need to have some artistic sensibilities, too, because blending sparkling-wine *cuvées*, well, that's like sculpting . . . with your palate."

As serious as the art of creating fine sparkling wines is, their selling occasionally requires a bit of whimsy. Two examples from the Gloria Ferrer collection. One is a print ad, showing a young man musing, "Gloria Ferrer, Gloria Ferrer, Gloria Ferrer. I went to school with her. I had a crush on her. Fifth grade. We were in Mrs. Peterson's home room. One day Gloria set her desk on fire. This couldn't be the same Gloria Ferrer." Then there's a button: "A Brut Named Gloria." Fun stuff. Serious wine. Good combination. *RPH*

An aerial view looks southwest toward the hills between the Sonoma Valley and the Petaluma plain. The land was given over largely to cattle before the invasion by wine people, who quickly planted it to the vine.

Arched windows and arched doorways repeat the Spanish theme throughout the winery, where much of the cellar space is actually underground, where it's easier to keep temperature and humidity at levels beneficial to the aging wines.

FIELD STONE WINERY

Wallace J.S. "Wally" Johnson first came to the southern end of the Alexander Valley in 1955, when he moved his registered Hereford ranch there from the Santa Cruz Mountains. Ten years later he expanded his ranch through the acquisition of an adjoining plot.

The new plot had a cherry orchard and a ten-acre block of Petite Sirah that had been planted prior to the turn of the century. Johnson replaced the cherry trees and put in a new clone of Petite Sirah adjacent to the ancient head-pruned vines. He then planted 15 to 20 acres of new vineland each year — with vineyard names like Hoot Owl Creek, Turkey Hill, and Home Ranch Vineyard.

A native of Fort Dodge, Iowa, Johnson earned his degree in mechanical engineering from the California Institute of Technology in 1935. In Berkeley, years later, he founded UpRight, which initially manufactured portable aluminum scaffolding and portable radio towers (used for the DEW [Distance Early Warning] Line), then created and manufactured a mechanical harvester for wine grapes.

At first, Johnson sold his grapes. When he opted to make wine in 1977, a trench was cut into the north-facing slope of an oak-studded knoll, in a slot where no trees grew. A concrete building was erected, then covered by earth, so that temperature control within requires limited energy expenditures. The only visible part of the winery is the fieldstone entrance which lent the winery its name. On August 12, 1979 Johnson fell victim to an unexpected stroke, succumbing at just 66 years of age.

The winery and vineyard operations were taken over by Johnson's son-in-law, John C. Staten, a Presbyterian minister with a doctorate in the philosophy of religion from the University of Chicago. "I was teaching at Mills College when Wally died," recalls Staten, who had married Katrina Johnson shortly after they graduated from Stanford University. "At first, I contin-

The late Wallace Johnson was the first modern winemaker to consider the energy efficiencies of an earth-insulated winery. He cut a trench in a low hill, built his winery, then covered most of it up with the dirt he had excavated. The part that shows above-ground is handsomely faced with native field stone.

When founder
Wallace Johnson
died, Field Stone's
operations were
taken over by his son-
in-law, John Staten,
who is an ordained
Presbyterian minister,
a professor of
theology, and the
author of Conscience
and the Reality of
God. Here Staten
and his wife, Katrina
Johnson Staten, salute
the winery's tenth
anniversary in 1987.

ued teaching a couple of days a week, and then spending the other five days up here. That got to be wearing after two years, but I discovered how fascinating the wine business could be."

Staten worked with industry analyst Jon Fredrikson to develop a long-term marketing and business plan for Field Stone. The family corporation divided the vineyards while John and Katrina kept the winery and its 42 acres, of which 24 were planted to Cabernet Sauvignon and Petite Sirah. Another 15 acres were planted to Merlot and Cabernet Sauvignon in 1991. (Curiously, since many of the vines are now cordon trained, Field Stone no longer employs the mechanical picker designed by its founder. His machine is used mostly on cane-pruned vines.)

"Early on, we had made a lot of white wines, but now our focus has shifted more to the reds," says Staten. "We dropped Chenin Blanc and Johannisberg Riesling because the interest just wasn't there. But we have kept Gewurztraminer. First because we've got a winemaker, Mike Duffy, who learned, while at Balverne Winery, how to make a dry Gewurztraminer without the bitterness. Second, we're now getting our Gewurztraminer grapes from the Hafner Ranch, and they really make an excellent wine. So that varietal has remained strong for Field Stone." *RPH*

The vineyards of
Field Stone were
planted on flat land,
formerly used to
graze cattle.
Johnson gave colorful
names to his
vineyards sites:
Turkey Hill, Terra
Rosa (now Staten
Estate), Indian Ridge,
and Hoot Owl Creek.
This is a Petite Sirah
vineyard and the
historic house in the
background now
serves as the
winery's office.

FISHER VINEYARDS

Making the best Cabernet Sauvignon and Chardonnay in Sonoma County wasn't precisely on the mind of Fred and Juelle Fisher when they first planted their 20 acres of vines high above the Sonoma Valley in 1973. "I just wanted to find my place in the sun and to grow grapes," says Fred.

"But as we came to know more and more about the fruit we were growing, we felt it was truly excellent. What makes great vineyards isn't really clear. But we felt that the Chardonnay we were growing in the Whitney's Vineyard was really top notch." The Whitney's Vineyard was named for the Fishers' daughter,

who arrived at the same time the vineyard was growing its first shoots at the 1,200-feet level in these Mayacamas Mountains that separate Napa from Sonoma. The cool mountain climate, shallow rocky soils, and well-drained hillsides gave Fred the fruit he felt was comparable to the best anywhere.

The Whitney's Chardonnay is made only in tiny quantities; the winery's Coach Insignia Chardonnay is made in a similar style and offers rich flavors and earlier drinkability.

The Cabernet Sauvignon, also called Coach Insignia, has currants and herbs, reminiscent of the Napa Valley, where the Fishers

Most of the Fishers' estate vineyard is located on sloping hillsides, shielded from late-afternoon sunshine by ridges in the Mayacamas Mountain range. The exposure keeps the grapes on the vine longer than lower-lying vineyards, and makes for more mature flavors.

also own vines that add richness to the wines.

Fred discovered he liked wine when, in 1957, he was stationed with the Army in West Germany and traveled to Italy. He later went back to Detroit and joined a manufacturing division of Cadillac. His grandfather, Charles Fisher, and Charles's brother, Fred J. Fisher, founded Fisher Body in 1908 — a reason the term "Coach Insignia" is used for his best wines.

Later, Fred worked for the Data Systems Division of Lytton Industries in southern California, then in general management consulting before deciding he wanted to live in the mountains. He and Juelle bought land in June 1973

The reflecting pool and gazebo that Fred and Juelle Fisher built on a rise just above their home in the mountains is the spot where Fisher Winery often stages parties to unveil its new wines.

and planted it in 1974; and then Fred worked briefly at Cuvaison in 1975 as a crush and cellar worker to learn the business. That year, the Fishers bought two new vineyards in the Napa Valley, near Sterling off the Silverado Trail. They were named for their other children: the RCF vineyard for Robert Charles (born in 1978) and the Cameron Vineyard for Cameron Nelson (born in 1982). Now with 55 of his 75 acres of vineyard located in the Napa Valley, Fisher is using more and more Napa fruit in his Cabernet Sauvignon.

Fred hired Charles Ortman as a winemaking consultant in 1979. Then in 1983 Fisher hired Henryk "Max" Gasiewicz as winemaker, with Ortman remaining a consultant through 1988, when he left to become winemaker at Meridian in Paso Robles.

Gasiewicz does a tremendous amount of experimentation, and the Fisher wines showed great style in the latter years of the 1980s.

Fred Fisher is pleased with the decision he made to move to Sonoma County. "When I left Detroit I was dedicated to living someday in the mountains."

Honoring his mountain location, Fisher built his winery from Douglas fir and redwood timbered and milled on the hillside above the winery. The building was recognized as the best designed winery of the 1970s by a panel of the American Institute of Architects. *DB*

The Fishers' Whitney's Vineyard, planted to Chardonnay, yields winemaker Max Gasiewicz's most concentrated white wine.

FOPPIANO VINEYARDS

Prohibition was, in a sense, a backhanded blessing to California winemakers. The industry was reborn with a new science. While many wineries replaced acetobacter (vinegar) damaged cooperage, they were still playing to a house that, by and large, demanded rough, hearty wines.

"In the old days, immigrants drank nothing but heavy, 'dirty' wines, which they made themselves," says Louis M. "Lou" Foppiano, general manager of Healdsburg's Foppiano Vineyards.

Foppiano credits the brothers Gallo — Ernest and Julio — with changing American taste patterns. "They began to produce cleaner, lighter wines, wines that appealed to a much larger market. And, following that lead, people like my father [Louis Joseph Fop-

This old Northwestern Pacific caboose sits behind the tasting room at Foppiano Vineyards. Lou used it as an office when he first acquired it; though it sits empty now, it will one day be refurbished for private tastings.

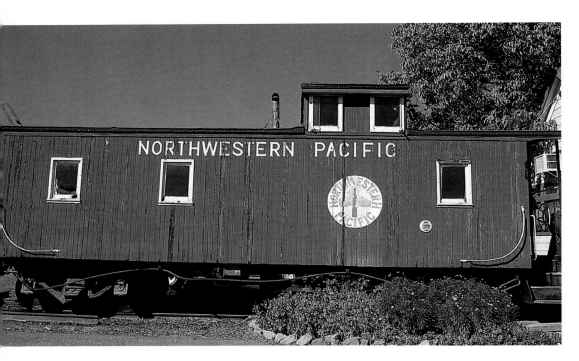

piano] also began to make cleaner, lighter wines."

The last decade has seen sweeping change at Foppiano, just a strong stone's throw south of where the Russian River crosses under Highway 101, south of Healdsburg. Founded in 1896 by Lou's great-grandfather, the winery has been almost completely rebuilt. Concrete fermenters and half-century-old redwood tanks

have been replaced by Yugoslavian stainless-steel puncheons and smaller barrels cut from French forests at Nevers and Limousin.

"My great-grandfather, John Foppiano, came here in 1864," says Lou. "He came from Italy with the gold fever, but found his life's work here, in the vineyards, instead. He built the winery in 1896. In 1910, his oldest son, Louis, took over the winery. In those days they sent the wines in horse-drawn wagons to San Francisco, where their customers brought their own jugs to be filled."

When Louis died, his son, Louis Joseph (Lou's dad), became winemaker. "By title, not by skills," recalls Louis J. "There were no wine schools then. You just talked to the old wine men, got what information you could, then went back to the winery and tried it.

"Most of what we produced was red. The red grapes — Zinfandel, Petite Sirah, and Carignane, with a little Alicante — were bottled either as Burgundy or Barberone. The difference was strictly in the color. You'd look at a tank of wine, and if it was heavy and dark it was Barberone. The lighter red was Burgundy."

Most of the wine was shipped to New York for bottling in those days. "But we always had some to sell in the retail room. We stacked 25-gallon barrels in there, shoved the spigots in and filled people's jugs for 45 cents a gallon. If you bought a lot, we'd let you have it for 35 cents a gallon. If you didn't have a jug, we'd sell you one for a dime."

Previously, Prohibition had put a healthy dent in the California wine industry. "We planted prune trees between the rows of vines," mutters Louis J. in disgust. "Let's not talk about prunes. I hated them. There's nothing worse than picking prunes. But we never did pull out the vines.

"You could tell Repeal was on the way. When Al Smith ran for President in 1928, he was for Repeal. And when Roosevelt was elected four years later, we were sure. As soon as it looked certain, we steamed and soaked the tanks and got ready. The winery had been

The old and new at Foppiano, side by side. The redwood tanks, on the left, have been used since before the turn of the century. Redwood imparts relatively little wood character to wine, while stainless-steel tanks are completely neutral.

TANK NO 12
STOR CAP
15150 GALS

empty all those years. When Prohibition hit we had 90,000 gallons of wine in those tanks and we dumped it all down the highway."

In the days after Repeal wines were fermented in concrete or redwood tanks. "The length of fermentation depended on how hot the weather was," says Louis J. with an ironic laugh. "In about eight or nine months the wine was filtered through paper pulp and was ready for sale. They were heavy wines, higher in alcohol than today.

"We were one of the first in the state to put wine in bottles. In those days, when you went into a restaurant, they'd set a bottle of wine on the table — freshly drawn from the barrel. Its quality depended on how long they had had it and where they kept the barrel, but it was free, and usually a good, sturdy wine."

Free wines are rare, if not nonexistent, today, but there are still wines that represent pretty good value. Foppiano has always put forth reasonably priced wines, but in 1982 they brought out a new, super-low-priced label, Riverside Farm. (Actually, the Riverside Farm label wasn't new, it just hadn't been used for decades.)

In 1986 Foppiano added another label, this on the other end of the winery's primary label, Louis J. Foppiano. Fox Mountain is, essentially, Foppiano's reserve line for Chardonnay and

"Old and new" is a recurring theme at Foppiano. Lou (left) might be called "new," while his dad, Louis J. (right), might resent "old," even though he celebrated his 80th birthday in November 1990. The concrete tanks in the background, though, are definitely old.

Cabernet Sauvignon, wine made from fruit set aside for special treatment. "Fox Mountain is the name of my dad's hunting retreat, a wilderness ranch the family owns up in Mendocino County," notes Lou. "Our first Fox Mountain Cabernet, the 1981, coincides with our winemaker's first vintage here."

Foppiano's winemaker is Bill Regan, who had assisted Rod Foppiano from 1981 until March 1984 when, tragically, Rod died at the age of 35.

The tall, soft-spoken Regan has crafted some very nice wines for the Fox Mountain label. The Fox Mountain Chardonnays consistently display pineapple and clove fruit of

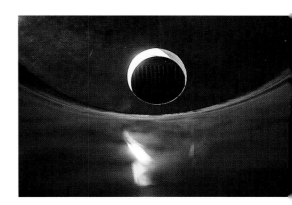

The pump in the foreground is a newer type, run by electricity. In the old days, hand pumps moved one quart per stroke, so you can imagine how many strokes it might take to empty a 40,000 gallon tank. (Guess 160,000!)

almost tropical intensity, while the Fox Mountain Cabs are big, with blackberry and cassis fruit showing off in most years.

As Fox Mountain offers a new direction, the Foppianos have a hard time leaving behind fundamental wines that made their past so strong. In 1990, for example, they introduced a Reserve Zinfandel under the Foppiano Vineyards label. "Though we almost completely replanted our 200 acres of vineyard during the '70s, the Reserve Zinfandel came from grapes harvested from old vines in the Dry Creek Valley," notes Lou. "After fermentation, it was clear that this would be a special wine. My father loves a good Zinfandel almost as much as his favorite, Petite Sirah."

As good as the wines are, perhaps the nicest thing you can say about Lou and Louis Foppiano is that they get along so well, that they work together so well. You can see the respect that Lou has for Louis J. in the 1987 Reserve Petite Sirah (released in 1990 to honor Louis' 80th birthday) and in the print ad campaign they ran the same year that, in a wry sort of way, spoofed the problems some family wineries — most families in general? — have had over the years. "Family Winery Rule No. 1:" the ad proclaims. "Your father is always right. (Rule No. 2: If your father is wrong, see rule No. 1.)" *RPH*

Looking inside an empty stainless-steel tank. Along with being able to monitor fermentation temperatures more accurately, the main advantage of using stainless steel is its absolute hygenic qualities, which, in turn, mean sounder wines bacteriologically.

FRITZ CELLARS

Fritz Cellars is not a household name, not even on Dutcher Creek Road in northern Sonoma County, where the winery is located. Yet David Hastings, the talented winemaker at Fritz, has turned out some of the most stylish wines in the County over the last decade, working in anonymity.

The winery is one of the most unusual you'll ever see. Owned by Arthur "Jay" Fritz, the winery is carved into a hillside on the northern tip of Dry Creek Valley — so far north that phone calls from most of Sonoma County are toll calls.

Production here is not large — rarely more than 20,000 cases a year divided among six or eight wines. And Hastings' works are not the showy, flashy models laden with oak and sugar that some producers make. Moreover, with Cabernet the hottest of the red wines, Fritz trumpets instead wines such as a sublime Zinfandel

Fritz was founded in 1981 by Jay Fritz, who runs a large, successful San Francisco-based customs brokerage and freight-forwarding operation. Hastings, who spent two years in Germany learning to make wine, joined in 1983.

The wine style here is lean and delicate. The two Chardonnays are from the Russian River and the Dry Creek areas . Both wines are fermented in barrels, but the differences in

The design of the Fritz Winery, off Dutcher Creek Road, is unusual in part because it is built into a hillside, making the tasting room naturally cool even on hot days. And it can get very hot in Cloverdale during the summer.

their growing regions show up in their character. They are subtly different: the Russian River wine shows slightly more spice and acidity, the Dry Creek a bit more complexity.

Fritz liked the Russian River wine from one vineyard so much that he invested in the vineyard to guarantee a perpetual supply of its fruit. He also owns 90 acres of vineyard in Dry Creek Valley.

The best red in the Fritz line is Zinfandel, produced from ancient vines planted in West Dry Creek just after the turn of the century. The flavors are typically Dry Creekish, with raspberry, plum, and spice wrapped around a core

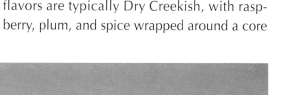

The design of the winery is essentially gravity-flow, with the crush pad located at the top of a hill. The trucks laden with grapes drive to the top, drop their load into the crusher, and then the juice or wine is dropped into a press. The next stop is the aging cellar, well below the top of the hill.

of richness. The oak treatment is modest and the wines are often fairly dense.

Hastings' German training gave him the skill to make truly exceptional dessert-style white wines, when the weather permits. His late-harvest Rieslings, Sauvignon Blancs, and even Chardonnays are some of the best around.

Fritz Cellars is blessed with a classic gravity-flow winery. The facility, designed by Jay Fritz and assembled by a local structural engineering firm, looks like a Hobbit's abode; Hastings refers to it as bomb-shelterish.

There is a crush pad at the top, where grapes or field crushed "must" are trucked. Gravity drops the wine to the press on the second level, which also has juice tanks. The resulting wine then flows by gravity down to the main floor of the cellar for barrel fermentation and aging. This minimization of handling makes for wine fresher than that from facilities where the juice must be pumped from place to place. Aging here is in French oak barrels and puncheons, the latter for better control over the oak character the wine will receive.

Hastings says both he and Fritz like the leaner style of wine. "We like a style of wine that shows the inherent fruit quality, but which has the acidity to complement a meal. So with that in mind, we refuse to over-oak them, or make them flat and flabby." *DB*

It is not just remoteness that has made Fritz Cellars a well-kept secret. It is also that production here is rarely more that 20,000 cases divided among a half dozen or so wines.

GALLO SONOMA

The E. & J. Gallo Winery, based in Modesto far to the south, uses more than a quarter of all the grapes grown in Sonoma County, processing them at its huge Frei Brothers plant in Dry Creek Valley. This "tank farm" is hard to see from the road, however, because it is hidden by a hillside.

Ernest Gallo phrases the question carefully: "How do we get the public to recognize Sonoma as a great wine growing region?" Then he ponders for a second and adds: "We know it's a great region, but how do we promote it?"

Coming from the man whose television commercials are some of the most brilliant in the history of the wine business, the question sounds rhetorical. Yet the answer lies partly in the simple fact that of all the regions in the world where it could plant its future, the world's most powerful wine company chose Sonoma County.

Gallo Sonoma, the world's largest winery, with sales of more than 70 million cases a year and with dollar volume estimated at about one and a half billion dollars annually, could well

have leaped into any wine region in the world to make superior wine. It could have carved out a parcel in the Napa Valley. It chose Sonoma. And how.

The Modesto-based company that made its billions selling sweet wine, jug wine, sparkling wine, cheap fortified wine, and everything but super-premium wines, today owns more than 2,500 acres of land in Sonoma County, about

2,000 of it prime vineyard land. This makes Gallo the single largest vineyard land owner in Sonoma County, and all of this land is aimed at making one thing: super-premium wines under the Gallo name.

The program that Gallo has set for itself has not been an overnight success, but it was never intended to be. (The phrase that comes to mind was made famous by a Gallo competitor — a line about releasing wine before its time.) In fact, it took more than 15 years before Gallo established an image of any kind for fine wine, and it may take the decade of the 1990s to make it reality in the mind of the American consumer.

Gallo's first vintage-dated varietal wines came out in 1982, with the 1978 Cabernet Sauvignon, but it wasn't until the early 1990s that the public began to take this program seriously. And plans set in motion in 1989 won't generate a quality statement for more than a decade.

Still, Gallo was prepared to make this commitment because of its faith in the soil of Sonoma County. The plans were set into motion by the octogenarians Ernest and Julio in 1989 when they acquired another 1,000 acres of land that once had been attached to Italian Swiss Colony in Asti.

Gallo had earlier developed significant holdings in Dry Creek and in the Sebastopol area, and had then made its first varietal wines from Sonoma County fruit in the late 1970s: a Cabernet Sauvignon and a Zinfandel.

Gallo's plans in fine wine country actually began long ago, in 1948, when the Gallo brothers entered into an agreement with the Frei family to use the Frei Bros. winery founded in 1885 — the oldest operating winery in Dry Creek Valley.

Gallo subsequently bought more grapes from Sonoma County than any other winery, and used this premium fruit as the backbone for such wines as Chablis Blanc and Hearty Burgundy, the widest-selling wines in the world. Through the 1970s, Gallo used its Frei facility for crushing and fermenting the grapes

Gallo processes such enormous quantities of grapes at its Sonoma County crushing facility that it uses huge stainless-steel crushers. But handling of the large quantities is done in a "small winery" manner, keeping all the lots separate. Wine is then taken to Modesto for final aging and bottling.

With well over 2,000 acres of vineyards here, Gallo is the largest vineyard landowner in Sonoma County. Its acreage in the Sebastopol area includes this large Dry Creek parcel, as well as another block planted entirely to Chardonnay. In addition, more than 1,000 acres were planted in 1991 in the Cloverdale area.

harvested here, and then the final wines were trucked to Gallo's massive Modesto winery for blending, aging, bottling, and shipping.

In 1977, the Frei family left the wine business and Gallo acquired all its holdings. It then planted its Sebastopol acreage (it had been an apple orchard). Heading up the development team for the Sonoma properties was Julio, with son Bob coordinating. Later, Bob's son, Matt, joined the team, in 1990, to help in development of the new ranch at Asti. (Ernest and his sons, Joseph and David, directed the sales and marketing of all Gallo wines.)

The Dry Creek property and the adjacent Canyon Creek vineyards were planted to Cabernet, Zinfandel, and Chardonnay. The Sebastopol vineyard, located in the cooler, Russian River viticultural region, was converted to Chardonnay in 1990 and 1991. Cabernet, Merlot, and Sauvignon Blanc are some of the varieties being considered for the Asti Ranch, a huge 1,000-acre parcel that sits just west of Highway 101.

Gallo's planning for these properties has, typically, been slow and cautious. Expertise like none other in the world was involved in their development.

First, hills and rills had to be cleared and leveled to make way for the vineyards, since much of the land Gallo bought was unusable

Julio Gallo in his omnipresent, wide-brimmed, straw hat, looks over grading plans for the new 1,000-acre vineyard project, the shining jewel in the winery's super-premium plans, with (from the left) Gary Patterson, Gallo's north coast viticulturalist, Bob Gallo, Julio's son, and engineer Andy Anderson.

in its form. To create this place, the Gallos acquired a large amount of earthmoving equipment at bargain-basement prices following completion in the mid-1970s of the Alaskan oil pipeline project. Ernest at one point joked: "We have so much equipment up there we have to keep buying land to keep it all busy."

The top layer of topsoil was scraped off and stockpiled, and the earth movers swept in to create a gently sloped land without the gullies that had scarred the land before. To insure no erosion, a network of drainpipes was installed below ground, and then ponds, lakes, and indigenous trees and plants were added to make the landscape look natural.

In this portrait photo of the Gallo brothers taken years ago by their winery photographer, Ernest Gallo is appropriately in the foreground, since, as winery president, it is he who makes all the major decisions, especially in marketing. Julio is head of the winery's vineyard operations and has spearheaded the Gallo drive to become a super-premium winery brand.

Then, after the land had been fumigated to eradicate pests and was finally ready, the topsoil was mixed with compost and placed back into what would become the new vineyard. Lime was then added in areas of high soil pH. In planting the vineyards, only the latest viticultural techniques were used, from the best rootstock to the top-quality clones of each variety — a costly and painstakingly slow project that would not reap benefits for a decade.

However, the Gallo Sonoma project will, by the mid-1990s, produce a line of estate-bottled, vintage-dated wines. "We will take the best of the best of these vineyards, and we'll make ultra-premium wine," says a company spokesman, who adds that Gallo plans to build a bottling room at its Sonoma winery, and to create a line to be marketed with the best wines in the state.

Before that, he explains, a wide variety of vineyard experiments will be conducted to see which growing systems make the best wines. *DB*

Gallo's ranch in Dry Creek Valley, up against the hills leading to Alexander Valley, is one of the most perfect spots in the state for growing Zinfandel. But the Gallos get excellent Cabernet Sauvignon and Sauvignon Blanc from here, too.

GAN EDEN

Tall, gleaming rows of stainless-steel fermenting tanks stand silently behind equally glittering strands of barbed wire. Why such security around a winery? Gan Eden produces kosher wine, so entry into the facility is strictly regulated under Orthodox Jewish law.

Next to a grove of apple trees and an old sawmill pond, choked with cattails, stands a pair of stark, steel buildings surrounded by chain-link fencing, topped by barbed wire and guarded by padlocked gates — which seems incongruous. Craig and Jennifer Winchell, who own Gan Eden, have the security to preserve rules laid down by the ultra-Orthodox Jewish sects for the making of kosher wines. If non-Orthodox Jews touch the wine, these sects no longer consider it to be kosher and will not drink the wine.

But Craig was not always so strictly observant. Born in Philadelphia and raised in Louisville, Kentucky, Craig is the son of a doctor who was a lover of fine wines. "I recall having wine since I was about eight years old," muses the bearded, young winemaker, who

sports a dry sense of humor. "If I could convince dad that I had finished my homework, I got to have a little wine with dinner. We drank a lot of Bordeaux, white Burgundies, and German whites."

Winchell started college at the University of Louisville, spent some time at Haverford College, did research work in nuclear medicine, managed a wine shop in Greenwich Village, and even worked as a flight attendant for a short time (one month, to be precise). Finally deciding to turn his love of wine ("wine was a gas") into a career, he applied to U.C. Davis, earning his BS (with honors) in fermentation science in June 1981.

He spent the '82 harvest at Tucker Cellars in Sunnyside, Washington, then worked a couple of crushes at Vina Vista, near Geyserville, before setting out to create his own operation.

"What I learned, working for other people, is that to keep my sanity it's best for me not to work for other people," he explains with a grin. "Also, I had met Jennifer. When she decided to convert to Judaism, I studied with her. There was a lot to it that I had never learned — we were not very religious at home — and I found it fascinating. At Vina Vista, I wanted to be Sabbath observant, but it was difficult. It turned out that the only way I could be Sabbath observant — and drink the wines I made — was to have my own winery."

Craig does bemoan the fact that, now observant, he can no longer drink the great wines of the world. "I have some '75 Lafite and '70 Beaulieu Reserve in the winery, and I can't drink it," he grumbles softly.

In February 1985, he traded his house "and some money" for 20-plus acres of apple orchard, pond, and home between Sebastopol and Forestville. He had a hard time with zoning officials who, for some inexplicable reason, didn't want to allow a winery in an apple orchard. "We even told them that we might make a little wine from the apples," he shrugs. "Fortunately, the county board of supervisors said, 'Big deal,' and approved us. So, we crushed some Chenin Blanc, one dry, one sweet, and Gewurztraminer. The next year, we also made Chardonnay and Cabernet Sauvignon."

The latter earned Gan Eden ("Garden of Eden" in Hebrew) national attention in a big way. Their 1986 Cabernet Sauvignon won the American Wine Competition and then won *Wine and Spirits* magazine's "American Wine Champion" for Cabernets. *RPH*

Owner/winemaker
Craig Winchell
stands on the spiral
stairway of one of
his large, stainless-
steel fermenting
tanks. The cooling
jackets that encircle
the tanks allow for
precise temperature
control during
fermentation —
cooler for whites, to
retain fruitiness,
warmer for reds, to
increase the
extraction of
flavor and tannin.

GAUER ESTATE WINERY

The Gauer Estate winery started life as a custom-crushing facility called Vinwood, a place where growers who had no equipment could have their grapes crushed to their specifications. In 1987, it also began making wine from Ed Gauer's top-quality grapes under its own label, Gauer Estate.

ountain-grown grapes, it is widely believed, yield a higher concentration of flavors, which makes for more flavorful wines. But it's more costly to plant and tend such vines. Much of the farming must be done by hand; slopes often don't allow tractors access. Vineyard owners who decide to terrace the slopes get even smaller yields per acre because of the amount of land needed and because of the good drainage, which results in a small, highly concentrated crop.

Yet Ed Gauer was ecstatic about his Gauer Ranch vineyards, which ran from a bench just off the Alexander Valley floor to 6,000 feet, some of the highest vineyards in California. The small yield was of no concern to Gauer, an octogenarian. Quality was his main concern, and he could afford it: he had owned the Roos-Atkins chain of apparel stores, which he had sold for $16 million, retiring to this ranch.

Moreover, Gauer was still making money from the land, even though he was "retired." Gauer profited from the sales of firewood, shale, and spring water and he leased the land to cattle ranchers for grazing of their stock.

The vineyard's grapes made award-winning wines in the hands of Chateau Souverain and Chateau St. Jean. Gauer's regret was that he owned no winery. In 1986, he decided he should have one so he could make great wine under his own label.

Allan Hemphill, former president of Chateau St. Jean, was hired as a consultant and he persuaded Gauer that at his age, building a winery was a project he might never live to see completed. Instead Gauer bought Vinwood Cellars near Geyserville, which had been one

The Gauer Estate Winery in Geyserville, now owned by a division of Chevron, is one of the most modern wineries in California. It does much of the custom-crushing in the state for a wide variety of contractors who bring fruit to be made into wine.

of the state's most modern "custom crush" wineries, where growers could go to have their grapes made into wine for a fee.

The name of the winery was changed to Gauer Estate and Hemphill hired Kerry Damskey to be its winemaker. The main goal was to turn the Gauer grapes into top-quality wine. Damskey, from a north coast grape-growing family, had made excellent wines at San Pasqual in San Diego before moving north to become winemaker at Stephen Zellerbach Winery.

Gauer's first wines were, predictably, excellent. The crusty gentleman was on course to see his dream become reality — a truly great wine made from his mountain-grown grapes.

Alas, circumstance has a way of changing things. Gauer had no heir who wanted to run the winery, and he felt it best to settle his personal affairs by selling the project. The winery and ranch, never officially on the market, generated quiet offers from Hong Kong and Japan. Gauer finally sold the 600-acre ranch to the Huntington Corp., the land and development division of Chevron, the oil firm.

Gauer Estate wines are often unveiled on a private railcar that attaches to commercial Amtrak trains and goes along for the ride.

Guests on the "Sonoma Valley" often sup on gourmet food in the dining room of the car. With wheels clacking, it's a romantic throwback to an earlier era when such sumptuous living was a treat reserved for the wealthiest citizens. *DB*

Gauer Estate vineyards, covering some 600 acres, range to a height of 6,000 feet and make some of the most concentrated wines in Sonoma County. Because of the depth of the red wines, winemaker Kerry Damskey vowed to hold them in the winery cellar four years or more, allowing them to mellow before releasing them.

GEYSER PEAK WINERY

The Geyser Peak Winery had been through a number of owners when the Trione family purchased it in the early 1980s and renovated it. The joint venture between the Triones and Penfolds of Australia, begun in 1989, changed the fortunes of the property dramatically.

Although the Geyser Peak Winery has a long and varied past that is rich in Sonoma County history and lore, the large winery that sits on a ledge on the western side of Geyserville is today creating an even more exciting future for itself.

The difference has to do with the erratic nature of the wines of the past and the greatness of the wines of the present and future. This upturn in fortune has come about largely because of the impact on Geyser Peak of a wine culture that is fully 50 years older than the wine industry of the United States. And for those who are into guessing games, it is not a winery from a European country that is providing this impetus.

Geyser Peak began as a winery in 1880, founded by wine pioneer Augustus Quitzow.

After Prohibition, the property went through several hands, but rarely did its image have much reach or national impact. One of the owners was the Bagnani family, which made vinegar here.

In 1972, the Schlitz Brewing Co. (now Stroh) acquired Geyser Peak and invested heavily in the property. Its biggest development was a clever way to market jug wine — a bladder filled with wine that was sold in a cardboard box with a spigot as the dispenser. It was the so-called bag-in-box, and it was marketed under the name of Summit. It was a new idea in marketing jug wines, for home use and restaurant use, and the idea was wildly successful in terms of dollar volume and profitability. However, it was not a wine of high quality and it didn't help the Geyser Peak image as a quality wine producer.

In 1982, Henry Trione, one of Santa Rosa's most successful businessmen, bought Geyser Peak from Schlitz. Trione, who had been with Wells Fargo Bank and was a successful real estate investor, aimed to make Geyser Peak a producer of world-class wines.

Trione and his sons, Mark and Victor, already owned more than 1,000 acres of prime vineyard land. The vineyards included acreage in the Alexander and Russian River valleys. The former is noted for its warmth, which ripens a Cabernet so well; the latter is cooler and known for a long growing season that is so beneficial in ripening Chardonnay and Pinot Noir.

Over the years, however, under winemaker Armand Bussone, the winery had only erratic success. Bussone, who had worked before at giant Almaden making wines in much larger quantities, produced wines at Geyser Peak with less consistency than the public sought.

Also, there was a bit of confusion in the brand names. Some of the wines Geyser Peak sold were called Reserve; others went out under the Trione label; still others were sold under the name Summit. Soon the Summit brand was sold and the Triones tried to disconnect it from the image of Geyser Peak.

But the image of the property still failed to find a home with connoisseurs until 1983, when the winery developed the Reserve Alexandre wines. These red wines — blends of Cabernet Sauvignon, Cabernet Franc, Merlot, Malbec, and Petit Verdot — were fine Bordeaux-style wines that fit into the so-called Meritage classification.

The red wines from Geyser Peak, starting with the 1989 vintage, are spectacular efforts largely because the new winemaker for the project, Daryl Groom, has the experience of having made Penfolds' famed Grange Hermitage wines for five years.

It wasn't until 1989, however, that a major change in Geyser Peak's fortunes occurred. That's when Penfolds, an Australian company, acquired 50 percent of the winery and immediately injected new life.

Australia, interestingly, has a wine history dating back a half century earlier than that of northern California. One of the oldest wineries in Australia, Penfolds began in the 1820s when Dr. Christopher Penfolds planted vines he had brought with him to Australia from England. The doctor made wine to give to his anemic patients for its mineral content. Over time, Penfolds became the largest winery in Australia and one of its most quality-conscious. Among

the great wines it makes is the world-famed Grange Hermitage, probably the most famous red wine in all Australia and a wine recently in such worldwide demand that it has become expensive and is allocated strictly.

No Australian wine company had invested in a California winery before the Penfolds investment in Geyser Peak, but Penfolds liked the opportunities it saw here.

Beginning with the harvest of 1989, Geyser Peak had a new regime. Daryl Groom, who had been responsible for making red wine for Penfolds, came on board to make the wines, and he brought with him some of the technology that had made Australia one of the world's

Geyser Peak is one of the most modern wineries in the county. Under Groom, the wines, both whites and reds, have improved dramatically.

fastest-growing fine wine regions. The result was a dramatic change in style for the winery. The white wines were fresher and more complex; the reds showed more extract, yet without excess astringency or bitterness.

Groom, who made Penfolds' fabled Grange Hermitage for five years, says red wine is his pet project. "We don't baby-sit the red wines," he says. "We knock it around, beat it up, and aerate it when it's young. A lot of that air tends to soften the tannins." He is proudest of the fact that his red wines from the 1989 vintage onward show far more depth and concentration of fruit than anything that came before it.

The Trione family's vineyards are now truly

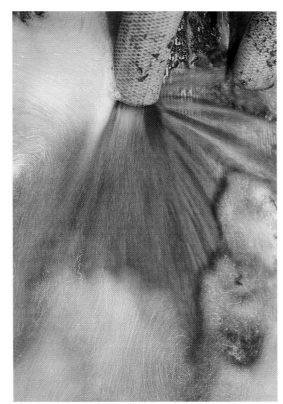

After Daryl Groom took charge as winemaker at Geyser Peak, he radically changed some of the winemaking procedures.

Geyser Peak's treasures. Groom says he keeps all lots of wine from each of the vineyard properties separate and spends a lot of time with his staff going over which lots make the best blends. In 1991, Geyser Peak introduced a new brand, called Canyon Road, a "second label" wine made from lower-quality grapes. It is a project that may permit Geyser Peak to find a use for lower-quality lots of wine, making the Geyser Peak brand that much greater.

Another project about which Groom is proud is the development of a wine called Semchard, a blend of Semillon and Chardonnay. Though it may strike some Americans as odd, the combination of the two grape varieties makes a most intriguing wine — complex and spicy without the need for overt oak character.

Soon after Groom moved to the United States, he discovered the Petite Sirah grape variety. Petite Sirah is little more than Durrif, a minor blending grape grown in the Rhone Valley, but Groom likes its complexity, and he makes the wine "exactly like I made the Grange," he says.

Groom is also fascinated with the Riesling he sees growing in Sonoma County. He uses it for softer, picnic wines of lower alcohol and for late-harvest wines of high residual sugars that can be marketed as dessert wines. *DB*

The Trione family, owner of half the Geyser Peak project, also owns almost 1,000 acres of prime vineyard land in a range of areas in Sonoma County, giving Geyser Peak winemaker Daryl Groom a great amount of top-rate fruit with which to work.

GLEN ELLEN WINERY

The story of Glen Ellen Vineyards and Winery, and the Benziger family that runs it, warms the cockles of your heart. It is the story of a family that has survived tragedy; of a family that lives and works together, growing good fruit and making great wine.

The impetus for this quiet, little success story came from the family's late patriarch, Bruno Benziger. Bruno carried the New York twang in his speech like a badge, so it was not a surprise to discover that he grew into his father's wine importing business there.

As successful as his business was, Bruno's passion was gardening, which prompted the move to California. "I love the out-of-doors," he confessed. "Helen and I love to ski, and I used to hike and hunt in Maine, the Adirondacks, and Canada. Deer, bear, moose, and a little fishing. I once spent a month hiking through northern Canada and Quebec with a friend. We had a canoe and lived off the land. We covered nearly 1,000 miles, as the crow flies.

"I always had a garden, two acres in White Plains, including a greenhouse and a rose garden. I'd grow trees from seedlings. Just puttering around was so restful and relaxing. I came close to buying a nursery once. That's probably why I came here. That, and my son."

Gardening was Bruno Benziger's passion, and one of the reasons the family moved from New York to California.

Bruno's eldest son, Mike, is a Holy Cross graduate who wasn't interested in going straight into the family business. At least that business. Mike Benziger first came to explore the West in 1973, spending two years working and learning about California wines at Beltramo's, one of the great California wine shops.

"Tony Wood, who ran Beltramo's then, is a real gentleman, and he taught me well," recalls Mike, now the managing partner of the winery. "I really got the wine bug. I went to Europe for a year and a half, traveling, working, and learning. Then I came back and worked for my dad for nine months. Well, I hated sales."

The quaint old home typifies the family spirit and closeness that continue to be framework and foundation of Glen Ellen's success, despite dizzying sales and production increases.

So, it was off to California again, this time working in the cellar at Stony Ridge Winery and scouting the state from Santa Barbara to Mendocino and east to the Sierras, looking for a place to plant vines and grow wines. "I was on my way to close a deal for a piece of land in Mendocino County's Anderson Valley in 1980, when I spent a night with Dr. Patrick Flynn, who owned this wonderful, old piece of vineyard just down the hill from the Jack London State Park."

He bought Flynn's 100-acre place instead, brought brother Jerry west to erect a neat, blue-trimmed, white barn/winery that conforms to the historic old houses on the former resort property, and with brother Joe began making wine. With a little help from the whole family — Bruno, Helen, and Mike's and Joe's three other brothers and two sisters.

"Our ranch sits on the eastern slopes of Sonoma Mountain," notes Mike, who, like his father, has a special interest in the farming side of things. "It boasts a staggering array of soil profiles, ranging from red, lean volcanic aggregate to deep bowls of rich, black humus. Each soil type is best suited for specific grape varieties."

Dedication to good farming is the foundation of great wines, and the Benziger family's efforts had an almost immediate payoff. They made their first wines in 1981. The following year, on September 24, 1982 — before crush

The Benziger boys recognize 21 separate vineyard blocks on the estate, but most of the plantings are to Bordeaux varieties like Cabernet Sauvignon, Sauvignon Blanc, and Semillon.

had even been completed — 15 judges were working their way through hundreds of entries to pick the sweepstakes winner at the Sonoma Harvest Fair.

As the judges sifted through the 13 gold medal winners to select the best of show, talk drifted to the rains of the weekend before and the rot problems Chardonnay had undergone earlier in the month. They finally narrowed down their choices to two. Second place: Glen Ellen's 1981 Chardonnay. Sweepstakes: Glen Ellen's 1981 Sauvignon Blanc. The first two wines the Benzigers ever made.

"Some guys like producing thoroughbreds, race horses," reasoned Mike at the time. "But you can't ride a race horse every day. We're not looking for race horse wines. We just want to emphasize the fruit with a cool fermentation. We're so concerned about that fruitiness that we inspect every cluster of grapes on a sorting table to remove imperfect fruit. It takes about an hour per ton, but we put impeccable fruit into the fermenters, and that means less racking, less handling, and a fruitier wine."

(Racking is the most common form of clarifying wine as it ages. The wine is transferred to other tanks or barrels every so often, leaving behind the sediment that has settled to the bottom. Cleaner fruit produces less sediment.)

With the same suddenness of their success,

Success has spoiled many a family firm, but it hasn't made the slightest dent in the Benziger tradition. The five Benziger brothers — (from the left) Joe, Jerry, Bob, Chris, and Mike — are living proof.

the Benzigers lost their patriarch on July 10, 1989, when Bruno, weakened by an earlier bout with pneumonia, complicated by a weak heart, died quietly in his sleep from heart failure. He was just 64 years old. But Bruno left a legacy of quality wines at reasonable prices, especially with his extremely popular Proprietor's Reserve wines, which made the "fighting varietals" a lively category and spearheaded the winery's growth from less than 10,000 cases in 1982 to some three million cases the year of his death.

The year before Bruno died, the family introduced the "Benziger of Glen Ellen" label for wines from the estate and selected Sonoma

There are quiet spots, among the trees and vines, to sit and meditate . . . and perhaps sample a bit of bread and cheese, a glass of wine. It is in such places that terms like "bucolic beauty" are born.

County vineyards. And, in 1989, they introduced the "Imagery Series," a still smaller selection of wines that might seem almost whimsical to the outsider.

"The Imagery Series gives our winemakers an artistic outlet," explains Mike Benziger. "They get to pull special lots out of the cellar, or make a completely unique wine from a special vineyard, then have an artist render his impression for a label that will only appear on a few hundred cases, at most, of wine that will be released only in our tasting room, a few local restaurants, and to a list of collectors."

"These are such small lots that, normally, it wouldn't be economically feasible to bottle them," notes head enologist Bruce H. Rector. It is an intriguing notion, and the examples thus far given rate appropriate attention. One wine, a barrel-fermented Aleatico Blanc de Noirs, has to be the only one of its type, with a perfumed nose of rose petals, peaches, spearmint, and nutmeg.

While Mike and Joe Benziger know their way around a cellar — brothers Bob and Jerry handle sales — they've not been bashful about bringing in other talented winemakers, from head man Bruce Rector to former Round Hill winemaker Jim Yerkes and Haywood's Riesling expert Charlie Tolbert. *RPH*

GRAND CRU VINEYARDS

Grand Cru is among the older "new" wineries in the Sonoma Valley, getting a new start in 1970 when a pair of engineers, Bob Magnani and Allen Ferrera, built a tiny A-frame over some old stone walls.

The walls had some historic value, having been put there in 1886 by a young Frenchman, François Lemoine. He built a mansion, called Villa de Amores, and had some 90 acres planted to vine by 1890. Prohibition forced the closing of the winery, which was reopened for a time in the 1950s.

Grand Cru was the first winery to make Sacramento Delta Chenin Blanc as something special, though it was more fortuitous accident than master plan. "In 1975 one of our distributors needed a house wine," laughs Magnani, Grand Cru's first winemaster. "A Napa grape grower told us about a grower over in Clarksburg. So we bought 20 tons, sight unseen. Three days into the fermentation I began smelling the juice, and it was nice stuff! It was about the best Chenin Blanc I'd ever seen, and the fruit wasn't even ripe!"

In 1981 Grand Cru was acquired by Walt and Tina Dreyer. A Stanford graduate who spent 21 years with Oroweat Foods, Walt sees several similarities between bread and wine.

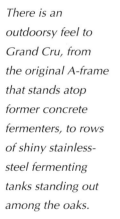

There is an outdoorsy feel to Grand Cru, from the original A-frame that stands atop former concrete fermenters, to rows of shiny stainless-steel fermenting tanks standing out among the oaks.

"In bread, you must begin with good ingredients. Your manufacturing process, a fermentation, really, must be sound. Finally, you must create a beautiful, aesthetic product."

A philosophical sort, Walt sees Grand Cru's success as being analogous to the stability of a three-legged stool. "The first leg is my agricultural background. My parents had wine grapes in Kern County and a cattle ranch in Nevada, where I spent most of my summers. The second leg is my business background, from my degree in economics to my career with Oroweat, starting in production and working my way through sales, marketing, and

management — eventually handling $250 million in sales. At one point I was running eight companies. One is so much easier!

"The third leg is that this business is an extension of my own experience as a home grape grower and winemaker. We first planted vines at our Woodside home in 1972. After looking at 50 wineries in 1979 and 1980, we found what we wanted here."

But the vintage of 1989 really tested Grand Cru. The lowest point was the murder of assistant winemaker Tracey Toovey by a fellow worker. That happened just when Bob Magnani was on the point of retiring to a hobby-turned-business in the electronics field. Added to that, the harvest season was riddled with rain. Fortunately, Magnani agreed to consult, and Barbara Lindblom slid into the winemaker's spot effortlessly.

"In the U.S., we decide what style of wine we want, then select grapes and use various vinification techniques to create that style," notes Lindblom, who spent two years in French wineries. "In France, they're more inclined to interpret what the vineyard has to say, and carry that through the winemaking process. Also, we pay a lot of attention to detail, do more analyses, give more weight to the numbers. The French approach is more holistic, more traditional, more intuitive." *RPH*

These newly planted vines appear to struggle for survival as autumn approaches. In truth, it is very difficult to kill a grapevine, which typically sends down a tap root 25 to 40 feet into the ground. These "children" will survive the winter and, in another year or so, begin to produce grapes for wine — and will continue to do so for 25 to 50 years.

This stainless-steel auger is used to move freshly picked grapes out of the receiving hopper and on into the crusher and destemming machine, which will separate the berries from the stems and break them open.

GUNDLACH-BUNDSCHU WINERY

"There are only two lasting bequests we can hope to give our children," argues social analyst Hodding Carter. "One is roots; the other, wings."

James Towle Bundschu's ancestors gave him abundant roots. More than a century and a quarter ago, Jim's forebears founded J. Gundlach & Company, planting 400 acres of European grape plants on the swell of land, cooled by afternoon breezes, rising gently out of the San Pablo Bay, east of Sonoma.

On November 10, 1850, Jacob Gundlach set sail from Hamburg, Germany bound for "the fervently desired land" of California. One

year later to the day — surviving shipwreck in the Cape Verde Islands, 162 days at sea, and being stranded in Rio for six months — he sailed through the Golden Gate strait (no bridge then, remember?). A native of Bavaria, he had established himself as a brewer in San Francisco by the following June. In 1855, just married to his Bavarian sweetheart, Eva, and now an American citizen, Gundlach moved north to the small pueblo of Sonoma.

That year he began planting 400 acres to vine on the tract he called Rhinefarm, named for the chilly, south-facing slopes along the River Rhine, west of Mainz and Frankfurt. He

A harvest scene, part of the 120-foot mural commissioned by Jim Bundschu to honor the contributions of Mexican-American workers to the California wine industry. The mural was done by two Hispanic artists.

cut into a limestone hillside and erected a stone winery that would keep barrels of wine cool and humid through the warm Sonoma summers. In 1858 Gundlach gathered his first harvest of grapes, making wine "that gladdens the hearts of God and man." Four years later, in 1862, he took on a partner, one Charles Bundschu who, a decade later, would marry Jacob's daughter Francesca.

Fine wine was the first order of business, and Gundlach and Bundschu worked so well together that they won awards at fairs in Philadelphia and Paris, had a 150,000-gallon stone winery tucked into a limestone hillside at

This segment of the mural pays homage to the joys of Mexican cuisine, which is prevalent during the harvest season — especially the red and green peppers, which are washed down with the main beverage of the harvest: cerveza, beer.

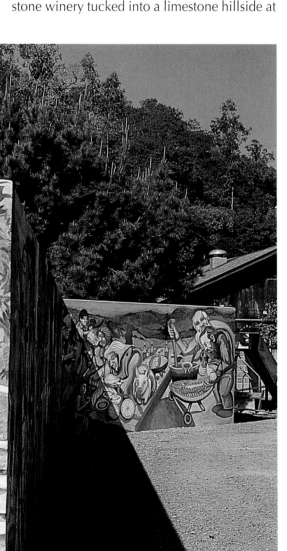

Vineburg, and had established a large cellar (and offices) in San Francisco.

Identified in the Sonoma Valley in 1873, phylloxera threatened to wipe out the wine industry before a means of prevention was discovered. But worse disasters were waiting in the wings. Early on the morning of April 18, 1906 the earth shook and the sky burned in San Francisco. Offices and inventory were destroyed. But Gundlach-Bundschu rose from the ashes, only to be dealt the still more devastating blow of Prohibition in 1919. It would be more than half a century before wine was again made on the Rhinefarm.

In the meantime, the vineyard was farmed, first for the burgeoning home winemaking market that came out of Prohibition, later for the benefit of wineries like Almaden, Louis Martini, and nearby Sebastiani. During those years Jim's grandfather, Walter, and father, Towle, maintained, even expanded, Rhinefarm. Those were the roots that came then to Jim. Along with those roots were wings, wings based on the Germanic principles of hard work and the farmer's ethic of eternal patience.

"I always felt lucky to grow up on the ranch," says Jim Bundschu, president of Gundlach-Bundschu. "It's a lot tougher for parents today, a lot more challenging with all the distractions of organized sports, television, and video games. My two boys got teased for hav-

Ancient photographs and silver cups speak of the history and the success the descendants of Jacob Gundlach and Charles Bundschu are able to look back on with pride. But it all came at the price of dedication and hard work, no strangers to any success story.

ing to work in the vineyard with a hoe and shovel, but that's the only way to get a feel for the vines and for Mother Nature." Jim got his feel for Mother Nature's pace in much the same way. "Knowing that vines have been on this land for more than 100 years allows me to react more slowly, more patiently than many grape growers might to new, occasionally faddish, cultural methods."

The transition from vineyard to winery began on Halloween evening 1969. Jim was sitting around tasting some homemade wines with then-brother-in-law John Merritt Jr. and soon-to-become brother-in-law Barney Fernandez.

"One of us suggested that our hobby was getting a bit expensive," remembers Jim, "and that perhaps we ought to call it a business. At least then our losses would be deductible." The idea, born of idle conversation, created its own reality: a three year restoration of the original three stone walls into a winery building. The reborn Gundlach-Bundschu held its first crush in 1973 with a redwood fermenter and a handful of used stainless-steel milk tanks, one of which carried the legend "Make Mine Milk!"

Today, Gundlach-Bundschu makes a broad range of wines, from crisp Chardonnays to powerful Cabernets, from a unique tart Kleinberger Riesling to some of the finest black currant and cherry-laden Merlots made anywhere — all crafted by winemaker Lance Cutler. A tenacious, driven, dedicated wineman, you can see his style in the wines Lance likes best

Lance Cutler (left) is the hard driving, energetic winemaker at Gundlach Bundschu. Jim Bundschu (right) honors his ancestors with hard work and a pixieish sense of humor that seems to spur Cutler's own. Together, they are the Abbott and Costello of vinous humor.

— dense, intense wines that make a clear and undeniable statement.

If they wanted, Bundschu and Cutler could easily earn their bread on the comedy circuit, for they are as unlikely a pair as Laurel and Hardy ever were — the quiet, almost studious, farm boy and the energized, fast-talking wine-maker. They have collaborated on some hilarious wine posters. (One shows Jim's mom, Mary, in a classic auto, pulled over by an old-time motorcycle cop, with a slogan suggesting that you shouldn't drive if you can't pronounce "Gundlach-Bundschu Gewurztraminer.")

And, in May of 1990, Cutler and Bundschu led a group of Sonoma vintners on a madcap raid on the elegant, high-toned Napa Valley Wine Train, serving a selection of Sonoma Val-

The small picnic area in front of the original stone winery looks out on vineyards and a vineyard pond. Water is not just for nurturing young vine plants; it can also be used to prevent frost damage by covering new shoots with a thin coat of insulating ice.

ley wines to a startled but game group of passengers.

The following month, the pair showed off a 120-foot winery mural that portrays the cycle from vine to wine (including the annual pig roast and beer-can-smashing ritual at Gundlach-Bundschu). The mural was designed and executed over an eight month period by San Francisco artists Ray Patlan and Eduardo Pineda, and its display honors the efforts and input of Hispanic vineyard workers. "These people are out there all day, working hard to get the grapes in, and we get all the credit," sighs Bundschu.

"There wouldn't be a California wine industry without Hispanic workers," adds Cutler bluntly. "These people put their sweat into planting, pruning, cultivating, and harvesting our grapes, yet they rarely get the credit they deserve for their contribution." They do at Gundlach-Bundschu, a winery known for deep roots and strong wings . . . and just plain caring. *RPH*

SONOMA VALLEY SOBRIETY TEST #1

If you can't say
"Gundlach-Bundschu Gewurztraminer"
you shouldn't be driving!

GUNDLACH BUNDSCHU

A good example of the Cutler-Bundschu sense of humor. That's Jim's mom, Mary, driving the classic auto, and trying hard to say Gundlach-Bundschu Gewurztraminer without slurring her words.

HACIENDA WINE CELLARS

Hacienda Wine Cellars typifies, in many ways, the hundreds of new wineries founded in California since the early '70s. Like most, it started small, then grew based upon economic necessity. Like most, it was founded in a building originally constructed for another purpose. And, like most, its early reds were big, brusque, bear-like wines that gradually evolved into balanced beauties of individuality and complexity.

Hacienda was founded in 1973 by the late Frank H. Bartholomew, the former president of United Press International. "Bart," as he liked to be called, had purchased the rundown Buena Vista Winery & Vineyards in 1941 at a state land auction, then restored both to full operation after World War II.

In 1968, Bartholomew sold the winery but retained the historic vineyards, originally planted by the rapscallion Hungarian "Count" Agoston Haraszthy in 1857. At first Bart sold the fruit to Buena Vista, but winemaking was thick in his veins.

So, in 1973, he turned the former Sonoma Valley District Hospital building into a Spanish-styled winery of modest size. "This is an experiment in quality, and nothing else," he said then. A few years later, as the winery grew

Set against the broad sweep of Buena Vista Vineyard is the modern reconstruction of the Pompeian villa built on the same site by Agoston Haraszthy in 1857. In October 1864 the villa hosted Sonoma Valley's first formal vintage festival, a masked ball at which General and Señora Mariano Vallejo were the guests of honor.

and demands on his time became more intense, Bartholomew sought out an old family friend's son, A. Crawford Cooley, who came to Hacienda first as manager, finally as owner.

The genial Cooley's roots dig deep into California soils. "My great-great-grandparents came here in the 1840s," says Cooley. "The Elliotts came out of the South in the second overland party in 1845. The Cooley side arrived from Ohio, lured by the gold rush in 1849, and settled in Sacramento. By 1853, they had moved to a farm in Cloverdale, planting prunes, citrus, and grapes."

A native of southern California, winemaker

The building that houses Hacienda Wine Cellars, on the eastern edge of historic Sonoma, was once a hospital, later a home for delinquent girls. The Spanish styling is typical of California wineries, most of which still rely upon largely Mexican crews for tending and harvesting their vineyards.

Eric Laumann interned at Hacienda while working toward his degree at Davis. But his first winemaking job after graduation was at Zaca Mesa, in Santa Barbara County. After a year and a half there, he returned to Hacienda, taking over as winemaker in March 1987.

"As a winemaker, I'm trying to produce distinctive wines, wines that show their varietal personality," he says. "I put a lot of emphasis on 'mouth feel,' and want each wine to paint a complete picture of smell, taste, and feel."

The best example of that "complete picture" is Hacienda's proprietary red blend, Antares. "The name we chose comes from the brightest star in the Southern hemisphere," notes the dark-haired, blue-eyed Laumann. "Antares is a red star, in the constellation Scorpio. It is so bright that it is used for navigation."

Hacienda's Antares may well be used for navigation by wineries trying to emulate this soft, but centered, red wine, which fills the mouth with red currant, blackberry, and violet flavors. "We didn't set out to make a proprietary wine, but rather this came about as a result of extensive tasting through the cellar," notes Laumann. "The Cabernet Sauvignon portion gives the tannin backbone and the cassis fruit; a spiciness and firm acidity comes from Cabernet Franc; and Merlot gives cherry fruitiness and soft tannins." *RPH*

Alongside the colorful entry to Hacienda's tasting room is a small demonstration vineyard. There you can see how the leaves of Cabernet Sauvignon (5-lobed, medium size) differ from those of Chardonnay (more whole and larger).

HANNA WINERY

An old joke says that if you want to make a small fortune in the wine business, start with a large one. Hanna Winery isn't exactly a case example of that apothegm, but neither did the Hanna Winery make it to fiscal splendor in its first half-decade of life.

Yet the owner and founder of Hanna, Dr. Elias Hanna, is one of the world's most successful cardiac surgeons, and a man for whom establishing a winery was not, at the outset, a financial burden. He entered the wine business in 1985 by acquiring vineyards in two of

Sonoma County's best regions, Alexander Valley and Russian River Valley.

The winery originally had goals of making superior-quality wine, establishing itself as a 30,000-case winery, and building a handsome estate in Alexander Valley, called internally "Hanna II." The first step was achieved as early as 1987 when Hanna's first wines hit the market. They were excellent.

Hanna had hired Merry Edwards, the long-time winemaker from Mt. Eden and Matanzas Creek, as consultant. Edwards worked with

A small pond faces the functional Hanna Winery, on Occidental Road just east of Sebastopol. The property is owned by Dr. Elias Hanna of San Francisco, one of the world's most renowned heart surgeons.

Hanna winemaker Linda Porter to establish a style of wine that would make Hanna one of the top producers of Sauvignon Blanc and Chardonnay in the state almost overnight.

However, reaching 30,000 cases was a chore. By 1990, production was barely over 15,000 cases, and growth and sales were slow. Moreover, construction of a large Alexandra Valley winery had been put on hold indefinitely.

Says Hanna candidly, "I love nature and farming, and I started the winery for those reasons, but the huge winery project wasn't a

The modest home that Dr. Hanna uses for those days when he's not required in San Francisco will have to serve as the winery's headquarters for the time being. Plans for a major new winery to the north have been put on hold because of its excessive costs and the lack of cash flow.

smart business idea. It's a very expensive privilege, owning a winery."

He said the costs of doing business as a tiny winery are manageable, but reaching 15,000 cases of top-quality wines raises some costs rather quickly. "We acquired the finest grapes and made the finest wine, but we are not well enough known to charge the highest prices," he explains. "I still love the beauty of what I am doing there, but it is expensive."

Hanna owns vineyard land in two of the best growing regions of Sonoma County: a 30-acre parcel with 16 acres planted in the cool West Russian River Valley (plus a 60-acre parcel there that will be developed); and a 75-acre vineyard in the warmer Alexander Valley. A fourth 300-acre parcel of land, acquired in 1989, is above the Sonoma Valley.

The style of the Hanna wines under Porter was fresh and crisp, with penetrating fruit characteristics. These wines were produced in Hanna's small winery off Occidental Road east of Santa Rosa. Porter left in 1989 to pursue a career in another field, and Hanna hired Steve Sullivan as winemaker. He had come from Buena Vista, and was assistant winemaker at Kenwood Vineyards for 10 years before that.

Hanna gained as much fame for his unusual label design as for anything else. The inverted staircase design is unique in labeling. It was designed by San Francisco artist Mike Manwaring. *DB*

HANZELL VINEYARDS

anzell Vineyards is a jewel of an estate. This tiny, picture-book winery, perched high on a southwest-facing slope above the Sonoma Valley, evokes philosophic and romantic feelings.

Its conception came from the mind and money of J.D. Zellerbach, board chairman of the giant paper company, Crown Zellerbach, and Ambassador to Italy during the Eisenhower administration. Living in Europe in the 1940s, he came to treasure the great Montrachets and Romanée-Contis of Burgundy's Côte d'Or. His romantic side had been touched by the physical and architectural beauty of the Clos de Vougeot Château. So he attempted to replicate what he had seen there.

In 1952 he began sculpting terraces into the hillsides of his 200-acre Sonoma estate, planting them to Chardonnay and Pinot Noir, the varieties of Burgundy. He then fashioned a miniature winery, borrowing from his memory of the inner courtyard at Clos Vougeot (in particular the north-facing facade). He even went to the extent of equipping it with sapling-hooped, French oak barrels to capture that elusive complexing agent that had previously been missing in California white wines. While many thought that Zellerbach was indulging

The main winery building at Hanzell was designed to replicate the northern courtyard facade of Burgundy's famed Clos de Vougeot. Founder J.D. Zellerbach was a great fan of Burgundian wines, and at the outset Hanzell produced only Chardonnay and Pinot Noir.

himself with his "play" winery, actions and wines belied that conclusion.

Not only had he spent a small fortune to build the winery and import French oak, but he hired one of the finest winemaking minds extant to give birth to his pet project. R. Brad Webb, now a top consultant (and part owner of Freemark Abbey), presided over the first California winery to be "furnished in French oak" at Hanzell, but also did pioneering work on malolactic fermentations (his pickup truck bears the license plate "ML 34," the malolactic bacterium he first identified) and introduced stainless-steel fermenting tanks.

This was an open meadow with a lovely view toward San Pablo Bay when winemaker Bob Sessions first came to Hanzell in 1973. A few years later he was able to plant five acres each to Pinot Noir and Chardonnay, and another five acres to Cabernet Sauvignon.

Though Zellerbach died in 1963, he had the chance to show off his wines to connoisseurs worldwide, most of whom picked his Chardonnay as being from the Côte d'Or but were unable to pinpoint the vineyard. Ha! Sadly, his wife, Hana, (the winery name is a contraction of her name) didn't care for wine, and sold out two years after her husband's death. A decade later it came to Australian-born heiress Barbara de Brye, who visits the winery each August with her son Alexander.

To her credit, Mrs. de Brye has been cautious about fiddling with the legend of Hanzell. The major change has been a small, new planting of Cabernet Sauvignon at the upper vineyard, which has a panoramic view of San Pablo Bay, San Francisco, and Mount Diablo. J.D. Zellerbach loved his Burgundies; Barbara de Brye fancies her Clarets. Fair enough.

A fixture at Hanzell for nearly two decades, and quietly responsible for the winery's continued success, is manager/winemaker Bob Sessions. Like his mentor (Webb), Sessions is modest enough to fade into the wallpaper. "He is an un-pushy fellow," assesses Webb, "but he is very resourceful. He was definitely the right man for Hanzell. Of course, I'm flattered that he has such respect for my procedures that he continued them. I can still walk into the lab and find things in the same drawers they were in 25 years ago!" *RPH*

Though production is still quite small, Hanzell owner Barbara de Brye added this modest wooden building to house more barrel storage when the vineyards were expanded to include Cabernet Sauvignon and a smattering of the other Bordeaux varieties.

HAYWOOD WINERY

The year was 1973. Peter Haywood was a successful building contractor and developer in Marin County who liked being out in the fresh air with a hammer and blueprints.

"But I was getting tired of not doing what I really wanted to do," explains Haywood. "The more successful I became, the less time I could work on job sites. I found myself constantly in the offices of bankers or at night meetings of the planning commission. I really liked the physical work and I wanted to leave what was becoming an overly congested urban environment." So Haywood bought a 300-acre parcel of land deep in the Sonoma Valley, behind the town of Sonoma, to have a project he could feel comfortable with.

"Grapes were the only small-scale farming that made economic sense at the time," he says. "I wanted to get back to more outside work, so I thought I'd start an agrarian business."

By 1976 the first vineyards were planted to Cabernet and Riesling, and in 1977 Haywood added 30 acres of Chardonnay. The next year, he added a hillside vineyard of Zinfandel.

The original vineyard was called Chamizal. "The early survey maps, dating back to 1864, had that word written across

Peter Haywood began to plant his vineyard in 1974 on a rocky point of land up a small canyon behind the town of Sonoma. The winery was constructed in 1980. A decade later Haywood sold this brand to Racke, the U.S. division of a large family-owned German firm, and moved to Buena Vista Winery. The old Haywood winery building was then leased by Ravenswood.

many locations," he says. "Chamizal was a kind of hillside growth, a type of ground cover that grew here. It's a hardwood bush that had been used for kindling."

In 1980, Haywood bought 25 more acres of land south of the valley, at the entrance to his property, including 11 of Chardonnay and three of Gewurztraminer.

But farming and making wine are two different things, and when Haywood wanted to build a winery on the front of the property, he formed a new company with Rudy Tulipani, who had been his partner in other ventures. They would jointly own the winery.

The etched glass at the Haywood Winery — a depiction of a worker pruning the vines — provided the design for Haywood's label.

The partners built a 12,000-square-feet winery, and the first Haywood wines were made in 1980. Headlines greeted Haywood Rieslings, made off-dry with peach-pear fruit and a spice component rarely found in California. Haywood attributes their quality to the east-facing position of the vineyard, the cool climate, and especially the extremely rocky soils on that side of the hill that rises in the center of the little valley. The rocky soil yields more of that Germanic character, he says.

The next Haywood success was Zinfandel, a raspberry-and-pepper-scented wine that lacked the astringent tannins of some producers' Zinfandels. Later, as the vineyards matured and as winemaker Charlie Tolbert began to understand them, Haywood made marvelous, long-lived Chardonnays and Fume Blancs. The Cabernet Sauvignons were a bit tannic when released, but aged nicely. Tolbert left in 1990 and was replaced by Sara Steiner, who previously had been at Chateau St. Jean.

Production was at 20,000 cases by 1990, when the partners came to a crossroads. "Rudy wanted to reduce his investment in the wine business," explains Haywood, so the partners divided the winery business. Haywood subsequently sold his brand to Buena Vista and Steiner joined the Buena Vista team to make estate-bottled wines from Haywood's vineyards. *DB*

Even though he moved his base of winemaking, Haywood retained ownership of his Chamizal Vineyard, located behind his former winery site. Haywood makes some of the best Zinfandel in the state with fruit from Chamizal.

HOP KILN WINERY

Over in the Napa Valley in 1976, Stag's Leap Wine Cellars' 1973 Cabernet Sauvignon won a major blind tasting — by French judges in Paris — against top-growth Bordeaux. The victory put Stag's Leap on the wine map.

L. Martin Griffin Jr., tells of a similar upset scored by his Hop Kiln Winery in 1984. Griffin, a physician who owns 240 acres in the western Russian River foothills, had always made a bold blended red wine from grapes on his ranch. He called this wine Marty Griffin's Big Red, and it was a wine that sang the glories of the pioneers of northern Sonoma County,

Italian farmers who planted red grapes without regard for varietal integrity. The idea was simply to make good wine.

In 1984, Griffin entered his 1981 Big Red in the Orange County Fair wine competition. A blend of Petite Sirah, Napa Gamay, Zinfandel, and other traditional varieties, the wine was bold and many-faceted. The judges gave Big Red the sweepstakes award. It beat out famed Opus One, the Napa Valley superstar.

"That put us on the map," says Griffin. Big Red sold, at the time, for about $8 a bottle and Opus One for $50. Red wine was the focus at Hop Kiln from day one. Its Zinfandel is annu-

The classic Hop Kiln Winery with its rock construction and redwood turrets was, in fact, just that — an old hop kiln — when it was built nearly 100 years ago. It was used to dry hops used in the making of beer, which was a major business in Sonoma County before Prohibition.

ally one of the best in the state; its Petite Sirah rates as one of the most flavor-packed in the country; its Napa Gamay has won wide acclaim.

Griffin, a specialist in public health living in Marin County, bought this ranch in 1961 and farmed it from afar for years. "I never had the money to start a winery," he says. "But then I retired in 1974 and I moved up here." To fund the winery, Griffin took a "temporary" job as public health officer at Sonoma State Hospital in Sonoma. The job lasted 15 years, Griffin explains, because he needed the salary to keep funding the winery.

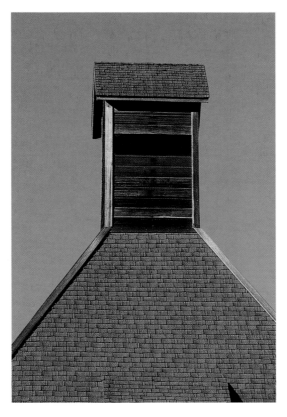

Dr. Marty Griffin has restored the old kiln, and from its upper level visitors can see the expanse of vineyards he has growing out here in the cool Russian River area. Also left in place are some of the accoutrements of the brewing era, so visitors can learn about the growth of two fermentables at one time.

The winery was founded in 1975 inside a restored barn that had been a kiln for drying hops in the days when Santa Rosa was a major beer-producing city. Hop Kiln is located in a region cooler than the rest of Russian River, where Petite Sirah, Zinfandel, and Napa Gamay vines ripen well. The vines, planted in the 1880s, were unirrigated and on hillsides.

One of the wines Griffin makes is a Zinfandel called Primitivo, a name he trademarked. Winemaker Steve Strobl also uses the fruit off the cool benchland to make a superb dry Gewurztraminer, a fresh Chardonnay, an herbal Sauvignon Blanc, and a flowery Riesling. Another wine of charm is called A Thousand Flowers, an off-dry blend featuring Gewurztraminer and Riesling. The winery also makes a fresh and fragrant sparkling Johannisberg Riesling, called Verveux.

Steve's wife, Joanne, is Hop Kiln's business and sales manager. Griffin and his wife, Joyce, live in the Victorian house next door to the winery, which is in the huge, towered hops barn that's now a National Trust. Griffin retired in 1989, but he devotes his free time to defending the area from what he perceives as an unhappy incursion for gravel mining. Griffin is an activist with public agencies trying to promote regulations that protect the land for purely agricultural uses. *DB*

IRON HORSE VINEYARDS

Barry and Audrey Sterling, who live part-time in France, still regard their Sonoma County ranch as home. Their Iron Horse property is as well known locally for its flower, herb, and vegetable gardens as for its great wines.

California winemakers have the best of all possible worlds: they have one of the most hospitable climates in the world in which to grow grapes for fine wine, and they have laws that do not restrict wineries from growing any variety they see fit in any location.

In Burgundy, for example, French law limits the white and red grapes to Chardonnay and Pinot Noir, respectively, and little else. Cabernet Sauvignon and Riesling are forbidden. Moreover, a property in Burgundy couldn't buy grapes from another region and market it with anything but a *vin de table* designation.

In California, however, there are any number of properties that grow Chardonnay, Pinot Noir, Cabernet, and Riesling, all within a few feet of one another. And wineries that make 20 — even 30 — different wines, much of it from grapes brought in from other regions.

The successful California winemaker is one who doesn't simply plant all the grapes for many varieties on the same soil and pray. Sometimes it's best to get cool-climate varieties from the cooler climates, and the grapes that like warmth from more temperate zones.

Rather than let fate and the grapes make the decisions for them, determining which of

their wines are excellent and which are not, Barry and Audrey Sterling have employed a unique concept for their Iron Horse Vineyards, the small estate winery located ten miles west of Santa Rosa on 350 acres of gently rolling hills.

Here in Sonoma County's lush Green Valley, the cool, occasionally frigid climate seems best suited for the Burgundian varieties and for sparkling wine grapes, not Cabernet. So it was here that the Sterlings planted 55 acres of Chardonnay and 55 of Pinot Noir, divided by a creek that meanders toward the Russian River.

And yet the Sterlings wanted to make a

Patrons of the arts as well as socially conscious, the Sterlings have made their ranch outside of Sebastopol and Forestville a sybaritic spot, filled with antiques and modern sculptures, not to mention wonderful wine.

Cabernet Sauvignon too, so it was pure serendipity that, after they brought in Forest Tancer as a partner and winemaker, they had access to Tancer's family vineyard of Cabernet Sauvignon grapes. That property is located in the warmer Alexander Valley 30 miles northeast — a plot of ground that would be rather dicey for Pinot Noir and would make a decidedly different style of Chardonnay.

In the Green Valley location, Iron Horse has one of the most westerly vineyards in Sonoma County. It is 12 miles from the Pacific Ocean, in a pocket where fog creeps in nights year-round and stays around covering the vines until noon, even on days when the afternoon temperature reaches 90 and above.

Still, the high temperature is, on average, 10 degrees cooler than at Tancer's Alexander Valley property, and this makes for the longer growing season that helps Tancer fashion a most delicate style of Chardonnay, one more reminiscent of Chablis than of Montrachet. Over the years, Tancer has refined his method of making this wine, and the result is more fleshy in character than Chablis, but without the fatness that makes so many California Chardonnays clumsy oafs.

The Pinot Noir here, lighter in color than many others that grow in warmer regions, produces a more delicate wine, with rose petal, tea, and clove characteristics that require intro-

Iron Horse is one of the few properties in California to reach the pinnacle in terms of both sparkling wines and still wines. The winery's Chardonnays and Pinot Noirs are most Burgundian, and its Cabernets, from grapes grown in another region, are a stunning achievement.

spection to understand. It is not blockbuster wine. Yet with bottle age, the Pinot Noirs usually come around to show their true Burgundian charm. The 1980 Pinot Noir, a case in point, was a delicate, feathery thing on release, a wine so light in color, some reviewers panned it as being little more than a dark rosé. Yet in 1990, a decade after the harvest, the wine was sweet and redolent of Near East spices and fruit, a penetratingly fine wine.

Here, too, are the grapes that make great sparkling wine. Iron Horse has developed a reputation for being one of the best in the state with three types of Champagne look-alikes, and a fourth showing amazing promise.

The best of them? That's a matter of taste. Some prefer the Chardonnay-spiced Blanc de Blancs, others like the rich, gutsy Blanc de Noirs, and others the more delicate, but in some ways more complex, Brut. Since 1986, the winery's Rosé has been the wine on the ascendant, deeply fruity and rich with Pinot-cherry character.

Iron Horse's Cabernet Sauvignon, from Tancer's Alexander Valley estate, was good on its own until the mid-1980s when a newer planting of Cabernet Franc came into full bearing. It was then that Tancer blended the Cabernet Sauvignon with the Cabernet Franc to make a more sublime wine than either variety could yield on its own. And the resulting wine was semi-proprietarily named Cabernets, reflecting the two different Cabernets that were used in the blend.

Barry Sterling (left) is an internationally known and respected attorney. Audrey (right) is renowned for her amazing gardens. Their daughter, Joy, is the director of marketing for the winery, and their son-in-law, Forest Tancer, is the winemaker.

The winery also makes a handsome Fume Blanc, one of the finest in the state.

In 1990, the ties between the Sterlings and Tancer became even tighter — the winemaker married Joy Anne Sterling, Barry's and Audrey's daughter, a former newswoman who headed up the Iron Horse sales team.

Then, just weeks after their marriage at the estate where Audrey's and Barry's fruit, flower, and vegetable garden is a matter of local pride and renown, the Tancers and Sterlings announced an exciting joint venture with the French Champagne house of Laurent Perrier.

The new partners said they would produce a classic sparkling wine in the French manner from a vineyard they would develop on a ridge overlooking the Iron Horse property in Green

In 1990, the winery announced a joint venture with Laurent Perrier to make a premium sparkling wine from a vineyard to be planted in early 1991. The partners say the first wine will be ready to sip in the 2000.

Valley. And Laurence Sterling, son of the owners and a Los Angeles attorney, agreed to become a partner in that project with Forrest and Joy. Laurence and his wife, Terry, moved to Sonoma County in 1990.

The joint venture, which began with the planting of the vineyard in 1991, was aimed at making its initial release in mid-1999 — "A wine that you can use to celebrate the next century," said Joy Sterling at the unveiling of the project.

Relatively low-key in image, Iron Horse is one of the few wineries in California to tackle super-premium Chardonnay, Pinot Noir, Cabernet, Fume Blanc, *and* sparkling wine — and hit the mark with each one. *DB*

The emblem of the Iron Horse is seen not only in the garden ornamentation found on the western Sonoma County property, but also in the subtle name selected by the Sterlings for their second label — Tin Pony.

JORDAN VINEYARD AND WINERY

Greatness in winemaking can come from the serendipitous good fortune of accidentally planting the right grapes in the right compost, but most often it is the result of design. And the story of Jordan Vineyard and Winery owes more to design than to chance, primarily because of the efforts of one man.

Andre Tchelistcheff is his name and his dominion originally wasn't Sonoma County at all, but the Napa Valley. Yet the impact this Russian-born, French-trained enologist has had on the American wine industry is incalculable. Though his name is well known, many wine lovers know little of his contributions to far-flung wineries like Firestone in Santa Barbara, Clos Pegase in Calistoga, Chateau Ste. Michelle in Washington, and Jordan in the remote hills north of Healdsburg.

The Jordan odyssey started decades ago when Tom Jordan discovered wine one summer. On holiday from the University of Minnesota, he followed a classmate home to France. There, Jordan was introduced to French cuisine, which he enjoyed, and wine, whose Bordeaux style appealed to him.

Years later, and now a successful oil-and-gas developer and president of Denver-based Trend Exploration Ltd., Jordan had developed

Tom Jordan gives interviews only rarely. Daughter Judy, who handles marketing and is a managing partner in the sparkling-wine project, is more visible. On their home property, which is not open to the public, the Jordans have designated more than 1,000 acres as a wildlife refuge. They've even planted grains for the migratory birds who pass by.

quite a taste for great wine and was a collector of the great wines of France. This was possible because of successful Indonesian oil projects, which permitted Tom and Sally Jordan to explore their lifelong dream to buy a chateau in France and make great wine. But the mid-1960s was a turbulent era in France and, after some consideration, they tabled the idea.

In the late 1960s, a chance occurrence gave Jordan a different idea. He and Sally were in San Francisco on vacation, at an elegant restaurant. They ordered a great Bordeaux. The sommelier suggested instead a California Cabernet Sauvignon, one Tom had heard of.

Rob Davis, the winemaker at Jordan since the start of the project in 1976, was hand-picked by consultant Andre Tchelistcheff while Rob was still a student at U. C. Davis.

The name was Beaulieu Vineyard Georges de Latour Private Reserve Cabernet Sauvignon. The taste was magical.

Jordan thought that if California could make wine like this, he could establish roots on the West Coast instead of having to go to Bordeaux. So in 1972, Jordan contacted the man who had made the wine that had made such an impact on him: Tchelistcheff.

Andre was, then, head of winemaking at Beaulieu Vineyards in Rutherford, but he was restive, looking for greater challenges. BV had been acquired by Heublein and Andre felt its family spirit evaporating. He longed to move on.

As a consultant, Tchelistcheff helped Jordan locate property, a 1,500-acre plot above Alexander Valley for the home and winery and 240 acres for the vineyard. And he even helped set the style of wine.

It is a style not unlike that of BV. The wines were initially aged in American oak casks, as BV does. And like BV, the wine was silky and elegant from the outset, more drinkable than competing Cabernets.

The Jordans and their three children moved to California to pursue the winery lifestyle. In 1974 Jordan sold Trend, though later he would re-enter the oil-and-gas business, forming Jordan Oil and Gas, which filled office space in Healdsburg.

By 1976, the young vines produced a small crop; to make the wine, Tchelistcheff suggested young Robert Davis, one of the top students in the U.C. Davis enology department. Davis graduated in the spring of 1976, and within days he was working at Jordan.

The winery was placed on top of an oak-covered knoll above the Alexander Valley. Its design was patterned after a Bordeaux chateau, with handsome guest rooms and an elegant formal dining room whose double doors face into the winemaking facility.

When Tom and Sally Jordan built their French-style chateau in the hills of the Alexander Valley, they included a series of terraced areas where visitors could sit and sip wine while watching the sun set.

The formal setting was Jordan's way of showing that the image of a fine wine could be enhanced by a good meal. And dining in sight of the barrels was that much more sybaritic. Pouring Jordan Cabernet into crystal and serving it with great food imprints the wine on the mind of the taster far more dramatically than serving the same wine in a plastic cup to someone sitting behind the tuba player at a high school football game.

Cabernet Sauvignon was the winery's first success. The 1976 wine stunned connoisseurs because of the delicate nature of the fruit and the fact that it was so approachable at such an early age. Later, Davis experimented with various styles of Chardonnay, Jordan's second wine.

Over the years, Jordan Cabernet was more and more aged in French oak while the Chardonnay more and more took on classic proportions. Production at Jordan rose by 1990 to 45,000 cases of Cabernet Sauvignon and 25,000 cases of Chardonnay. They were made entirely from 275 acres planted in 1972, on a low-lying Alexander Valley parcel located below the winery.

Years later, a new idea was conceived. When Tom and Sally Jordan entertained, they liked to serve Champagne to guests, and for some functions they chose Iron Horse sparkling wine. Jordan wanted to make his own sparkling wine, so in the mid-1980s Tom and his daughter, Judy, formed a new compa-

ny. Jordan Sparkling Wine Co. produces just one product, made by French and American experts in the *méthode champenoise*.

Because of their appreciation of the Iron Horse style, the Jordans hired former Iron Horse sparkling-wine maker Claude Thibaut to make the *cuvées*, starting with the 1987 harvest.

To make the project a true sparkling-wine estate, the Jordans bought land on Eastside Road near the Russian River, west of Windsor — land that includes another oak-covered knoll. The Jordans have built a sparkling-wine facility in the Russian River Valley, next to the Pinot Noir and Chardonnay planted to make the wine.

The name of the new sparkling wine is simply "J." The idea is that when people ask for Dom Perignon, they usually say, "Let's have Dom," or D.P. Jordan hopes people someday will simply order, "A bottle of J."

The bottle shape selected by Jordan for this project is unique. And the wines will always be blends of Pinot Noir and Chardonnay, fermented at least three years in the bottle.

The Jordans live a quiet life, never throwing lavish parties or doing splashy promotions, though members of the wine trade often stay overnight in the lavishly appointed guest rooms and dine in the Jordan manner in the Jordan manor. *DB*

The cask-filled aging room at Jordan is attached to the dining room. There guests can sit at tables adorned with silver candelabras and dine on classic cuisine within a few feet of the glass doors showing where wine is made.

To ensure there would never be any cramping of the winemaker, the Jordan winery building was made larger than needed for the small quantity of wine that would be made. The building was then integrated with spacious guest quarters.

KENWOOD VINEYARDS

This old barn houses one of the warmest tasting rooms you'll find. On weekends you're likely to find tasty food items, prepared by the Kenwood staff to demonstrate how different wine and food pairings work.

In an era when there are more horn blowers than deeds worth blowing about, it is refreshing to find folks whose work stands forward, framed by the very shadows of their own modesty. Given a two-decade track record of excellence, you might expect the folks at Kenwood Vineyards to stand up and crow. But no. You will not find these folks on a fence post warbling at the moon.

Kenwood's unprepossessing winery sits well back from the road, a covey of warm, wood buildings framed by silent vines in front and whispering oaks behind. But what comes away from there, in bottle, speaks persuasively. The rich, toasty Beltane Chardonnay has been a standard for years. A creamy, lemon-fruited Chardonnay defines the rocky, clay-loam vineyard called Yulupa (the Miwok Indian term

meaning "ever-flowing"), named for an all-year spring on the property.

Kenwood's silky-lean Sauvignon Blancs, with apple and lemon fruit, have won trunks full of medals.

Then there are the pepper-spiced Jack London Zinfandels. The rough-hewn Jack London Cabernets. The refined Artist Series Cabernets. Even the Vintage Red and Vintage White have

a vocabulary that leaves "leftovers" far back in the dust.

The Artist Series Cabernets have given Kenwood recognition well beyond that which the wines earn on their own merits. The concept got off to an unintentionally wild start when the winery was ready to release its 1975 Cabernet, the first of the Artist Series. The original label, featuring a reclining nude on a hillside, was painted by Berkeley poster artist David Lance Goines, whose works are included in the collections of the Museum of Modern Art, the Smithsonian, and the Louvre.

But the Bureau of Alcohol, Tobacco, and Firearms (ATF) rejected the label saying, "The Bureau regards the picture as 'obscene or indecent.'" Said Goines to Marty Lee, the head of winery marketing who dreamed up the Artist Series idea, "I've never gotten anything past those blue-nosed bastards the first time yet. Just to comfort you, they're all going to hell when they die."

Goines redesigned the painting, this time replacing the reclining nude with a reclining skeleton. Same hillside, same cloud background. "The bureaucrats must have scratched their heads a few times before they could come up with a reason to reject that one," laughs Marty. "They finally came back with the note: 'Rejected — particularly in light of current opinion on the fetal alcohol syndrome and alcoholism.'"

The final version showed a bare hillside, with the clouds moved to the far right hand side. Said Goines, "We'll just have to imagine the girl is still on the hill, but on the other side where we can't see her and be morally offended by her pretty figure."

Subsequent Artist Series labels have ranged from a color still life (Nell Melcher, the '76 vintage) to a New England sailboat and lighthouse (Joseph Neary, the '79), and from the realistic (Golden Gate Bridge, Joseph Eidenberger, '81) to the impressionistic (Painted Door, James Harrill, '82). There's even a multimedia label — Eventide Sonata, '83, by Marcus Uzilevsky,

A glass of Kenwood Sauvignon Blanc, perhaps the most recognized Sauvignon Blanc in the country. The Kenwood style features an herbaceous perfume with sweet lemon fruit, a hint of smoke from the oak, and a finish that combines lime and fresh grass flavors.

which includes a cassette tape of Bob Hogins' piano interpretation of Uzilevsky's painting.

Kenwood Vineyards occupies the entire Lee family (including brother-in-law John Sheela, president); they scraped together savings in 1970 to purchase the "rustic" (read "falling apart quickly") Pagani Winery on the east side of Highway 12, just north of the russet slopes of Wildwood Vineyards. The Paganis had produced, since 1906, the hearty reds known best by their Italian ancestors. The Lees had different notions.

One key vineyard for Kenwood is Jack London's former ranch, now owned by Milo Shepard, a shirttail relative of the famous writ-

er. "This vineyard has most of the right ingredients for great Cabernet Sauvignons," notes curly-haired winemaker Mike Lee. "On the west side of the valley, it's a very temperate spot and doesn't get the extremes of heat, because the sun is in the trees by early afternoon. The vineyard has beautiful, rich soils, but Milo doesn't overcrop the vines, so we end up with highly distinctive tastes in the wines."

Originally, the London Ranch fruit was slated to go to Chateau St. Jean, Kenwood's nearest winery neighbor to the north. "I had started reading about Jack London when we bought the winery," recalls Marty, Mike's older brother. "I got to be a real buff, collecting first

Kenwood's handsome wooden warehouse is tucked in a grove of oak trees, set back from Highway 12 on the eastern flank of the Sonoma Valley. The little village of Kenwood hosts the immensely popular Pillow Fights every Fourth of July.

editions. So I met Milo when he began planting vines in 1972, and asked him if he had a home for his fruit.

"He wasn't too sure about our chances, but he let us share in his first vintage. That was 1976, which was the hundredth anniversary of Jack London's birth. So, when I promised to emphasize the historical aspect of the vineyard, Milo agreed to sell us all of his fruit. That's why we give that wine a vineyard designation and put London's signature on the back label, along with a quote from his tract against drink, John Barleycorn, and the wolf's head for London's 'Wolf House'."

Marty likes living in the Valley of the Moon

The dejuicing tanks on top allow free-run juice to be drawn off before the rest of the skins, pulp, seeds, and juice are emptied into the presses for further separation. Pressing too hard leaves too many solids, which can make a wine coarse.

as much as London did. "Coming over the hill into the valley, it's like a time warp," he says pensively. "It's quiet, and the pace of life is slow." Thus, Marty is pleased with his family's decision to level off at 175,000 cases per year, reached in the last decade. "We make a comfortable living at that size. I'd hate being a personnel administrator, which is what I'd have to be if we got all that much bigger."

Downplaying his family's dedication and hard work, Mike Lee lays much of the credit for the winery's success to timing and location. "You'd have to say that we lucked out a little," he explains. "We bought a winery that happened to be near good grapes. We bought it a time when there wasn't the rush to wine country, so we had the chance to get to know the good growers well."

This is quite typical of the modesty of the Lees and their kin. You can see it when Mike talks of his winery's public image. "I don't know if people perceive us as we do. It's important to have a high quality image these days, but we don't set out to use superlatives in describing ourselves or our wines. I think we have a good image with consumers. In fact, it may be better than we think it is." The wines of Kenwood speak to that musing better than anything anyone else might care to add. *RPH*

The Beltane Ranch, a few miles south of the winery, arguably grows the finest Chardonnay Kenwood bottles. "The ranch gets a lot of sun, so you wouldn't think it would be good for Chardonnay," notes Mike Lee. "They must have the perfect clone for that site."

KISTLER VINEYARDS

early three and a half twisting miles up Nun's Canyon is a small vineyard and winery that one might call "Two Guys Winery." Such a moniker is not meant to demean seasonal help. Nor is it to diminish the early contribution of Steve's brother, John. But, truth to tell, the existence of Kistler Vineyards today is mirrored in the faces of its prime founders, former writer Steve Kistler and one time chemistry prof Mark Bixler.

Bixler doesn't have the severe, emaciated look of the prototypical chemistry professor. His soft face, fleshy build, curly brown hair, and sunshine smile make you think more of a chef

pursuing the pleasures of new vistas in cuisine. "Actually, I do like to cook," confides Bixler, an MIT graduate who taught organic chemistry at Fresno State for seven years. "I lean toward Chinese cuisine; Szechwan to be specific. I like to do a dried, shredded beef, wok-fried in oil and ginger, with celery, carrots, and red peppers. It's unsauced, but its vegetable flavors are subtle and really come through."

Ah, what wine do you serve with that? "Beer," laughs Bixler. "Okay, maybe a Gewurztraminer, or perhaps a Johannisberg Riesling. But beer is preferred."

Mark's initial interest in wine had been

Kistler Vineyards is set near the crest of the west-facing flank of the Mayacamas Mountains. There is iron in these reddish hills, so Cabernet Sauvignon is well-suited to the slopes. Chardonnay is also grown at Kistler.

sparked by trips through the Napa Valley while he was doing his doctoral work at Berkeley. It took fire when he helped guide a tasting group at Fresno State. "In the late sixties, our Berkeley research group had been tasting '61 Bordeaux and the occasional Chateau d'Yquem," he considers. "The wine that really fired my simmering interest was Martin Ray's 1948 Cabernet Sauvignon, which wasn't released until the late '60s. Here was a California red wine, nearly 20 years old, and yet as intense as its flavors were, it was smooth and drinkable."

It was at Fresno State that Mark and Steve met. "I had done my undergraduate work at

Stanford," says Steve, whose light green eyes are shaded by a dark shock of tousled hair. "I was an English major, creative writing, so I tried for four years to write fiction. You know how crazy that is!"

So Steve returned to school, attending Davis and Fresno for theory, then working two years at Ridge Vineyards, the prototypical mountainside winegrowing estate. The Kistler property covers more than half a section (a section is a square mile, or 640 acres) on the southwest slopes of the Mayacamas Mountains, just miles away, as the crow flies, from Mount Veeder and Mount St. John. Brush covers most of the 360 acres of the Kistler property and, due to the steepness of the terrain, barely 30 acres have been terraced to accommodate vines. Chardonnay, the mainstay of Kistler Vineyards, accounts for 18 acres; the remaining 12 acres are planted to Cabernet Sauvignon.

"When I got out of school, the only thing I knew for sure was that I wanted to handcraft something," says Steve slowly. "A short story. A wine. I wanted to be a craftsman. I've found that here. I like taking care of the vines. And I like having a place where the winemaker actually makes the wines, and is not relegated to being a mere administrator. You see, I like being in the middle of a problem . . . trying to solve it." *RPH*

Chardonnay is the mainstay of Kistler Vineyards, and accounts for 18 acres of its vineland. The remaining 12 acres are planted to Cabernet Sauvignon.

Though the property of Kistler Vineyards covers more than 360 acres, only 30 acres have been recovered, through terracing, for the vine.

KORBEL CHAMPAGNE CELLARS

Getting the spent yeast cells out of the bottle of twice-fermented wine is the key problem in making sparkling wine by the French *méthode champenoise*.

To make classical-method sparkling wines, one first makes wine without bubbles, puts it in the bottle with additional yeast and sugar, and caps it. The yeast converts the sugar into carbon dioxide and alcohol. Since the bottle is sealed with a steel crown cap, the carbon dioxide — the bubbles — have nowhere to go, so they remain in the wine, in solution.

However, after the bubbles are created, there is sediment, essentially the dead yeast cells, remaining in the wine. This residue must be gotten out of the bottle, but it is a fine, almost powdery substance that resists removal. You must invert the bottle and jostle it gently to get the sediment down into the neck of the bottle. Then the neck is immersed in a freezing brine solution, and when the sediment freezes into an ice plug, the cap is popped off and the sediment goes flying out of the bottle.

Getting the sediment down into the neck is the trick, and the traditional method calls for the inverted bottles to be "riddled" — turned a quarter-turn daily by a worker. This is costly.

Adolf Heck, who with his brother, Paul,

Winemaker Bob Stashak and a large crew make a wide range of sparkling wines. Most of the products are non-vintage wines blended from vines growing here and in other viticultural regions. Stashak is developing a vintage-dated appellation sparkling wine.

bought the Korbel winery in 1954, invented the first automated riddling device to get the sediment down into the neck of the bottle. It was a system of parallel templates with holes cut in them. Bottles placed upside down in the twin rack were automatically moved backward and forward until the sediment was in the neck.

Heck was awarded two patents on his idea in the 1960s, and Korbel used the labor-saving device — as well as skilled marketing and a top-quality product — to develop one of the fastest-selling sparkling-wine brands in the United States.

The entrance to Korbel, open to visitors, is 12 miles west of Highway 101. Visitors may take a tour of the facility, see a special multimedia presentation on the winery's history, tour its famed rose garden, and taste some of Korbel's sparkling and still wines.

F. Korbel and Brothers actually was founded as a wood-products company in the mid-1850s by Czechoslovakian brothers Joseph (a gunsmith), Francis (a cigar maker), and Anton (a locksmith) Korbel. They logged the redwoods well west of Santa Rosa, and when the lumber was played out, the brothers switched to other agricultural crops. However, they found that only grapes made any economic sense, and thus began the saga of sparkling wine in western Sonoma County.

The descendants of the Korbel brothers sold the winery to the Heck family only after assurances that the new owners would maintain the quality the founders had developed, and the Hecks did just that. Over the years, the Korbel winery made strides in quality by exploring different viticultural areas and different grape varieties.

After the Heck brothers bought the winery, the quality of the sparkling wine was also improved by more modern methods of production. In addition, a small amount of still wine was produced. It remains part of the Korbel line, but for sale at the winery only.

In the late 1970s, Heck invented an even better system of riddling the bottles. It called for the second fermentation to take place inside the boxes in which the wine would be shipped. The bottles with the added yeast and sugar were put into the boxes, neck down, and

Some of Korbel's vineyards are located in a low spot along the Russian River. In the spring of 1986, heavy rains flooded the area and the Korbel vineyards were under eight feet of water. But vines are hardy and they recovered by harvest time to produce an excellent crop.

the boxes placed on a giant pallet that had pneumatic lifts and springs on either side. On a set schedule, the pumps would raise one side of the pallet a few inches and then drop the side of the pallet down onto the springs. The result was automatic shaking of the sediment into the neck.

Adolf's son, Gary, who also held a part-time position as a deputy sheriff, joined the winery in 1965, soon working his way up to executive vice president. In the early 1980s Gary became president, as Adolf reduced his activities with the winery.

The most controversial aspect of the Korbel winery in the 1980s was the almost *Falcon Crest*-like intrigue surrounding Adolf Heck and his constant companion, Veronica Miramon-tez. Adolf Heck remained married to Richie C. Heck, the mother of their four children, but Miramontez often accompanied him at social events.

When Adolf died unexpectedly in 1984, Miramontez filed suit to challenge Heck's will, but was largely unsuccessful.

In 1985, with Gary Heck now president and chairman of the board, Korbel hit one million cases of *méthode champenoise* sparkling wine. Korbel persisted in calling its product "Champagne" even though use of the term irritated French producers, who claim that anything using that term must come from the Champagne district in France.

Korbel owns some 3,000 acres of land out here in the heavily wooded, western Russian

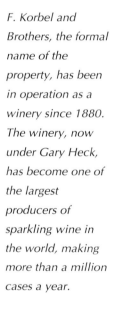

F. Korbel and Brothers, the formal name of the property, has been in operation as a winery since 1880. The winery, now under Gary Heck, has become one of the largest producers of sparkling wine in the world, making more than a million cases a year.

River wildlands. The winery buys grapes from Sonoma County and other areas of the state, including Santa Barbara County and the central San Joaquin Valley.

The company also makes a top-selling brandy of high quality. Brandy was first made here by the Korbel family and shipped in 1889. Brandy production stopped in 1919 at the start of Prohibition and now the brandy is made in the San Joaquin Valley.

The classic tower that once was the production center for brandy on the Korbel property still sits in the middle of the facility here, a picturesque reminder of an earlier era.

Korbel's brandy sales reached 375,000 cases in the late 1980s, and the company was third in national brandy sales to E. & J. Gallo

The sprawling Korbel ranch in Guerneville has a number of older buildings on it that are used for guest quarters, offices, storage, and other mundane activities.

and The Christian Brothers. Meanwhile, sparkling wine sales were level at just over 1.1 million cases by 1991.

Over the years, winemaker Bob Stashak has developed a following for the winery's Brut, Blanc de Noirs, and especially the Korbel Natural, an essentially dry wine. All Korbel wines were non-vintage.

However, in 1991 Korbel was making plans to release a line of vintage-dated sparkling wines. *DB*

The older buildings evoke the feel of an earlier day and are so charming that they have been renovated.

LA CREMA

When first opened as La Crema Vinera ("the cream of the vintner" in Spanish), this winery bragged of being the first winery in Petaluma since Prohibition and boasted Burgundian wines from individual vineyards. Today, La Crema no longer makes single vineyard wines and, indeed, is no longer in Petaluma. In fact, everything, from ownership to winemaker, is new, save for the Burgundian leaning.

The winery was founded in a Petaluma industrial complex in the spring of 1979 by winemaker Rod Berglund and partners John Bessey (an Optical Coating Lab engineer), Bob Goyette, and Rick Burmester. Berglund, who later took over winemaking at Joe Swan, made some excellent, if eclectic, wines.

In June 1985, a group of East Coast wine enthusiasts, headed by rare-wine specialist Jason Korman, bought the winery and moved La Crema (figuratively and literally) from its experimental mode into a more commercial stance. The winery now resides in a spartan steel building between Sebastopol and Forestville, across a gravel road from Gan Eden.

La Crema's winemaker is Philadelphia-born Dan Goldfield. His ruddy complexion

Winemaker Dan Goldfield stands among hundreds of white oak barrels in his broad barrel cellar. You need a lot of barrels if you're going to barrel ferment white wines. "Yeah, we barrel ferment everything here," he shrugs. "Chardonnay, Sauvignon Blanc . . . even our Chenin Blanc!"

suggests the out-of-doors, and indeed he's a kayaker and backpacker who once trekked through Alaska near the Arctic circle with his equally adventurous wife. Goldfield studied at Brandeis University, where he double-majored in philosophy and chemistry.

"I like concepts," Goldfield says with a shrug. "I loved the theory of physical chemistry, but found that I didn't want to spend my life sitting in front of a computer screen."

He took a year off, spending half of it at the University of Utah doing computer models in theoretical chemistry, half doing underwater research at Woods Hole studying diurnal

A worker is cleaning out small, open-top stainless-steel fermenters. These fermenters are used specifically for Pinot Noir, whose fermentation temperature must be controlled carefully — a task that can be done more easily in smaller tanks.

migrations. "I love to sail, so I headed for Berkeley, where I spent two years at the Lawrence Berkeley Lab doing energy research, then two and a half years at the U.C. Medical Center in San Francisco doing toxicology research. For the first time, I was making money like a real person, and I spent it sailing on the bay and buying French Burgundies."

His brother had turned him on to wine in college, and Goldfield was lured by the sensual attributes of Burgundies and Italian Barolos. "These are wines that have a lot of flavors, but they still talk to you!" he stresses. "For a Bordeaux or Cabernet to be a great wine, it has to be perfect. But a Burgundy can have all sorts of problems . . . and still be wonderful!"

Seeking to turn hobby toward career, he enrolled at U.C. Davis, earning his master's in December 1986. He worked at Robert Mondavi and Schramsberg before joining La Crema in May 1990 to make Chardonnay, Pinot Noir, and a barrel-fermented Chenin Blanc.

"Our owner, Jason Korman, is a young guy — he was only 25 when he bought the place — with a great palate," says Goldfield. "He had already had a lot of experience with the Eastern wine establishment, so he had some great contacts when he came here. It's a long way from Long Island to Stockton, where he lives now, but he's doing a great job of marketing and selling our wines." *RPH*

A bucket of whole berries is dumped into the press, where juice will be separated from solids. The grape solids, called pomace — skins, seeds, pulp — will later be tilled into the vineyard to enrich the soil.

LAMBERT BRIDGE

Gerard Lambert III didn't know in 1969 that the one-lane bridge he crossed to view property northwest of Healdsburg in Dry Creek Valley was called Lambert Bridge, named for C. L. Lambert, an early pioneer here.

"One reason for naming the winery Lambert Bridge was the coincidence — Lambert was my name," says Jerry. "Also, when we bought this place, it was the only man-made structure visible from where the winery is, and today, if you're on the bridge, the only man-made structure visible is the winery."

Lambert bought 119 acres here to grow grapes; winemaking was secondary. "When you start something like this, you're trying to grow the best fruit that you can," he says. "Then it just seemed to me to lack fulfillment not to process the fruit I had grown. So we built the winery to make wine."

The winery was designed by Lambert and was built in 1975, five years after the vineyards were developed.

Lambert's first winemaker, Ed Samperton, set the style here, making wines of finesse and elegance. After Samperton left to open his own winery nearby, Nick Martin became winemaker, but he left to join his brother, Tom, at Martin Bros. Winery in Paso Robles. Jamie Meves then

The aging cellar at Lambert Bridge provides a peaceful respite from the hectic life Jerry Lambert has led in the last decade. Today, with a solid winemaker on board, Lambert is making excellent wines.

146

came on board, but he left to work for Pat Paulsen and then for Chateau de Baun. Finally, in 1979, Lambert hired Ed Killian and his wines became increasingly excellent.

The all estate-bottled winery, which made just 9,000 cases in 1982, soon hit a flat spot. In 1983, Lambert signed an agreement with Joseph Seagram and Sons to market Lambert Bridge wines under its Seagram Classics Wine Co. division. It was a decision Lambert would grow to regret.

The agreement spurred Lambert to produce more wine than he ever imagined — 31,000 cases a year at one point. He later admitted that

Jerry Lambert had a number of different winemakers in the early years of his winery; then he was kept occupied by a major lawsuit, in which he and other wineries were pitted against the giant Joseph Seagram and Sons. At last, in the late 1980s, stability, excellent wines, and good marketing righted the Lambert Bridge ship.

sales never reached the target and by the spring of 1986, Lambert Bridge's sales had suffered so much that the agreement between the winery and Seagram was terminated.

Lambert and two other wineries eventually sued Seagram for not acting in good faith, claiming their wines were being "dumped" at prices that permitted the Chardonnay and Cabernet to be sold at $3 a bottle. "Not only didn't I have a marketing system any more, but my own wine was out there at prices so low they were competing with me," says Lambert.

After the break with Seagram in 1986, Lambert Bridge's debt rose to more than $1 million. "Some of the land I had bought had to be sold off to pay debts," said Lambert. However, the quality of the wines soared under Killian. And by 1988, production had dropped back to a manageable 25,000 cases a year. Then the winery began to get a string of gold medals at major wine competitions. That success, plus critical acclaim elsewhere, helped the winery regain all of its original luster.

"We've come back thanks to Paul Schofield, our marketing director, and an exemplary staff," says Lambert. "He's done a creative marketing job."

Lambert was an heir of the family that founded the Warner-Lambert company, but Jerry's ancestors sold their ownership in the company quite a while ago. *DB*

The Lambert Bridge wine label has on it a drawing of the steel bridge that coinci dentally was called Lambert Bridge when Jerry bought this property. The bridge crosses Dry Creek. When Lambert first visited the property, the bridge was the only man-made structure within view.

LANDMARK VINEYARDS

There was the old Landmark; now there is the new Landmark. And, while the new sits not at the end of a row of stately cypresses in Windsor, neither is it immediately threatened by housing developments.

Instead, nestled at the base of Mount Hood, the new Landmark Vineyards is surrounded by vineyards, and its neighbors are not houses and a shopping center, but a pair of saintly wineries (St. Jean and St. Francis).

"We had hoped to stay in Windsor forever," recalls William "Bill" Mabry III, whose family founded Landmark Vineyards in 1974. "But we knew our stay was limited when Raley's came in with their food store. Windsor was no longer a sleepy, two-block farming community. The zoning had been changed to residential and, wham, we were looking at a sewer assessment of a million dollars!"

There being a time to fight and a time to flee, Mabry took the opportunity of selling high and buying low. "The question we faced was, Where to go? We have vineyards in Alexander Valley and Sonoma, but to have built at either of those sites, we would have had to tear out more vines. And I'd already watched them tear out the vines we had at the original winery. That hurt quite enough, thanks."

Landmark hews closely to California's Spanish traditions with this central courtyard, which looks out to Sugarloaf Mountain. The earth-toned stucco finish of the walls recalls the hand-plastered adobe used in haciendas of old.

So, after inspecting some 30 sites all over the county, Mabry stumbled upon the perfect solution, practically splitting the difference between his two vineyard loci: Kenwood, in the heart of the Sonoma Valley.

"We wanted to keep the early California flavor of the old winery, finished in 1976, and villa, built in the late '20s," says Mabry. He has done just that. Built around a courtyard that features a carved fountain — and a pair of 40-year-old live oaks that were lifted into place by crane — are three wings: The hospitality center, complete with tasting room, kitchen, dining room, guest cottage, and a tower room for pri-

A blazing fire takes the chill off of winter mornings in Landmark's inviting tasting room. In the old days, most wineries held tastings on a board supported by a pair of barrels stood on end, in the cellar — which could get pretty chilly in winter.

vate tastings, sits on the south side; the west wing houses offices; the north wing is the working winery.

With the move, completed in 1990, came a change in ownership structure. The winery had been founded by Bill's dad, Air Force pilot and architect Colonel William Mabry Jr., and other partners. But when it became evident that the winery would have to leave Windsor, most of the partners wanted out. Which worked out fine, since one wanted all the way in.

Bill Mabry stayed on as winemaker and managing partner, but the largest part of Landmark is now owned by Damaris Deere Wiman Ethridge, an original partner in Landmark and no stranger to ventures agricultural. Mrs. Ethridge, you see, is the great-great-grand-daughter of John Deere, the man who invented the steel plow and founded Deere & Co.

Ethridge was quick to put her mark on Landmark, first in the label redesign necessitated by the move (the old label featured the twin rows of cypress trees leading up to the villa at the original winery). She bypassed the usual wine label artists for New York designer Tom Richardson, who had created logos for Ivory Soap and Arrow Shirts. His label features "Landmark" in black, slashing diagonally up the center, with a ragged border of bright raspberry-violet across the top. It has a presence. *RPH*

This newly planted vineyard took the place of a dying walnut orchard. As wine increased in popularity in the 1960s, the farming focus of Sonoma County shifted from grains, prunes, apples, and walnuts to Chardonnays, Sauvignon Blancs, Zinfandels, Pinot Noirs, and Cabernet Sauvignons.

LAUREL GLEN VINEYARD

When you see red leaves in the vineyard during the fall, don't assume that it's the change of colors. It usually indicates fan leaf virus. This is not fatal to the vine, but it does decrease fruit production. This, however, may only serve to improve and intensify fruit flavors.

The air about Laurel Glen Vineyard has a sweetness to it. There is even a pastoral air about Patrick Campbell as he clumps around his vineyard and winery. There is noise to his clumping, but it is noise not heard. The distinct air of serenity at Laurel Glen might best be laid at the door of Patrick's almost spiritual focus on Cabernet.

"The role model for Laurel Glen is a composite of the Bordeaux estates," begins Campbell, a one-time English major who later took a masters in the philosophy of religion from Harvard's Divinity School. "I believe in the concept of an integrated system where you concentrate on a single product from beginning to end.

It works here for a lot of reasons. Cabernet Sauvignon has always been my favorite

wine, and that was what was planted here when we bought the property in 1977. Cabernet Sauvignon is a variety that is conducive to blending, and blending makes it more fun to make as a wine.

"I like making one wine for the simplicity of it, the efficiency, the concentration of it. The bookkeeping is easier, glass [bottle] orders are easier, and you have a better focus

in selling the wine. It also helps with our identity in the marketplace. When people think of Laurel Glen we hope they'll think of Cabernet.

"I planted an acre of Chardonnay at one point, to see how it would do. But a couple of barrels in a corner of the winery got to be a pain. I was always having to move them to get to something else."

"I also believe that it's a good thing to take your product from start to finish," admits Campbell. "It's impossible to make a living by farming 40 acres of quality grapes and then giving the fruit to someone else. That's like giving your kid away at age ten, after having raised him halfway.

"We were getting paid at the highest level for Sonoma County Cabernet Sauvignon by wineries who gave our fruit vineyard designation. But unless you're not servicing any debt, unless your land is paid off, it's not economically feasible to grow quality Cabernet and let someone else make the wine . . . and the profits."

As persuasive as the economic push was, the philosophical motivation toward unifying the process was equally powerful. "First off, to exist as a small winery, you have to have the topmost quality, and get a price for it. I made a big effort to get my name out to the press and public. I'm not real aggressive or pushy, but I do enjoy meeting people."

Campbell made one wise choice in defining Laurel Glen to his customers: he hung his reputation on the vineyard. "I learned early on that this vineyard had achieved something of a name for itself, so I decided to develop its following. When I first went out to visit major California retailers, and the top wine writers, I tried to show the similarity of winemaking techniques and the consistency of character and style in the wines from year to year."

As a winemaker, Campbell tries to accentuate the natural fruitiness of his grapes, and prop it up with a solid acid spine. "With

The poetry of wine
lies in putting
together flavors that
either contrast or
complement. You
can almost imagine
the flavors of these
grilled filets — laid
out so delectably at
Sonoma Mission Inn
— matching up
beautifully to Laurel
Glen's violet-filled
Cabernet Sauvignon.

Cabernet, there is a spectrum from vegetal to berry. We're not at the herbal, olive, bell pepper end of that spectrum; we're closer to the berry end. We field-crush the fruit, which helps retain that natural berry-like quality; we've trained our pickers over the years so that they know to put only clean, ripe fruit into the crusher. We ferment in open-top fermenters, which tends to blow off alcohol. That means we can pick fairly ripe fruit without getting high, out-of-balance alcohol levels."

(That said, Campbell has set out a small test plot of Syrah [a Rhone variety], Tempranillo [a Spanish variety], and Mataro [another Rhone] to see what they might add to his Cabernet Sauvignon.

"If any of them grow well and add a positive dimension to my wine, I'll try them out in my second label, Counterpoint, for a couple of years, and even consider them for Laurel Glen.")

The Laurel Glen Cabernets are firmly structured, ageable wines with plush, well-defined fruit — usually in the blackberry, black cherry, and violet range. As such, they are in high demand in the marketplace; Patrick is able to sell a fair portion of each new release in the "futures" market.

"The theory of futures, for the consumer, is

The sages note that the most important tracks in a vineyard are the footprints of its owner. Patrick Campbell, shown here with his vineyard consultant, Spike, spends a good deal of time monitoring vine growth and fruit development throughout the growing season.

that you get the wines at a much lower price than you'd have to pay when the normal release date finally rolls around," explains Campbell. "The idea is that the wines will appreciate in value over time.

The main advantage to me is the publicity this market entails. There are big tastings on the East Coast, with a lot of fancy people, a lot of important people."

For all his seriousness about the business, Campbell does have a sense of the serendipitous. One year, when the fall was cool and damp, and a fair amount of botrytis (the noble rot) stalked the vineyards, Patrick made a small quantity of late-harvest dessert

High on the flank of Sonoma Mountain, Laurel Glen Vineyard overlooks the upper Sonoma Valley. This view is toward Kenwood and the vineyards on the western flanks of the Mayacamas Mountains.

wine, dubbed Cochino de Oro. The literal translation from the Spanish is "the pig of gold." Something of the silk purse from the sow's ear is what you might imagine, for the wine, though made from rotting grapes, was rich with honey and melon flavors.

"Actually, 'cochino' has more the connotation of gross, or pig-like behavior," says Campbell with a laugh. "The pickers, when they were harvesting the fruit, which was covered with the greyish mold of botrytis, kept saying, 'You sure you want this cochino fruit, hombre?'"

If there is a sweetness that permeates the rural quiet of Laurel Glen — Patrick, his wife, Faith, and their three lovely daughters live surrounded by vines and family dogs, far from the madding crowd — there is nothing saccharine about the place, the people, or the product.

Just as dogs seem to take on the look of their owners, so too do wines follow the precepts of their producers. Patrick Campbell is a lean, wiry, almost spartan fellow. (How else do you explain the fact that he gets up at 5:30 a.m. to practice on the viola?) So are his wines. "I'm obviously not an opulent person," he agrees. "Otherwise I would be making Pinot Noir!" *RPH*

Gnarled, maturing vines of Cabernet Sauvignon — grown in the shallow soils of a mountain regime — can be expected to yield wines of character and definition. At Laurel Glen, winegrower Patrick Campbell takes full advantage of that intensity, but tempers it in a style that is at once powerful and subtle.

LAURIER

Hidden in a green glen in the hills north of Forestville, Laurier once was a vine-filled retirement estate for Barbara and Jacob Shilo.

Polish-born Jacob Shilo was a youth in summer camp in 1939 when the German army invaded. He fled through Russian-held land and just two weeks before Germany invaded Holland, Shilo escaped to Israel. He got a degree in water engineering and after World War II solved a number of key problems for that arid country. In appreciation, the government gave him a trip to New York, where he met Barbara, whom he eventually married.

Jacob, who had become president of an electronics company, commuted between New York and Tel Aviv until 1978, when he left the whirlwind life. It was then that the Shilos founded Domaine Laurier to make fine wine. Jacob and Barbara, a renowned artist, designed and built there one of the most attractive homes in Sonoma County and a small 3,000-square-feet winery. They hired Steve Test to make wine and his age-worthy wines won numerous awards.

The sudden death of Jacob in 1988 of a heart attack ended the dream the Shilos shared. Soon Barbara sold the winery to a Santa Rosa

Laurier was a tiny winery until Vintech acquired it and built this estate-sized winery, complete with guest quarters, on the back edge of the property, set well back from the road. Here Merry Edwards makes the Laurier wines that have received praise.

partnership, which spent more than $3 million in constructing a gorgeous, state-of-the-art winery covering 29,000 square feet. The winery's name was changed to just Laurier and Merry Edwards was hired to make the wine.

Edwards, who has a master's degree in winemaking from U. C. Davis, had an extensive background in wine. She was winemaker at Mount Eden in the Santa Cruz Mountains from 1974 to 1976, then joined Matanzas Creek in 1977, making the wines there through 1984. That year she also started her own winery, The Merry Vintners.

In creating a bolder style of wine for Lauri-

Winemaker Merry Edwards operates out of Laurier's carefully designed "in place" barrel storage room, in which each barrel sits on its own rack. This arrangement makes handling of the oak casks easier than configurations where barrels sit on barrels.

er, Edwards -- always a lover of very ripe Chardonnay fruit -- says she's excited about the Chardonnay growing nearby in the western Russian River area. "There is an intensely spicy character to the fruit here," says Edwards, "so when I find a lot that has that character, I'm careful about whether that lot goes through malolactic fermentation, and about the choice of yeast, and what kind of oak I use [in aging]."

The Pinot Noirs likewise need care to capture the delicate fruit the grape has, but which it yields grudgingly. Steve Test made some wonderful Pinot Noirs here. They were light in color, but packed with flavor and often were compared with Burgundy of Beaune, France.

Because the 15-acre vineyard provides such dramatic Pinot Noir fruit, Edwards tore out all the Chardonnay and planted the entire estate to Pinot Noir, a bold move.

Production under the Shilos had been 15,000 cases. Edwards immediately targeted 45,000 cases and said the winery would top out in the mid-1990s at 60,000 cases. But in late 1990 the owners were forced to declare bankruptcy on Laurier.

Edwards remained as the winemaker, however, and Laurier's wines continued to improve. And Barbara Shilo still lives, paints, and sculpts in the mountaintop home she and Jacob built. DB

The sloping Laurier ranch hidden behind a ridge in Forestville is now planted entirely to Pinot Noir, the grape variety that seems to do best here. The winery's Chardonnay is blended from grapes purchased from a variety of cool-climate vineyards located nearby.

LYETH WINERY

There is a wonderful focus that has grown out of the estate the late Munro "Chip" Lyeth Jr. founded in 1972. The best evidence is a bottle of the estate red, which has only the word "Lyeth," a spare outline of the chateau, and the vintage date — all silk-screened in 14-karat gold! That's the whole front label, and it's a stunningly simple, yet effective package.

Yes, the feds do require that that trivial "other" stuff —appellation, address, alcohol content, Universal Product Code, and all the mandatory warning garbage — exists on a paper back label. But what the public sees, standing on a wine shelf, is a packaging purity that speaks of the fundamental of making just two wines, a red and a white, that need be identified solely by the producer's name.

Lyeth (pronounced "Leeth") had been a world traveler after serving a hitch in the Navy as a linguist, became an adept stunt pilot, then studied photography at the Brooks Institute (Santa Barbara). "Photography taught me to acknowledge excellence," Lyeth once told me, "that you can't do a half-ass job in any business and be successful."

When a European sojourn turned his passion to wine, he bought a 285-acre parcel,

The winery's tri-peaked facade gives the feeling of an English country manor. Inside is a dining room featuring a massive stone fireplace, a fully equipped kitchen, and elegant private guest suites.

north of Geyserville, from Russ Green (then owner of Simi). It had a Victorian house, an old winery (built by the Brignole family just after the turn of the century), three barns, and 25 acres of vines. What Lyeth did — before he was killed piloting his stunt plane in 1988 — was establish a winegrowing estate based strictly on the Bordeaux mold: a red made from Cabernet Sauvignon, Cabernet Franc, Merlot, and Malbec; and a white blended from Sauvignon Blanc, Semillon, and Muscadelle du Bordelais.

"Chip sold the grapes for nearly a decade, and the winery wasn't started until 1981, when

Lyeth ages its red wine 14 months in small barrels made of oak grown in central France. The wines are then removed to these larger, upright, French oak tanks for a year to soften out and prevent oak extraction from becoming dominant in the finished wine.

Chip Sr. sold his banks and told Chip he had 'a little spare change,'" chuckles Bill Arbios, Lyeth's founding winemaker.

The winery is a tri-peaked edifice that recalls an English country manor, with a flagstone court-yard. There are also an English country dining room featuring a massive stone fireplace, a mag-nificent kitchen for chef de cuisine Donna Wegener, and elegant private guest suites.

Like Lyeth, Arbios was committed to the blending ideal, aiming for wines that do not expose the elements from which they were constructed. "I like to have a wine that is har-monious, one that's so integrated that no one component jumps out of the glass. And I prefer fruit flavors to the herbal, grassy flavors that a lot of people get with Cabernet Sauvignon, and even Sauvignon Blanc."

Cabernet Sauvignon provides the frame-work for the red. Fatness in the middle comes from Merlot. Cabernet Franc adds a wonderful raspberry-and-strawberry spice, especially evi-dent in the aromatics. Malbec lends a green olive fruitiness, good color, and firm tannin.

The Lyeth White is built around a skeleton of Sauvignon Blanc. Semillon gives the wine breadth, richness, and roundness in the middle, much as Merlot does for the red blend. The Muscadelle du Bordelais, like Cabernet Franc, adds a floral, spicy sense to the nose. *RPH*

The entryway at Lyeth leads to a central courtyard, covered with flagstone. You'd think you were in an English castle, where the click of a boot heel carries a hundred yards with perfect clarity.

LYTTON SPRINGS WINERY

Oak barrels are employed for aging by everyone serious about making red wines, and increasingly for whites. The smaller the barrel, the greater the oak extraction. American oak is considered by many to be coarser, more obvious than French oak.

Lytton Springs' vineyard was first planted prior to the turn of the century. Owned today by Dick Sherwin, it has been known as one of the great Zinfandel vineyards of California since the early 1970s, when its fruit was the "Lytton Springs" Zinfandel of Ridge Vineyards (1972 to 1976). In 1975, Sherwin, Walt Walters, and Dee Sindt (*Wine World* magazine) began producing wine under their own label. "We made the first two vintages down the road at Vina Vista Winery," remembers Sherwin, now the primary owner of Lytton Springs. By 1977 we were ready to set up and bond our own winery."

Raised in Los Angeles, Sherwin got into publishing with *Sports Car Journal* in the '50s. Later his work evolved into the graphic arts ("that's always been more interesting"). He

started *Wine World* in 1971, then moved into the more lucrative field of girlie magazines. "I miss the money, but wine and pornography are not terribly compatible," he laughs.

It is hard for Dick to speak of the winery without crediting his partner, winemaker "Walt" Walters, who died of heart failure in 1986. Walt was more than partner and winemaker to Dick; he was like an older brother. "I

met Walt in 1969," recalls Dick quietly. "He was married to my wife's aunt — a Mississippi farmboy with a slow, Southern sense of humor and a simple, down-home honesty that quickly made you feel at home.

"He had just retired from the Navy, where he had spent most of his time in food services. He liked the idea of being outdoors and doing physical work, so he was delighted when I asked him to take over the vineyard. He jumped into it with a passion: he took courses at Davis, consulted with other farmers, and each year we made our 200 gallons of wine from our vines. We made pretty good wine, and knew that we had stumbled onto an exceptional vineyard."

The vineyard, sitting on a rolling plateau midway between Dry Creek and Alexander Valley — right down the road from the Healdsburg Airport where Dick keeps his airplane — is about 50 acres, of which some five or six percent is planted to Petite Sirah. "The Petite Sirah adds a little spice to the wine," concedes Sherwin with a wink.

As the winery grew, Walt Walters slid from grape grower into winemaker. "We did give him additional help, but he loved his work to a fault," says Sherwin. "One year, in 1982, his car caught fire, and he suffered a severe heart attack. I used to demand that he leave the winery and go down to the house and rest, but he didn't want to. He wanted, more than anything else in the world, to participate in everything that was going on in the winery."

The early wines were brilliant, which only served to highlight a combination of events — an off year (1981), coupled with the addition of fruit from other vineyards — that yielded a markedly less-than-brilliant wine. "Was that an error in judgment!" states Sherwin frankly. "We bought a lot of grapes that year, expanding production to 10,000 cases, and over-blended the wine. We ended up with a very average wine. It was drinkable. But it wasn't memorable, and it didn't win any prizes. We learned a valuable, and very costly lesson." *RPH*

It is more crucial to Zinfandel than to any other variety that the vines be mature, even old. Young Zinfandel vines tend to ripen fruit unevenly, then go suddenly overripe. Older vines seem to settle down, maturing their fruit at a more even pace. The vines here have been around for more than five decades.

Stainless-steel tanks became a force in winemaking in the 1970s, especially in the production of white wines. By means of a cooler, longer fermentation — you see the thermostat here — a greater portion of the grape's fruitiness can be retained, even in red wine production.

MARK WEST VINEYARDS

Bob Ellis tried to put out of his mind the phrase "absentee owner." A pilot for Pan American World Airways, Ellis was also co-owner, with his wife, Joan, of Mark West Vineyards, a small Russian River Valley winery sitting on 116 acres of some of the most beautiful land in the county.

The couple bought Mark West in 1974 and things went well for the first few years. Joan liked making the wine and Bob could handle his flight chores and still see to the ranch, located a 90-minute drive north of San Francisco.

A number of Joan's early wines gained recognition for their intensity. And the winery grew, to nearly 25,000 cases a year by 1990. All seemed rosy. But during the latter part of the 1980s, things got strained.

"I think both Joan and I are 'nuts and bolts' people," says Bob. "Our background was real estate, and marketing was done when you bought a piece of property. The top three things about property are location, location, location. When you brighten it up, improve the property a bit, then you're in business. Well, it's exactly the opposite in the wine business. You have to have great wine, but then you have to create an image and you have to be consistent with it.

Bob and Joan Ellis began Mark West Vineyards in the mid-1970s, well before the Russian River was known as a fine winegrowing region, and they hit upon a couple of wines of Germanic/Alsatian origin that were widely accepted.

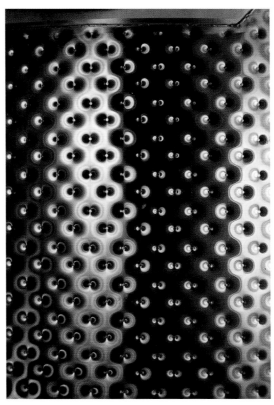

At Mark West both
the Reisling and
Gewurtztraminer
wines are fermented
in stainless steel and
made fairly dry, with
little residual sugar.

You have to promote constantly."

While he was flying, Bob wasn't around to market and promote the Mark West Vineyards brand. "Also, I think Joan got burned out, so we hired Norman Yost to be our winemaker." Yost came from Monticello in the Napa Valley. "And the style of wine did change, but not always to our liking so much. Sales weren't growing the way we hoped. The whole thing led to my retirement from Pan Am. We just needed more attention here."

Yost left in 1990 to work in the Australian wine industry. The Ellises hired David Hopkins to handle winemaking. Bob, meanwhile,

delved eagerly into farming. "We began doing much more work on the vineyards, with rootstock trials and clonal selections and so forth."

Mark West specializes in Chardonnay and Gewurztraminer from its own grapes as well as a stylish Zinfandel from the grapes of Robert Rue in Fulton. However, the winery is slowly gaining a cult following for its Pinot Noirs — excellent but limited in quantity — from the cool Russian River Valley. The Ellises are hoping to expand production of that variety by planting more of it. The property now includes 66 acres of vines, and also provides fruit for a small amount of sparkling Blanc de Noirs. Now and then, Mark West also makes a stunning late-harvest Gewurztraminer.

Hopkins, who had been an assistant at nearby DeLoach Vineyards, had also worked at Paul Masson. It was immediately evident that his style of Chardonnay was more delicate than that of his predecessors. "My style of Chardonnay emphasizes the fruit we get here in Russian River Valley. It has real grapefruit tones and we want to emphasize that."

Mark West also has helped others win plaudits for their wines. Fellow Pan Am pilot Jerry Dion, who grows Chardonnay on his small Sonoma Valley ranch, used to have his wine made at Mark West. And San Francisco art supply dealer, Phil Flax, has Chardonnay

Mark West
Vineyards was
named for an early
Sonoma County
pioneer whose name
now identifies
a meandering creek
that borders
the ranch.

MARTINI & PRATI WINES

A mile and a quarter north of Guerneville Road on Laguna brings you to the crest of Vine Hill. On your left is a silver water tower with big, black, block letters: MARTINI & PRATI. Next to the tower are a pair of ancient, diseased fir trees that will almost certainly come down soon.

In 1881, however, those trees gave a fledgling wine operation its name: Twin Fir Winery. "It was built by a woman writer, but I don't know her name," ponders Elmo Martini, current president of Martini & Prati. It was Elmo's grandfather, Rafaele Martini, who purchased the winery in the 1890s.

Rafaele Martini was born in Lucca, Italy, and came to the United States in the 1860s. He settled in Montera, near Half Moon Bay (south of San Francisco, along the coast), where he farmed vegetables. "He introduced artichokes to San Francisco," says Elmo, with obvious pride.

In 1910 — the year of Elmo's birth — Rafaele's five sons took over the R. Martini Winery. "We never stopped making wine during Prohibition. In fact, we opened a second winery in New York City. Rabbis could buy 50 gallons a month for religious purposes, and there were a lot of rabbis in New York in those days!"

This silver water tower stands as a beacon atop Vine Hill, attracting visitors to Martini & Prati. The winery exists as if in a time warp, harking back to days when consumers still brought their own glass jugs and wooden casks to be filled at the winery.

Elmo was graduated from St. Mary's College in 1933 and immediately sent to New York to run that winery. Four years later he returned to take over the home winery from his father. The winery was handling a lot of wine in those days, especially when Hiram Walker owned it in the '40s. "Oh yeah, we were bottling wine from Seghesio, Frei Brothers, and Ferrari here, and also from many of the valley co-ops. We had 600 employees then, and an inventory of 30 million gallons."

In 1950, Elmo went into partnership with the veteran wine man Enrico Prati, who had played a masterful part in bringing Italian Swiss

Low-slung buildings conceal an extensive facility, capable of storing more than 2.5 million gallons of wine. "We do a lot of crushing and storage for other wineries," notes Elmo Martini modestly. He still makes 100,000 cases under Fountain Grove and Martini & Prati labels.

Colony to vinous prominence. When Enrico dropped dead two years later, his son Edward succeeded him in the partnership.

Martini & Prati remains a good-sized winery today, with a storage capacity of more than 2.5 million gallons, much of that in concrete fermenters and large redwood tanks. The small oak barrels and stainless-steel tanks you see belong to Glen Ellen Winery. "We do a lot of crushing and storage for other wineries," says Elmo. "Three-quarters of our production is for other wineries." Which still means that he's putting out 100,000 cases under his own label and that of Fountain Grove, a label purchased in the mid-'50s when that justly famed champagne-and-table-wine facility went out of business.

Elmo's sons, Tom and Jim, work with him. Ed Prati's son, Pete, handles the necessary book work. The winemaker is Frank Vanucci, a native Santa Rosan, who worked a crush at the old Petri plant in Forestville before hustling off to England to fly ball gunner in B-17s during the war.

Vanucci's brother Harley is in charge of maintenance at the huge winery, and loves to point to the forest of huge redwood tanks. And there are three great concrete tanks, used for cold stabilizing the wines, or chilling them to 24° F for three days to settle out tartrates. The tanks are insulated with six inches of cork. Harley will stick a pocketknife blade into the cork to prove it to you. *RPH*

MATANZAS CREEK WINERY

Bill and Sandra MacIver love to have "wild animals" around their property, so they've selected a number of modern metal sculptures to adorn their property. This one is a crane from sculptor Peter Busby of the neighboring Sonoma County town of Sebastopol.

Matanzas Creek Winery came into existence as a commune settled on hills that rolled beneath a mountain peak. The property was located on the arid benchland of Bennett Valley, a quiet, seldom-traversed enclave on the other side of Sonoma Mountain from the heart of the Valley of the Moon.

Founder Sandra Stern envisioned and planned Matanzas Creek to be a quiet place, a utopia of sorts, where grapes would be grown and peaceful lives would be lived.

Today Matanzas Creek Winery is one of the top producers in California, a winery that has made some of the state's finest wines -- both white and red, and one whose wines are in wide demand. The development is due to Sandra and her husband, Bill MacIver.

Sandra began her existence in New Orleans, the great-granddaughter of Julius Rosenwald, one of the founders of the Sears-Roebuck department store chain. Contrary to public misconception, however, there really was no vast wealth on which the owners of Matanzas Creek could rely. Bill and Sandra knew they'd have to work night and day to make the small winery successful.

Bill understood what hard work was. He grew up poor, the son of itinerant cotton pickers, and he quit school in the tenth grade. He wound up spending 21 years in the armed forces before he moved to California, where he met Sandra.

It was 1974 when Matanzas Creek planted its grapes and three years later when wine began to be made. Sandra and Bill knew they had to get a good start, so they hired one of the best winemakers around -- Merry Edwards, one of the first women in California to operate a major winery. Edwards had been trained at the University of California at Davis and had made spectacular wines at Mount Eden Vineyards in the Santa Cruz Mountains.

In 1979, before the first wines were bottled, Sandra and Bill were married. They decided to make the winery a lifetime project. The ranch seemed capable of growing excellent grapes for top-notch wine and Edwards' first wines were mind-blowing: big, rich, powerful wines that connoisseurs loved. The Chardonnays won gold medals at major wine competitions and seemed to age beautifully in the cellar. And the red wines were deep, dark potent things with years of potential.

Included in this array were such wines as deeply rich Pinot Noirs, dense Merlots, and even such oddities as dry Semillon, a magnificent wine that, tasted a decade later, was a miracle of fruit, finesse, and rich flavors. One reason for the depth of the wines was that the MacIvers used some fruit from the marvelous Sonoma Mountain vineyard of David Steiner, Sandra's former husband. The vineyard is on a remote ranch that typically yields densely scented, concentrated fruit.

In the early 1980s, Edwards and the MacIvers had some differences and Merry left in 1984 to make wine under The Merry Vintners label, jointly owned by herself, her parents, and her husband. Matanzas Creek hired David Ramey to make their wines, and he changed the style somewhat, soon making strides with a Chardonnay that underwent a

A fountain sculpture by local artist Bruce Johnson graces the front of the modest Matanzas Creek property. Johnson entitled the sculpture Izumi. The MacIvers, in addition to being supporters of the arts, are both politically active and have opened their winery's doors to many wine industry meetings.

complete malolactic fermentation. Meanwhile, some of the wines, including Pinot Noir, Cabernet Sauvignon, and Semillon, were dropped.

Production remained at about 3,000 cases a year. Demand for the white wines was so great, however, that in 1984 the MacIvers built a new winery and installed (at the urging of Ramey) one of the county's most modern laboratories in which to analyze wine and grape juice. The building was designed by Santa Rosa architect Paul Hamilton, and set on a plateau a few notches above lightly traveled Bennett Valley Road.

Ramey, who had been assistant to wine-making-legend Zelma Long at Simi Winery, had conducted all sorts of experiments while he was at Simi. He continued that quest at Matanzas Creek, looking for better ways to grow grapes, gentler methods of bottling, the effect of different levels of charring on the inside of barrels, different fermenting and aging techniques, crushing and pressing methods, and even shipping and storage improvements.

Ramey's successes, starting with the 1985 vintage, created even more demand for Matanzas Creek's wines than there had been, and production rose to 20,000 cases. By early 1989 production had hit 30,000 cases a year, with 18,000 cases of that in Chardonnay.

Visitors to Matanzas Creek see first what appears to be a small, elegant building at the top of a hill. The winery is set into the side of the hill, and all the functions are at the rear and on a lower level, cooled in part by being partially underground.

Among the winery's major hits in the marketplace was a stylish, complex Sauvignon Blanc as well as an amazingly dense and complex Merlot that some people felt was more like a Pomerol, only better.

In 1991, Matanzas Creek's Merlot became one of the most expensive in California, selling at $27.50 a bottle; yet because of its amazing depth, concentration, and richness, the wine sold out almost instantly.

Ramey left Matanzas Creek in 1990, later to become winemaker at Chalk Hill Winery. The MacIvers then tapped their cellar crew to make the wines as a team. Sharing the task of crafting the wines were Susan Reed, who had

The vines growing on the Matanzas Creek ranch were planted in the mid-1970s on the slopes of Sonoma Mountain in Bennett Valley. The valley is technically part of Sonoma Valley, but is not well-traveled by visitors because it's not on the wineries' beaten path.

been laboratory director, and Bill Parker, who had been cellarmaster. Despite the changes, the standard of Matanzas Creek's wines has remained high due to the MacIver's commitment to quality.

Over the years Sandra and Bill, who both grew up in liberal families, have become active participants in the wider wine community. Both play leading roles in a group of family wineries which seek to promote their wines differently than California's larger wineries tend to promote theirs.

Bill also helped to form AWARE -- the American Wine Alliance for Research and Education, and has become deeply involved in a number of political movements aiming to protect wine from Prohibitionist attacks, unfair taxation, and excessive governmental regulation -- which he feels includes unnecessary warning label requirements.

The MacIvers have hosted numerous industry-wide affairs at their winery, and have also become supporters of wine-and-food pairing efforts staged by well-known restaurants. In recent years the former commune has even been the site of marketing symposiums. DB

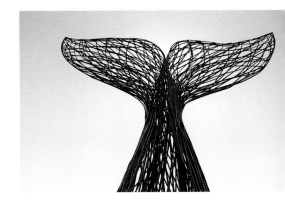

The sculpture of a whale was not chosen for any particular reason other than art, but chef Leonard Cohen of the Old Porte Inn in San Luis Obispo County, who regularly cooks dinners for the MacIvers at the winery, feels it was selected because of his commitment to great seafood.

MAZZOCCO VINEYARDS

It all looked too good to be true. Dr. Thomas Mazzocco, a world-famed Los Angeles eye surgeon, loved wine. He was already part-owner of a vineyard in Sonoma County. And there was a property off Lytton Springs Road in the county's Dry Creek area that was within a half-mile walk of Healdsburg Airport — and Mazzocco flew his own plane. This meant, he thought, he could continue his eye surgery and also make wine, using the grapes off his own vineyard. He imagined a rosy scenario: he could leave work afternoons, fly to Sonoma in a couple of hours, and walk to the winery in five minutes. A short commute.

Thus was Mazzocco Vineyards born. The property was acquired in 1984 and wine was made and sold under the Mazzocco label.

The seeds of the project were actually sown earlier, in 1980, when Mazzocco entered into a joint venture with vineyard manager Kevin Barr and others in the purchase of a 20-acre Chardonnay vineyard in the Alexander Valley, on River Lane near the Russian River.

In 1985, the year after Mazzocco's first wine was produced, he built a winery up a rise off Lytton Springs Road, in the rolling hills between Alexander Valley and Dry Creek Valley. The 25-acre vineyard on the property was planted to

The black Zinfandel grapes growing near the Mazzocco Winery have given this Lytton Springs area in northern Sonoma County a degree of its fame. Mazzocco's winemaker, U.C. Davis graduate Nancy Steel, also makes excellent Chardonnay and Cabernet Sauvignon here.

Cabernet Sauvignon, Cabernet Franc, Merlot, Petit Verdot, and Malbec — traditional Bordeaux grapes that would be assembled into complex red wines. The first was a stylish Cabernet Sauvignon. Mazzocco also made wine from ancient Zinfandel vines growing nearby, and bought grapes from various regions for the winery's "regular" Sonoma County Chardonnay. Some would come from as far south as the Carneros, the cool region off San Pablo Bay. The River Lane Vineyard Chardonnay would be released as a separate wine.

After the first vintage, Mazzocco hired U. C. Davis graduate Nancy Steel to handle the wine.

Dr. Thomas Mazzocco, founded his winery here in part because it was near the Healdsburg Airport, where he could fly in his plane. He installed quality equipment including temperature-controlled stainless-steel tanks, and began making excellent wine.

Steel had done stints at Stag's Leap Wine Cellars and in Australia's Barossa Valley. An energetic and inventive winemaker, Steel immediately created a bold style of wine. Meanwhile, Barr, one of the state's top grape growers, entered into an agreement with U.C. Davis to plant a test plot of Chardonnay in the River Lane vineyard. The 16-acre trellising trial will, after a decade of research, prove which of a number of trellis systems is best used here.

The winery project seemed to be working well. But Mazzocco was one of the world's leading cataract surgeons (and the inventor of the soft intraocular lens used after cataract surgery). So he was in great demand. Running a winery and being on call for surgery was exhausting, and he finally had to agree that the combination was too stressful. (He also was an avid golfer and had invented a telescopic shaft golf club that was approved for use by the U.S. Golf Association. His winemaking and surgery both kept him away from golf!)

So in 1990, Mazzocco sold the winery to Vintech, aSanta Rosa company specializing in winery limited partnerships. Vintech had previously acquired Lyeth and Laurier, and later acquired Jekel in Monterey. In early 1991, Vintech, facing financial difficulties, placed Mazzocco under the protection of the bankruptcy court as it attempted to reorganize. *DB*

The first wines Mazzocco released were 1985 Chardonnays; no red wines were made that year. However, since the 1986 vintage, Steel's Cabernet Sauvignons and Zinfandels have been more impressive than her whites.

THE MERRY VINTNERS

The notion of getting into wine for the money is a mistake anyone could make. Coca-Cola made it on the grandest scale when they bought into the wine business in a big way in 1977, only to sell out six years later. That is not a mistake that Meredith "Merry" Edwards will make. She cannot afford to.

"You don't start a winery looking for big profits, for 'return on investment,'" reminds Edwards. "We're just here to make a modest living for our two families: my parents, Bill and I, and our two boys." A proponent of family wineries, Edwards wears a red sweatshirt that sports the caption, "Kiss French, Drink Californian!"

"Most people say that it takes ten years for a new winery to generate positive cash flow," notes Edwards, who built a reputation for rich Chardonnays while at Mount Eden and Matanzas Creek in the '70s. "I thought we could do it in three, but even doing much of the construction ourselves, five years was a more realistic goal. Success will be generating enough cash flow to pay our salaries — and selling our wine out in nine months!"

The Merry Vintners is a tiny operation, with Merry's folks taking care of finance and administration, and Merry's husband, Bill Miller, handling California sales and all equipment repair. (Miller is also a computer wizard.)

Starting any winery is capital-intensive, especially when you consider that much of the equipment is used barely two months out of the year. "We bought 18 acres west of Santa Rosa, with two houses on it, for $300,000 in 1981. It was a good buy. We built the winery building on a shoestring, in 1984, for about $70,000, with dad and Bill doing all the electrical work and plumbing. Bill used to have a wine-equipment repair business, so there isn't anything here he can't fix."

Then, of course, you add in crushers,

The entire crew at The Merry Vintners — a family winery extraordinaire: Bill Miller (sales and equipment repair — and Merry's husband), Merry Edwards, D.J. Edwards (administration — and Merry's mom), and Charles Edwards (finance — and Merry's dad).

presses, bottling lines, tractors, forklifts, pumps, and stainless-steel fermenting tanks. Not to mention a forest of French oak barrels that go for more than $400 a pop. "Sure, we could buy American oak cheaper," says Edwards." They're less than half the cost of French oak. But American oak imparts raw, intrusive, 'toothpicky' oak to white wines. French oak, on the other hand, is much more seasoned. It adds viscosity to the wine, and that subtle, pleasant, vanilla flavor."

As Merry is serious about Chardonnay, she requires more than 200 barrels, a third of which need to be replaced by new ones each year. In all, Merry figures she's got more than half a million dollars in the winery, equipment, and inventory.

Like any good winemaker, Edwards would much prefer to be making wine from grapes she grew herself. "It's a question of control," she says matter-of-factly. "The highest quality comes from getting the grapes in exactly the condition you want."

Making wine on a shoestring means doing much of the work yourself. "I make the wine and handle out-of-state sales," says Merry, who also serves as winemaker at nearby Laurier (good for cash flow). "Husband Bill [Miller] handles California sales and keeps our equipment in running order. My father, Charles Edwards, handles finance, and mom, 'DJ,' is in charge of all things administrative." *RPH*

MILL CREEK VINEYARDS

All too often excellence and subtlety remain their own rewards. Those capable of the extra effort required to reach a higher level of achievement are often unwilling to make any effort at all to publicize either effort or achievement. I suppose this attitude comes out of a purist's belief that the achievement should stand on its own merits.

In an ideal world achievement would stand and be recognized on its own. As fine a world as wine's world is, it does not always reach the ideal. Mill Creek Vineyards quietly goes about providing quality product without fanfare, without self-promotion.

You will find Mill Creek on the western outskirts of Healdsburg, out on Westside Road where a low rock wall and parallel columns of purple-leafed Thunderbird plum trees flank the entry drive.

Charles "Chuck" Kreck had been involved in the manufacture of industrial hardware when World War II came along and took the output of his factory for the Liberty Ships being built at nearby Long Beach Shipyard. A few years after the war, Chuck sold his interest to his brother and moved his family to the open spaces of Sonoma, intending to raise cattle.

"Dad was actually heading for Oregon,"

Mill Creek sits at the foot of the hills on the west side of Dry Creek, just west of Healdsburg. The Kreck family originally settled here to raise cattle, but grapevines proved the better bet economically.

laughs Chuck's son, Bill, who handles business and finance at the medium-sized winery. "But the roads were washed out by flooding just north of here, so we settled here. Dad quickly got into ranch development and real estate, having discovered that the only money in farming is in buying and selling farms."

Still, there was the urge to stick something into the earth. By 1965 the Krecks were poking Cabernet plants into an old prune orchard. "I can still remember an old Italian wine man telling me that Cabernet was the worst thing to plant," remembers Chuck with a chuckle. "It was really scary, because I was totally new to

A working water-wheel is the most notable feature of Mill Creek's tasting and retail room. Inside, it's airy but warm, with wooden walls and a wood stove that can really crank out the heat on a frosty morning.

grape growing, and all these old Italian farmers were telling me that I was committing suicide.

"Then this fellow from Cresta Blanca, then over in Livermore, came by and offered me $175 a ton for my grapes. Naturally, I jumped at the chance, because my Italian advisors were getting just $40 a ton for their Zinfandel and Carignane. Ha! A few years later, we really got on the gravy train, and Cabernet prices jumped to nearly a thousand dollars a ton."

But, as with all farming cycles, bust follows boom. By 1974 Cabernet plantings had outpaced demand, and prices dropped precipitously. "That year we took our grapes to Korbel and had them custom crushed for our account," recalls Bill. "By 1975 we had to decide whether to get out or get in. Being just a grower wasn't enough. You didn't have any control over your destiny. We decided to convert an old equipment barn into a winery so that we could handle the fruit from the 65 acres of vines we had planted."

The wine that really brought attention to Mill Creek was dubbed Cabernet "Blush." First produced in 1976, it is made from Cabernet Sauvignon juice that is drained off the skins after enough skin contact to give the wine a "blush" of color. The wine has a plummy pink hue, a fresh, plum-like fruitiness, and a delightfully oily, viscous mouth feel. *RPH*

The Krecks started their first grapevines in an old prune orchard, planting Cabernet despite the advice of veteran Italian winegrowers — and the bet paid off.

J. W. MORRIS

The winemaking history of J.W. Morris and the Black Mountain Vineyard really begins with the brand created by Jim Olsen — and funded by his father-in-law, yes, J. W. Morris — in 1975. Working out of Emeryville's People's Bakery, Olsen began by producing only ports.

Toward the end of the decade, Olsen had begun producing varietal table wines, mostly from fruit grown at Ken Toth's Black Mountain Vineyard. After an expansion and a move, J. W. Morris foundered when a new partner's health failed. In 1983, Ken and Tricia Toth bought the brand, and moved it to a small industrial park on the south side of Healdsburg, within two miles of Black Mountain Vineyard.

Framed by a graveled bend in the Russian River, at the southern end of the Alexander Valley, Black Mountain has 115 acres planted to vines. "We bought the 275-acre estate in 1976 from the Demostene family, who had farmed it from the late 1800s," says Ken. (The Demostenes now operate Sausal Winery.) "At that time the estate had 30 acres of old Zinfandel and Petite Sirah, planted near the turn of the century. We added Cabernet Sauvignon and Sauvignon Blanc on volcanic hillsides, some of which rise 300 feet above the river. Chardonnay is planted on flatter shale, nearer the river."

J.W. Morris' Black Mountain Vineyard lies at the boundary between Alexander Valley and the Russian River Valley. Here you can see the vineyard basking in sunlight, while the Russian River Valley (further west) lies under a shroud of fog.

A native of New York City, Toth was graduated from the Stevens Institute of Technology in 1956, then earned an MBA from the Harvard Graduate School of Business in 1961. He worked as a management consultant, moving to San Francisco in 1967. "I wanted to get into business for myself. One of the consultants who had worked for our company was Jack Davies, who had just founded Schramsberg. I took a long look at the vineyard business. It looked like a lot of fun, and I figured I could make a lot of money. I must say, it has been a lot of fun!"

When J. W. Morris faltered, Toth decided it was time to get into making wine. "At the time,

The Russian River flows in a horseshoe bend around Black Mountain Vineyard, exposing the heavily graveled subsoil that is a feature of this region. The loose gravel gives excellent drainage, important for grapevines which, say old farmers, "do not like wet feet."

we didn't have a lot of choice," he recalls. "We stood to make a better recovery of our assets by buying the winery — lock, stock, and all the barrels."

Today the J. W. Morris label is used for a line of generic and varietal table wines, while the Black Mountain Vineyard label covers just 10,000 cases a year of estate-grown Chardonnay, Sauvignon Blanc, Cabernet, Zinfandel, and Petite Sirah (half of the vineyard's production is still sold to other wineries). Very small quantities of Port, up to a thousand cases a year, are also made.

But these Ports are especially toothsome, with black walnut, black cherry, and black pepper aromas and flavors. "At a tasting once, people kept pouring it over Dreyer's French Vanilla Ice Cream," exclaims tasting-room manager Joan Hines. "It's also pretty good with chocolate-covered cherries and candied walnuts."

Toth notes that Port production has been scaled back a bit. "Nobody is producing premium Ports that are aged on release, so perhaps we are filling a niche that hadn't previously existed."

His Black Mountain Vineyard wines are also only a small part of production plans. "If I made only the style of wine I like, I'd have a very small winery," he says with a grin. "The Black Mountain Vineyard varietals are my expression, these are the wines that I like, but you can't sell large volumes of these wines." *RPH*

A former management consultant, Ken Toth initially got into wine with the intention of only growing grapes. But, when the winery buying his grapes suffered difficult times, Toth was forced to become winemaker as well. One of the wines he particularly enjoys is Port, which he makes mostly for himself. But it's okay if others buy some, too.

MURPHY-GOODE ESTATE WINERY

It's possible to grow great grapes and make fine wine, but doing one well does not necessarily mean it's possible to do the other well. Tim Murphy knew grapes: he was one of the top growers in the Alexander Valley. Murphy had superb grapes, and one of the best quality grapes he grew was Sauvignon Blanc.

But he knew little about the wine business. He was a skilled organizer, however, and that led to the success called Murphy-Goode.

Both Murphy and Dale Goode began growing grapes in the Alexander Valley in the mid-1960s. Murphy grew up in Berkeley; for three generations his family owned and operated a meat market across the street from where the famed restaurant Chez Panisse is now located. Murphy retains ownership of the property in the neighborhood now considered the gourmet mecca of Berkeley.

Goode has managed vineyards for Alexander Valley Vineyards (where he was a general partner), Hoot Owl Creek Vineyards, and Jimtown Ranch. He and Murphy formed a partnership in 1980.

Murphy had long thought about starting a sparkling wine brand, and had talked about it with marketing specialist Dave Ready and pub-

Grape growers Tim Murphy and Dale Goode founded Murphy-Goode as a hedge against the lean times when grapes sell for low prices. With the marketing skills of Dave Ready, the promotional talent of Rick Theis, and the winemaking of Chris Benz, Murphy-Goode became one of the bright new lights in Sonoma in the late 1980s.

lic relations expert Rick Theis. In 1985, as the sale of grapes slowed down, the winery idea looked more feasible.

"By 1985, there were a lot of grapes unsold, and Tim and Dale were looking to start a winery principally as a hedge, so they could move all the fruit they were growing," says Ready.

Murphy asked Ready to handle sales of the wine; Ready suggested that Theis handle PR and marketing. Theis had worked for Wine Institute and for The Wine Spectrum, Coca-Cola's short-lived foray into wine.

With no winery, the partners contracted with Rick Sayre at Rodney Strong Vineyards to

White wines, mostly Fume Blanc, were the first successes here. But as the operation grew, the partners added a large supply of (costly) French oak barrels, and the result was quality Cabernet Sauvignons and Merlots.

oversee making the wine, and with consultant Merry Edwards, one of the top winemakers in the business. The partners priced their 1985 Murphy-Goode Fume Blanc lower than most, and Theis then set out to market the new brand. "The market for Sauvignon Blanc was weak," recalls Theis, who was then president of Murphy-Goode. His campaign to make Murphy-Goode a household word was tireless. "I had been the wine columnist for The Minneapolis Star . . . so I wrote a personal letter to every wine writer in the country."

Ready and Theis traveled coast-to-coast to public tasting events and did interviews extolling the greatness of the wine. The partnership of Murphy, Theis, Goode, and Ready was an instant success. Some 7,000 cases of Fume Blanc were sold in the first six months.

By 1988, as Murphy was building a winery (to be leased to the partnership), frictions developed. Theis left to spend more time with the Grape Growers, to head the Meritage Association (a group of wineries that make ultra-premium wines from the classic Bordeaux varieties), and to become a political activist. Murphy then assumed the presidency of the winery.

Meanwhile, winemaker Christina Benz was hired. She added to the line a Chardonnay, a Merlot, and a Cabernet Sauvignon from Murphy's Alexander Valley ranch. By 1990 the winery was making about 40,000 cases a year. *DB*

The first few vintages of Murphy-Goode wines, made with the aid of consultant Merry Edwards, were produced under contract at Rodney Strong Vineyards. Later, the partners built their own winery and tasting room in the Alexander Valley, where they own vineyards.

NALLE WINERY

The Zinfandel grape has a mysterious history, one more uniquely Californian than any other variety. Some feel the master of this many-faceted variety is Doug Nalle.

Nalle has made other wines in his career, but recently he has concentrated on Zinfandel, gaining renown as the finest artisan of the variety. He has achieved this because he discovered a special region for Zinfandel — Dry Creek Valley — and a technique for aging it that makes a sublime wine. Some say Nalle's Zinfandel is the best in California each year. Others say the best comes from Quivira, but Nalle also worked there for three years, and left his stamp on Quivira's technique.

"I like the flexibility of Zinfandel," explains Nalle. "You can come at it from so many different styles, from white Zinfandel all the way to late-harvest."

Nalle makes his Zinfandel from a blend of grapes grown in three nearby vineyards, each contributing a note of fruit to the final blend. The wine is made to preserve the fruit, and to avoid gaining so much tannin that the result becomes astringent. The wine is aged in French oak barrels for about a year.

There once was a theory that if you aged Zinfandel long enough in the bottle it would taste like Cabernet Sauvignon. Nalle doesn't dispute this, but he adheres more closely to the concept that Zinfandel, properly made, tastes great when it's young and takes on bouquet for only a short time before it begins to decline.

"Zinfandel is not known throughout the world as a connoisseur's wine," he says, adding that some people equate great wine with how long it ages. "I doubt that Zin has the aging potential of Cabernet, but that doesn't

Doug Nalle started his winery by making wine in a tiny, old dairy barn that — when filled with barrels — was barely big enough to walk into. In 1991, Nalle's new winery on Dry Creek Road in Healdsburg was completed.

Nalle makes only
one wine, Zinfandel,
and he takes great
care in choosing the
vineyards the
grapes are from as
well as the condition
of the grapes. Nalle,
former winemaker at
Balverne, makes one
of the top Zinfandels
in the state.

matter very much, does it? I don't think a wine has to age 20 years for it to be great."

Nalle's Zinfandels seem to age well for about six or seven years, perhaps longer. He likes to consume them about that age or younger — and when matched with the right foods, such as Italian dishes, the result is a marvelous combination of flavors.

Nalle was the winemaker at nearby Balverne from 1979 through 1983. His Zinfandels there were appealing harbingers of his present wines. The Nalle brand began as a Zinfandel-only project in 1984, funded then by William Hambrecht, a San Francisco investment banking executive and an investor in other Sonoma County wine projects. The first Nalle Zinfandel was made at Belvedere; the '85 and '86 vintages were made in a tiny barn on Hambrecht's property above Dry Creek Valley; the 1987, 1988, and 1989 wines were made at Quivira, where Doug was then winemaker; and the 1990 was made at Hafner Winery in Healdsburg.

In 1989, Nalle bought Hambrecht's share of the Nalle brand and by 1991, his own small winery was completed next to his home. In addition to Zinfandel, Nalle also makes about 250 cases of Cabernet Sauvignon from grapes grown on Hambrecht's Bradford Mountain ranch. Nalle is a family winery. Doug's wife, Lee, and sons, Andrew and Sam, do much of the work during harvest. "I couldn't do any of this without their help," says Doug. "I'd be even more of a zombie than I already am." *DB*

Some of the grapes
Nalle gets for his
Zinfandel are grown
on the hillsides
rolling up off the
valley floor in Dry
Creek Valley.
The wind machine
stands ready to
defend the
vines against
a sudden frost.

NUNN'S CANYON

Nunn's Canyon, still in the formation stage, planted additional vineyards in 1991. Here workers lay down plastic sheets to help protect the young plants and maintain the integrity of the fertilization.

Unlike many fine-wine growing regions of the world that have no land left to plant, Sonoma County still has opportunities for winemakers, though the sites may be remote and hard to farm.

One of the newest ventures in the county is a remote property on the northwestern edge of Sonoma Valley, called Nunn's Canyon. It is located on hilly land that's perfect for intensely flavored red wines.

Getting to Nunn's Canyon is an adventure. Travelers drive up Nunn's Canyon Road a half mile, then turn left onto Nelligan Road and travel 2.3 miles through towering ancient oak trees, madrone, and fern-filled vales on an unimproved road.

The project is the dream of Frank McConnell, a businessman from Toronto and one of

the early investors in the William Hill Winery in the Napa Valley. He liked the idea of owning a winery.

"Frank and a small group of investors wanted a bigger piece of a smaller project," says Bill Henri, winemaker for Nunn's Canyon. "I found this piece of property, and they invested."

The 160 acres, located on sloping hills, had been a vineyard for nearly a century

when Henri found it in the early 1980s, but much of the planted acreage was gnarled older vines that had to be ripped out and replanted.

"This was a six-year project," he says. "I looked at this place back in 1982, when the property was first on the market, and it had great qualifications for fine wine. I majored in fruit science, but I had a minor in soil science, and I knew this place had the right soil and the right climate." The ranch is adjacent to Steve Kistler's Cabernet Sauvignon, the Beltane Ranch (which has sold excellent Chardonnay grapes to Kenwood Winery), and the Kunde family's Sonoma Valley ranch and brand new winery.

The Nunn's Canyon site is between 1,600 and 2,000 feet off the valley floor, meaning the drawbacks were obvious: a high cost of planting on the steeply sloped hills. But the benefits were obvious, too: intensely flavored fruit from stressed hillside grapes.

The deal was concluded in 1988, and Henri made wines that vintage. After removing useless vines, some 30 acres remained, and the first wines were made off old vines (planted some time between 1900 and 1920, as best Henri can figure) — yielding a potent, richly scented Zinfandel. An additional ten acres were planted to Pinot Noir, Zinfandel, and Cabernet.

In addition to being the winemaker here, Henri, former winemaker at William Hill, also is a general partner and vice president. About 85 percent of the investors in the project are Canadian.

The first wine from Nunn's Canyon, the 1988 Zinfandel, was made in a tiny quantity (400 cases); only 100 cases of a 1989 Pinot Noir were made. But with Cabernet Sauvignon its No. 1 varietal, the winery should be making 25,000 cases of wine by the turn of the century. McConnell intends to import Nunn's Canyon wines into Canada. To reach the partnership's 25,000-case target, about 100 acres in all will be planted here. *DB*

The partners in
Nunn's Canyon
winery chose their
vineyard land for
quality fruit, not
visitor access. Thus
the ranch is located
well off Highway 12,
up Nunn's Canyon
Road at the
northwest edge of
the Sonoma Valley.

J. PEDRONCELLI WINERY

The history of winegrowing at Pedroncelli mirrors the evolution of that art in Sonoma County. Like so many Sonoma wineries, it grew out of the Italian culture. Giovanni (quickly changed to John) Pedroncelli came to California from Lombardy as a teenager, with the will to make his own way in a new world.

After working for the railroad in the town of Dunsmuir, on the slopes of Mt. Shasta, John moved to Geyserville with his wife and young son, John Jr., in 1927. There he purchased a 55-acre vineyard in a high bowl between the Alexander and Dry Creek valleys. A winery, built circa 1904 by San Francisco groceryman John Canata, had been converted into a horse barn during Prohibition.

"Virtually everything was red wine in those days," says John A. Pedroncelli Jr., today's president and winemaker. "Dad made mostly Zinfandel, because it matured quickly and could be drunk young. We also had a little Carignane, Petite Sirah, Early Burgundy, and Burger, which were all blended together for our red wine. There were very few white varieties then."

There were no varietal wines then, not even rosés. Just red, and the smallest smattering of white. "Mother wouldn't drink white wine unless it was the only thing that was

In the old days, all the wines of Sonoma County were aged in large, redwood vats. But technology has given the winemaker a much better tool — for temperature control and cleanliness — in stainless-steel tanks.

available," laughs brother Jim, winery vice president. "Heck, dad was the same way. He'd have a glass of white at the ten a.m. break, but from the noon meal on it was nothing but red wine!"

Changes in the vineyard went hand-in-hand with winery evolution in Sonoma County. As bulk blends gave way to vintage-dated varietals, "vineyard blends" gave way to separate blocks of small-berried, low-yielding varieties with fancy French names: Cabernet Sauvignon, Chardonnay, Pinot Noir, Sauvignon Blanc. And the farmers who knew only "Petty Sarahs" and "Care-ig-nans" shook their heads

© 1983

Zinfandel

This colorful drawing honors Zinfandel, long a favorite with old-time Italian vintners in Sonoma County. At Pedroncelli, they make a white Zinfandel, a zesty, fruity Zinfandel Rosé, and some full-bodied red wines that remind us that Zinfandel's first duty is to be red.

in wonder at those who talked of "Puh-teet Sear-ah" and "Care-eehn-yown."

"When I was a young man, in the late '40s and early '50s, I was the delivery man," recalls Jim, a slender, wiry fellow whose black hair curls slightly around his ears. "I'd go to Eureka and San Francisco and drop off ten or 20 cases at a time to the Italian families who were our longtime customers. Many of them would take a 50-gallon barrel or two and bottle their wine themselves."

The big change came in the mid-'50s, when prices hit rock bottom. "Until about 1954 or 1955, most of our sales were in bulk, either to individual customers or to other wineries," continues Jim. "I think it was 1955 when we had another big crop, and grape prices dropped to $40 a ton [compared to Chardonnay prices that reached $2,000 a ton in the '80s]. At that point, bulk sales slumped markedly. You couldn't just sit on thousands of gallons of bulk wine, hoping somebody would buy it before you needed those tanks and casks for the following year's crush. Bottling wines under our own label gave us a way to move the wines — and stay in business."

Progress took many forms. Redwood tanks gave way to temperature-controlled stainless steel; tractors replaced horses. The demise of bulk blends led to varietal wines of all colors.

"Grey Riesling was the first white varietal we made," recalls Jim, "but we dropped it when we realized that it had no future. We added most of our whites in the late '60s. We've also renamed our generic wines from Burgundy and Chablis to Sonoma Red and Sonoma White, which tells the consumer something about where the wine came from."

John Pedroncelli Jr. is a short, solid fellow who loves trout fishing and traveling. As a winemaker, he is attuned to fundamentals. "In a sense, I'm a non-winemaker. Every time you put a wine through a procedure, you take something out of it. I try to tend wine more than make wine."

The wines show it. They are elemental wines, wines that unequivocally demonstrate the character of the grape. The whites, for example — with the exception of Chardonnay and Sauvignon Blanc, which are fermented dry — are finished with a bit more than one percent residual sugar. They're not sweet, yet there's just enough sugar to expose, almost frame, the natural fruit flavors. The Chenin Blanc shows a spritzy grassiness; the Johannisberg Riesling is nearly fragile in its apricot definition.

That said, the Pedroncellis don't stint on the oak where it's needed. The Chardonnays are aged in French and American oak barrels. "Some people think that oak is the varietal character of Chardonnay," laments John. "We want people to see the grape in the wine; we use the oak only for extra complexity."

One of Sonoma County's finest red wines is Zinfandel, a variety well suited to Sonoma County climes. Probably brought to California in the 1850s from Italy, Zinfandel quickly became a workhorse variety. The Pedroncellis have been making Zinfandel since their beginning; it is still an important part of their repertoire. "This is a good region to grow Zinfandel," notes Jim. "It gives excellent fruit-and-berry character, almost like blackberries." John

During harvest, gondolas full of ripe grapes will be driven up under the hoist, where this pickup truck is. The hoist will tip the gondola, dumping the grapes into the receiving hopper behind the truck. A helical screw will move the grapes from hopper to crusher-stemmer.

takes full advantage of Zinfandel's greatest shortcoming — its uneven ripening — by making a whole range of wine types.

"Sugar levels can rise very rapidly," says John. "One day they may be 21 Brix, and three days later they're at 24, or even 25. So we have to pay close attention to sugar levels to harvest fruit that is correct for each wine.

"I suspect that the popularity of Zinfandel in Sonoma County comes from all the Italian winegrowers who settled here. My parents and their neighbors didn't want to wait around for three or four years after the crush for the wines to mature. Zinfandel can be drunk within six or seven months of the harvest, but it can also age nicely over the years. That's the great thing about Zinfandel: you can have it both ways."

In a sense, it's Cabernet Sauvignon that really tells the Pedroncelli story, and in so doing reflects a lot of what Sonoma County wines stand for. For while they clearly show varietal heritage — with defined bell pepper and plum fruit — they are never overbearing in body or price. They are not trophy-case wines — over-oaked lovelies that win tastings but remain undrinkable for decades — but rather are wines that one can afford to buy, and afford to drink . . . today. *RPH*

Brothers Jim (left) and John Pedroncelli checking the ripeness of their fruit. While there are instruments to check sugar levels, the only way to gauge grape maturity correctly is by tasting the fruit. If the flavor isn't in the fruit, it will never find its way to the wine.

The low hills of Dry Creek Valley are an excellent place to grow grapes, especially the Zinfandel. In the old days, these hills would be worked by horses, like the Pedroncellis' Silver, but the advent of the tractor changed all that.

PIPER SONOMA CELLARS

It is a good reflection on Piper-Sonoma that fine sparkling wines go so well with the festive, out-of-doors lifestyle of wine country. Picnics are a way of life during warm summer days, while the grapes quietly ripen for the harvest season to come.

Piper Sonoma sits west of Highway 101, about midway between Windsor and Healdsburg, on the east bank of the Russian River. This sparkling-wine facility, with its horizontally parallel concrete lines climbing lazily out of the vineyard next door to the concrete cross of Rodney Strong Vineyards, was founded in 1980 as a joint venture by Piper-Heidsieck (France's centuries-old, Reims-based Champagne house), Sonoma Vineyards (nee Windsor Vineyards, now Rodney Strong Vineyards), and Renfield Corporation (Sonoma Vineyards' partner and distributor).

Piper-Heidsieck was the second major French player to join the hunt for great sparkling wines in California. (The first was Moët & Chandon, seven years earlier.) Its reasons were simple enough: the region of Cham-

pagne had no more room for expansion, sales of Champagne were sill skyrocketing, and Californian wines were improving at a remarkable rate. "It is stupid to compare French and Californian wines," said Piper's chairman, Marquis François d'Aulan at the time. "Each should be judged entirely on its own merit."

The joint venture's first vintage was crushed at Sonoma Vineyards, under the super-

vision of its winemaker, Rod Strong, and Piper-Heidsieck's veteran chef de cave Michel Lacroix, who continues to add his expertise. "Michel comes over two or three times a year, when we're making final decisions on the blends," says winemaker Chris Markell, who's been with Piper Sonoma since its inception.

The basic Brut blend is typically three-quarters Pinot Noir, with smaller amounts of Chardonnay, Pinot Blanc, and Pinot Meunier. "The Pinot Noir gives the berry aromas, a lot of structure, backbone, and a roundness in the finish," says Markell, who was raised in Berkeley. "From the Chardonnay we get fruitiness, that citrus-like quality, with lemon and apple character in both aroma and taste. Pinot Blanc has less obvious fruit, but contributes structure and roundness.

"We started using Pinot Meunier in 1987, and really like what it adds to the aromatics; it's particularly round and soft in the mouth. We're really interested in this variety, so we contracted with our growers to increase their plantings of Meunier."

Piper Sonoma's Blanc de Noirs, a consistently flavorful wine, is made strictly from the black grape varieties -- Pinot Noir and Pinot Meunier -- and with increasing amounts of the latter. "I can see us using anywhere from two to 25 percent Pinot Meunier, depending on the vintage," says Markell. "Our Brut Reserve and Tete de Cuvee are usually pretty evenly balanced between Pinot Noir and Chardonnay. The Reserve is blended to handle extra aging on the yeast -- it usually gets five years -- while the Tete de Cuvee is made only in the best vintages and from our very best lots. That also gets extended aging on the yeast, up to six years."

Markell is one of a rare breed who, though not raised in a winegrowing family, knew that he wanted to make wine from age 16. "I chose a career in wine after my parents gave me a winemaking kit," he says with a laugh. "They gave me some concentrate and a small oak barrel. It must have held five gallons. I also

This Piper-Sonoma poster hearkens back to the flapper era of the 1920s and the art-deco period of the thirties, when French Champagne was the only beverage worth considering. Nowadays, other winegrowing regions do pretty well with the sparklers.

remember going to visit wineries with my parents, and I loved the smells. I particularly remember visiting the old Buena Vista, out there under the trees."

So Markell headed straight for U. C. Davis after high school, taking his degree in 1976. "Dr. Olmo had suggested that I go to France for some direct, practical experience. So I took off, not knowing exactly where I would end up. I had never even drunk Champagne, but I worked for a small company there that didn't export. Because they were so small I got to do everything, from the vineyard to the disgorging line. In the year I was there, I worked through the whole cycle of Champagne."

Back in California, he worked at Simi, with Mary Ann Graf and Andre Tchelistcheff. In early 1980 he spent some time with the French Champagne producer Lanson, who was then investigating the possibility of starting an operation in California.

When Lanson decided against it, Markell signed on with Piper Sonoma in time for the winery's first crush. "I came on a Monday in mid-August, and we began picking grapes on Thursday. I was the winery's first employee," he says with pride.

Markell worked with winemaker Rod Strong through the '85 crush, and then was appointed head winemaker. Shortly thereafter,

After a sparkling wine sits on the yeast for two or three years, the dead yeast cells must be removed. The bottles are placed on riddling racks, where they are turned daily to move yeast cells into the neck of the bottle. Later the neck will be frozen so that the plug of sediment can be removed.

Piper-Heidsieck bought out its American partners, acquiring sole ownership in 1987.

"Since 1986 we've been harvesting a bit more mature fruit -- for more flavor, a little more roundness, and a longer finish," says Markell. "We're also taking a closer look at some older Champagne techniques. For example, we're barrel fermenting some of our Pinot Noir in different sizes of French oak, just to see how it affects the flavors we can get."

Piper Sonoma has some 250 57-gallon barrels, and ten 1,600-gallon foudres -- large wine tanks made of wood -- French oak in this case. Fermentation in oak adds something of a vanilla character to the wine, which as part of the

Winemaker Chris Markell is unafraid of trying new things to improve wine quality. "We're harvesting fruit a bit more mature than before, for more flavor, a little more roundness and a longer finish," he notes. "We're also barrel fermenting a little Pinot Noir."

blend will give a subtle complexity to the resulting sparkling wine.

"We're also trying to convince consumers that sparkling wines are great with food, and are not strictly aperitif wines or wines just for celebrations. Actually, we believe that sparkling wines match up better to a greater variety of foods than any single still wine."

Markell himself is single still, and loves the outdoors, from backpacking in Yosemite to sailing, swimming, and running.

In 1991 Piper Sonoma Sparkling Wine was named the official sparkling wine for the Royal Caribbean Cruise Line's Viking Serenade, the largest cruise liner in regular service on the west coast of California. Made especially for the christening was a Sovereign bottle, the largest of all oversized bottles, with a capacity if 20 liters (more than two cases worth of wine).

"We found the bottles, which were hand blown, in Italy," says the winery's managing director, Bernard La Borie. "The producer broke the mold because he was unable to make a profit on the bottles, even though the three we were able to obtain cost us a thousand dollars apiece." RPH

Piper Sonoma, halfway between Windsor and Healdsburg, boasts an elegant visitors' center. The approach to the winery is across a bridge that appears to cross a moat. In reality, it's a small creek that drains into the Russian River a few hundred yards to the west.

PRESTON VINEYARDS

ouis D. Preston comes from a north county farming family. His folks had a dairy, orchards, and vineyards near Windsor. After an Army stint, an MBA from Stanford, and a year at U. C. Davis, Lou turned to winegrowing. He bought a ranch near West Dry Creek Road, and converted a 1917 prune dehydrator into a 2,000-case winery in 1975.

At the beginning, like all winegrowers, Lou Preston assured one and all that 2,000 cases would be the winery's maximum size. Uh huh. And the budget — anybody's, from the federal government on down — will be balanced.

"Well, sales grew," laughs Lou. Enough that he had to build a whole new facility in 1982. "Our new winery was modeled after Trefethen's century-old wooden winery, and we built it for a capacity of 12,000 cases a year." And then expanded it. And expanded it again. Today's production? "Well, we're at about 26,000 cases in a normal year," says Lou with a cat-got-the-canary grin.

Lou used to sell most of his fruit, but he had pegged the land right and planted mostly Sauvignon Blanc and Zinfandel, which are perfectly matched to the deep, graveled soils and warm climate of Dry Creek Valley. "We knew this was the right place for those two varieties, but were very disappointed with the newer, heat-treated clones of Zinfandel," he says. "We really liked the flavors off of our old vines — some of which date to the turn of the century — so we selected the cleanest wood we could find and propagated new blocks from them."

As the winery grew, Lou found himself acting more as general manager than as winemaker. "I get involved in everything now," he says with a contented grin. "Mostly I tend my vegetable garden and bake bread for the crew's lunch." You've got to watch this guy. Yes, he does do those things, but he also does a lot more. Like head up the production team: himself, viticulturist John Clendenen, and winemaker Kevin Hamel.

You can see the resemblance to Napa Valley's century-old Trefethen in this angle of Preston's lovely wooden winery. Built to handle production of 12,000 cases in 1982, it has since been expanded. And expanded again.

One of the keys to the quality of Preston wines is its location. Here in Dry Creek Valley, the soils are almost all gravel, which means excellent drainage — perhaps the single most important criterion for a vineyard site.

"We've really got good people here," stresses Lou. "Clendenen's been here ten years, and has helped us to eliminate insecticide sprays. That's a quality-of-life and a marketing decision. Our cellarmaster Christopher Wirth. And Linda Villagomez, our crush-cellar supervisor. She runs our quality control and trains all our new employees." Lou's wife, Susan, creates inventive culinary matches for the wines.

Winemaker Hamel joined the team in January 1989. He's a lean and wiry fellow, with green eyes, a long but happy face, and outsized hands that remind one of a Labrador puppy's paws. Born in Maryland, Hamel grew up east of Sacramento, in Roseville. "My folks drank wine with some regularity," he says.

But he really developed an interest in wine after leaving Notre Dame, meeting wife-to-be Yvonne, and enrolling at U. C. Davis. "I had a great time studying under Roger Boulton, who taught the distillation class. I worked at the Corti Brothers wine shop, worked at Cockburn in Portugal for a year in production, then came back to Corti Brothers for six years."

In 1987 he took a job as assistant winemaker at Santino Winery, making many of the same wines he now makes at Preston. "When I looked at his resume, I asked him if he hadn't just copied our wine list," chuckles Lou. *RPH*

Stainless-steel tanks are vital to an industry where cleanliness is not merely next to godliness — it is an absolute essential. There seem almost limitless numbers of bacterium that will grow nicely in wine if you give them half a chance.

QUIVIRA VINEYARDS

The most difficult of disciplines is that of gaining perspective — perspective on life in general, on oneself in disarming particular. It is a rare and valuable ability, one that requires great honesty.

Those who run multinational corporations ought to be required — by moral law if by no other — to be well-endowed with this ability. For perspective yields insight, insight that translates into what might be called the "long view," with which we may survive the nuclear age and construct a future bright and beautiful for our grandchildren. Henry Wendt appears to possess this insight.

Wendt is chairman of SmithKline Beecham, at $7 billion per year one of the largest producers of health-care products on the third planet. He is also the proprietor of a small wine estate called Quivira ("kee-veer-a"), started in 1981 out on West Dry Creek Road, Healdsburg.

The name was that of a mythical kingdom of wealth and culture, located on 16th century maps on the Pacific Coast between Cape Mendocino and "Capo de San Francisco." Henry and Holly Wendt began Quivira as their retirement venture. "We wanted a dynamic and interesting way of life," says Wendt. "We're not the kind of people who can just lie on the

This handsome wooden winery, built in 1987, sits at a curve in the West Dry Creek Road, northwest of Healdsburg. Wisteria and olive trees surround the entryway. Inside, excellent Sauvignon Blanc, Zinfandel, and Cabernet Sauvignon are made.

beach. We chose the Dry Creek Valley because it's a good place to grow grapes, and we like the way Sonoma County has preserved its rural sense and agricultural heritage."

Quivira built its foundation upon Zinfandel, as crafted by founding winemaker Doug Nalle, then added a Sauvignon Blanc and a Cabernet Sauvignon, all drawn from 76 acres of estate vineyard. In 1990 Grady Wann, who has a Ph.D. in organic chemistry from Stanford, joined the team as full-time winemaker when Nalle left to run his own winery.

Wendt began working for SmithKline the day after he graduated from Princeton in 1955.

Winemaker Grady Wann checks a tank sample of Sauvignon Blanc. After earning a Ph. D. in organic chemistry at Stanford University, Wann worked with Bill Bonetti at Sonoma-Cutrer prior to joining the Wendt family at Quivira.

He introduced the cold remedy Contac to Japan, in 1966. "We were the first foreign health-care company to directly market in Japan," notes the lithe, tanned Wendt. "Fortunately, I had studied judo while working in Hawaii. This was at the YMCA, and our instructor was a Japanese carpenter. Judo is as much philosophy as it is physical, and it gave me a good introduction to the Japanese way of thinking.

"Later, I had spent nine weeks in Japan, the first of many trips, immersing myself in their way of life. Because of that, when we offered Contac, we offered a formula that was geared to their metabolic rate and stature. It was one of the best business decisions I ever made, because the Japanese believe themselves to be inherently different."

In operating SmithKline, or his 20,000-case winery in Dry Creek Valley, the key according to Wendt lies in "getting good people, giving them clear and proper guidance, and the authority to carry out their assignments.

"Essentially, good management is the recognition that people have to come first. It's like the Quakers say: 'Do well by doing good.' The wine business is no different than the health-care business in its attributes and virtues: we're both trying to enhance happiness, sociability, compatibility, to create a general sense of well-being. Both require strong artistic and creative capabilities." *RPH*

The lattice work on the east and west sides of the winery are more than mere trim in architect Michael A. Rubenstein's scheme. Set eight feet away from the building, the lattices will provide extra insulation . . . once the ivy reaches up to cover them.

A. RAFANELLI WINERY

There's little or nothing fancy about Rafanelli. This redwood structure houses the winery, and the wines are straightforward and plenty flavorful. Pretension is a word unknow here, and a good thing too.

David Rafanelli, tanned, with pale blue eyes and dark, wavy hair, doesn't quite look the part of the little, old Italian winemaker. "Grapes and vineyards are sort of my hobby," he says quietly, with a smile.

If so, it's a hobby he grew up with, in fits and starts. "Well, my grandfather, Alberto, a contractor, must have started making wine here before Prohibition," says Dave, who took over the A. Rafanelli Winery, on West Dry Creek Road, when his father, Americo "Am" Rafanelli, died in January 1987. "They had a rough time during Prohibition, selling grapes to home winemakers."

Alberto's winery was on a low slope on the north side of Healdsburg, and the town was planning a new high school. So, the Rafanellis sold their 30 acres of vineyard to the city for a

new Healdsburg High in 1954. Al and Am then purchased nearly 100 acres of land out west of town, and began putting in Zinfandel, Gamay Beaujolais, Early Burgundy (a crude red variety), and French Colombard.

In 1974 Am, who had continued making wine for the family, decided to expand into commercial production, focusing mainly on a hearty, flavorful Zinfandel. He also made a

Gamay Beaujolais that was equally packed with flavor, but somehow managed to retain the lighter body that makes Gamay so accessible to those not versed in wine.

Dave Rafanelli has a great love of the land. "Dad was that way, too," notes Dave. "He always claimed that good wines are made in the vineyards. He certainly proved that it doesn't take university degrees to make good wine — it just takes good grapes."

Still, David headed north for his formal education, attending Oregon State on a football scholarship (his dad had been named Healdsburg High's best athlete in 1938). "I was a halfback, and we upset USC one year when they were number one in the nation," he recalls with pride. "I came home on vacation and met Patty in Santa Rosa." They were married during Dave's junior year. He earned his degree in agronomy at OSU in 1971, then joined Jerry Lambert, supervising the construction of his winery (Lambert Bridge) and the planting of its vineyards.

"David was in charge of everything, from planting the vineyard to hammering nails into the building," Lambert said early in his winery's existence. But when Lambert and Seagram began to do battle in court over the breakup of their marketing agreement, things turned nasty in a hurry. That dispute, coupled with his father's death, meant it was time for Dave to leave and take care of his own business.

"We have 50 acres of vineyards today," says Dave. "We have 15 acres of Zinfandel, which is two-thirds of our overall production. The other third is now Cabernet Sauvignon, which comes from 12 acres of Cabernet and two of Merlot.

"We're pretty straightforward in our winemaking," he adds. "I grow the grapes and make the wine. I like ripe fruit. I put both the Zinfandel and Cabernet in oak uprights for about three months, then in small French Nevers oak barrels — about 15 to 18 months for the Zinfandel, a few months longer for the Cabernet." *RPH*

Old Zinfandel vines hug the ground in Dry Creek Valley, where the Rafanelli winery sits on a low western bench. Old-time growers felt that the closer the fruit was to the roots the better the wines would taste.

Religious icons are nothing new to wine cellars, and are as much a comment on the iffiness of winemaking as on the strong Italian influence in Sonoma County: the Ferronis, the Mazzonis, the Buchignanis, the Seghesios, the Passelaquas, the Rafanellis — to name a few.

RAVENSWOOD

This is the view the winemaker has looking through the oval port into an upright oak tank as wine is being racked into another tank or into barrels. Once the tank is empty, this oval is the cellar rat's means of entry into the tank so it can be cleaned.

It would be almost unfair to talk of the present-day Ravenswood without at least mentioning the "other" Ravenswood, the Livermore estate established a century ago by San Francisco politico Christopher A. "Blind Boss" Buckley. A colorful character, Buckley entertained his friends lavishly, if unusually.

On at least one occasion his guests, journeying to Ravenswood for a feast, were accosted by a highwayman. From all accounts, the "holdup" was the talk of a lively evening and none of the guests was particularly surprised when, at party's end, their valuables were returned by their gracious, sightless host.

Joel Peterson, founder of Sonoma's reincarnation of Ravenswood, had never heard of Buckley, but selected the name of the hero in Sir Walter Scott's novel *The Bride of Lammermoor*. That Lord Ravenswood fell off his horse to a death in quicksand only added to the appeal of the name. "In the wine business," quips Peterson, "one often has the feeling of going down in the quicksand."

If the blond-bearded Peterson doesn't entertain with quite the élan of a Buckley, he has a flair for making distinctive wines. When he founded Ravenswood in 1976, in the Russian River Valley, he began by making nothing but Zinfandel. (It still accounts for more than half of his production.) And Joel still takes his Zins seriously, to the point of aging them in French oak, about a third of which is new each year.

Peterson grew up tasting wines, his dad a longtime wine collector and friend of Santa Cruz doctor/winemaker David Bruce, his mom a writer of travel and wine newsletters. After an education in biochemistry at Oregon State — he had intended to become a doctor — and

In February 1991, Ravenswood moved into the former Haywood Winery facility on Gehricke Road, on the east side of Sonoma, where they open their tasting room to the public every day.

several frustrating years in cancer research ("people were still dying"), Joel decided to make better use of his wine knowledge.

Wanting to create a wine style — rather than "make what the grapes give you" — Joel apprenticed himself to the late Joe Swan for two years, then made his first Ravenswood Zinfandel at Swan. After leasing space for a time, he finally moved to Sonoma, where he is now ensconced in the former Haywood facility.

Peterson makes a fair amount of Merlot and what he calls his "self-defense" Chardonnay. "If you don't have a white wine, everybody comes to your table last at tastings. Plus, I was tired of the fruity, California style of Chardonnay. I was raised tasting Montrachets and Meursaults. So I make a Chardonnay that is barrel fermented, put through malolactic fermentation, and left for 11 months on the lees. Tastes good to me!"

Ravenswood's label features poster artist David Lance Goines' rendition of three interlocked ravens. "I can vividly remember picking those first eight tons at the Vogensen Ranch in 1976," says Peterson. "There were billowing rain clouds moving ominously in from the east, complete with lightning and thunder. I was try-

ing to get all the grapes in before the rains hit. Two huge ravens perched on a nearby tree, sitting there as if passing judgment. It was wonderfully surrealistic." Between that scene and Lord Ravenswood in the quicksand, how could he have chosen any other name? *RPH*

With all the technology available to winemakers, sometimes it's the simplest things that make it all work. One Sonoma winery uses a $10 hair dryer to secure labels on a $100,000 bottling line; here it takes plastic wrap to keep a bung secure and airtight.

RICHARDSON VINEYARDS

He is of the "Boomer" generation: born after World War II, educated in the crucible of the '70s, open in thought, and guided by the ideal of creating a more meaningful and less materialistic life for himself and his family in particular, and — at least theoretically — the world in general.

"My dad had been a career Navy man," says Dennis Richardson in reflection, "but with all the turmoil of society I never really gave much thought toward 'career.' At Cornell University, where I was a government major, they were geared toward a broad education. Actually, I usually tell people that I majored in demonstrations and waterfalls."

For miles around Cornell, and even in downtown Ithaca itself, waterfalls seem to drop out of glacially formed lakes everywhere, cascading over brown slate. "When I met [wife] Carrie at Cornell, I had no clear direction in my life," he recalls over a glass of Pinot Noir. "I had no training that qualified me to do anything. All we had going for us was intelligence, inquisitiveness, and an interest in supporting each

The view, in late afternoon, looking southwest over Sonoma's side of the Carneros district toward the San Pablo Bay and the setting sun. Being on the cool side, as far as wine grapes are concerned, the Carneros is the ideal place to grow Pinot Noir and Chardonnay.

other in something that would keep us close to one another and our soon-to-be family."

So, they came to the sunny Sonoma Valley, where Carrie took a job as a medical lab technologist and Dennis worked as a tour guide at Sebastiani Vineyards. While he thrived on his interaction with local grape growers and winemakers, he grew to dread the arrival of tour buses, unloading bored passengers who had little interest in wine and less in learning about winemaking. "It got to the point where I'd go into hiding when the buses pulled up.

A cluster of Pinot Noir grapes, hanging ripe and ready at the end of the growing season, look innocent enough. Yet Pinot Noir is the most difficult of grapes, both in the fermenting of its juice and the aging of its wines. But the rewards of the Pinot well-made? Ahh, there's the justification.

"Actually, a continuing nightmare for me is the fear that a busload of strangers will pull into my driveway — when I'm either shooting 'hoops' or walking up to our hilltop to enjoy the view it affords of the Bay and San Francisco — and expect me to show them around the winery." For Dennis, it is the privacy, and relative anonymity, that makes his livelihood so enjoyable. Part of that is location: Dennis and Carrie have a ten-acre parcel some miles southeast of Sonoma, out in the wilds of the Carneros district.

"What I did know when we decided to start our own winery was that I didn't want to go to a job in the city so I could live in the country," he says with feeling. "The only real option was to do it ourselves."

Dennis began as a home winemaker in 1974, leaning decidedly toward monster Zinfandels — the bigger, the riper, the better. Over the years his wines decreased in ripeness and tannin. "We're on a wave of changing tastes and philosophies," he grumbles good-naturedly. "But I still like substance in my wines, though my notion of the power that a wine has to possess has been reined in.

"Wine is not just that pastoral trip to the vineyard, watching balloons rising in the crisp morning air. Marketing and sales are necessary evils. But, "smiles Dennis," the fun of this business remains making that tub of freshly picked grapes into wine!" *RPH*

ROCHE WINERY

So many stories of fine wine started out with little more than a quest for peace and quiet. Such is the story of Joe and Genevieve Roche, but success came more rapidly to this couple because of a lucky meeting with Steve MacRostie, a winemaker in search of a winery.

The quest for peace started in the late 1970s. The Roches, both physicians and both in pathology (he sub-specializing in nuclear medicine), decided it would be nice to live part-time in the country. They looked at the southern end of Sonoma County; from here the commute wasn't bad. Wine wasn't on their minds at all.

The place that intrigued Genevieve most was a cattle ranch at the southern end of the Sonoma Valley, one of the most southerly areas of a region known as the Carneros. The size of the place was daunting — 2,480 acres — and for that reason the price was reasonable, an average of $400 an acre. But the views were breathtaking.

In 1982, at the suggestion of a local grower, the Roches planted five acres of Chardonnay and five more of Pinot Noir. The following year, a group formed to try to make the Carneros area its own approved viticultural appellation, separate from the Napa or Sonoma valleys. Joe was

When Joe and Genevieve Roche bought their property in the 1970s, no one knew that the area, just 32 miles from the northern end of the Golden Gate Bridge, would become the prime vineyard land called Carneros. It was Angelo Sangiacomo, owner of one of the Carneros's most prized vineyards, who suggested the couple plant grapes.

one of the leaders of the movement. Still, the Roches had only scant thoughts of making wine until they met MacRostie, former winemaker at Hacienda Winery.

"I called Joe in December of 1987 when I heard he was thinking of building a winery," says MacRostie. "We spoke briefly, agreed with a handshake, and I've been the consulting winemaker ever since."

Steve's first year with Roche, the 1988 harvest, was no picnic. The Roche wines were made at Sunny St. Helena Winery in the Napa Valley, meaning Steve had to put a lot of mileage on his car.

By becoming winemaker at the Roche Winery, Steve MacRostie found a home for his own brand of Chardonnay as well.

Meanwhile, Roche was continuing to plant more acreage (500 of his 2,450 acres are plantable). By 1990, he had 18 acres of Chardonnay and ten acres of Pinot Noir, as well as ten acres of Merlot, which the Roches believed would become a great wine in the cooler Carneros climate.

Roche Chardonnay is delicate and spicy, and its excellent fruit shows careful handling. MacRostie's own Chardonnay is a bit more creamy and textured than it had been at Hacienda, and richer than the Roche Chardonnay. MacRostie also fashioned from the Roche's fruit a stylish and complex, though lighter-styled, Roche Pinot Noir. It was a wine that gained early attention, showing dense flavors and a cinnamon-and-spice aroma.

The Roche Winery, a modest 8,800 square feet, was designed by Vic Conforti to look like a barn that might have sat on the very same knoll years earlier when the place was a cattle ranch. In fact, the smells of the cattle grazing next door waft through the air as one drives up the winding road to the crest of the hill.

A watercolor view of this place may be seen in the wrap-around label the Roches had designed by graphic artist Chuck House. A sweeping brush-covered hillside is brown like the hay that grows here, and off to the side of the label stands a lone cow, homage to the recent past. *DB*

The Roches' winery, which opened in 1990, isn't large, though it is big enough for two small operations like theirs and MacRostie's. The property faces San Pablo Bay to the south and east, and visitors will notice the cool marine breezes even on the hottest days of summer.

J. ROCHIOLI VINEYARDS

In France's Burgundy region, one red grape variety dominates: Pinot Noir. And it is this region that so intrigued so many of the great writers on wine of the past. The red wines were so amazingly sublime and packed with flavors that the character of red Burgundy became the standard against which the world judged any wine made from Pinot Noir. Thus did California get branded as a pretender: "[Pinot Noir] makes a comparatively undistinguished wine in California . . . [it varies] from producer to producer, but none, I think, makes a really fine one." So wrote Hugh Johnson in one of his first wine books, *Wine*, in 1966.

How times change. As worldwide demand for Burgundy pushed producers to ever-greater production, overall quality dropped. Meanwhile, people like Tom Rochioli were coming into the business in the Russian River Valley with the idea that great wine could be made from Pinot Noir in this cool region. In fact, some day it may well be that the Russian River Valley will be seen primarily as a great region for the Pinot Noir grape.

The J. Rochioli winery was founded in 1976 by Joe Rochioli Jr. His son, Tom, came into the business in 1983, so the Rochiolis' accomplishments have only recently been

The Rochioli family started planting their wonderful Russian River vineyards in 1959. Over the years the fruit has gone to such well-regarded producers as Dry Creek Vineyard and even Robert Mondavi in the Napa Valley.

seen. But the fact that Rochioli's vineyard is the prime source for three of the state's greatest Pinot Noirs is ample proof that what Hugh Johnson wrote decades ago has changed.

Today the best California Pinot Noirs are strong competition for the best Burgundy.

It all started here with a farm begun by Joe Rochioli Sr. in 1938. Then it was known as Fenton Acres. On the hillside were vineyards, in the flatlands were hops — nearby Santa Rosa was a beer-making town. Eventually, as beer production diminished, hops went by the wayside, and "dad and my grandfather [Joe Sr.] planted Cabernet and Sauvignon Blanc, in

It is the Pinot Noir grape that has made the Rochioli name so famous. On its own wines or on the wines of Williams-Selyem or Gary Farrell, the name Rochioli indicates a Pinot Noir of deep fruit and sublime character.

1959." Rochioli still makes both wines out of that vineyard. The Cabernet now makes a reserve wine, called Neoma's Vineyard for Tom's grandmother, who died in 1985.

Rochioli first gained industry recognition by selling grapes "to just about everybody in the county — even to Robert Mondavi in the mid-1960s." In the 1970s, Dave Stare at Dry Creek bought Sauvignon Blanc from Rochioli and made wonderful wine from the grapes.

Yet it was the Pinot Noir that excited people most. "Dad was the guy who started it. He saw this area's potential for Pinot. He planted the [now famed] Howard Allen vineyard and we farm it for him." The Rochioli vineyard, neighboring Allen's hillside ranch on the west side of Westside Road, is 130 acres, with 95 planted.

Today Rochioli's own Pinot Noir rivals those of Williams-Selyem and Gary Farrell, both of whom buy Rochioli grapes for their wines. Farrell was the first consultant to Rochioli, in 1985; he set up the winery production facility and assisted with the winemaking.

Rochioli began making Pinot Noir in 1973 "just for fun." The first vintage he sold was 1982. By 1984, the Rochioli name was already known as a growing star by connoisseurs. Today, "we have a waiting list for the grapes," says Tom. *DB*

J. Rochioli Vineyards and Winery is located out on Westside Road, south of Healdsburg. It is not a heavily-traveled path by tourists, but the Rochiolis are in good company, for out here are located such other excellent producers as Hop Kiln, Davis Bynum, Belvedere, Mill Creek, and Rabbit Ridge.

ST. FRANCIS VINEYARDS

This stone and wood archway marks the Highway 12 entry to the St. Francis Vineyards winery, just north of downtown Kenwood. The village is the site of the famed Fourth of July Pillow Fight.

Kenwood village is a throwback to another time. Situated on State Highway 12, it manages to retain its rustic charm and bucolic calm, clinging to traditions like the Fourth of July Pillow Fight. And, if there's something that resembles a shopping center, it's postage-stamp-sized and hardly counts.

Kenwood remains the only village in the Valley of the Moon still sans a single traffic signal. Yet, there are reasons to stop. Primary among them are wineries, four right on the highway. The only one on the west side of the road is St. Francis, built in 1979 by the burly Joe Martin. Born in Los Angeles, Martin was raised in Modesto, where his dad was a dairyman.

"After dad died, I lived in Los Banos with cousins, who raised row crops, hay, and also ran dairy cows," muses Martin. "But I finished high school at Mission High in San Francisco.

That was a rough neighborhood, even then." He liked it enough to stay for a quarter-century, operating the deli business he had started in high school, then running Modern House Furniture for 22 years. "My partner and I sold the business in 1971. My partner stayed in the furniture business, but I was tired of hearing telephones ring all the time, so I headed north and bought this 100-acre piece, which was then in walnuts and prunes."

In 1971 and '72 Joe tore out the orchards, replacing elderly trees with vine cuttings bearing arcane names like Merlot, Chardonnay, Gewurztraminer, Johannisberg Riesling, and Pinot Noir. The fruit turned out well enough to be bought by quality wineries. Realizing that every farmer exercises only limited control over perishable fruit, Martin decided to take hold of the processing part as well.

Owner Joe Martin came to Kenwood from San Francisco, and brought with him — in name and philosophy — that city's patron saint: St. Francis of Assisi, the friend to all living things.

"When we built the winery in 1979, we started out with a much larger building than we had intended," recalls Martin. "The county people had suggested that they wouldn't be happy to see us come back a few years down the road with expansion plans, and that we'd be better off to build to the size we were eventually anticipating. Fortunately, Acacia Winery was starting up and looking for space to lease until they were able to build their own facility. We also shared consultant Brad Webb for those two years."

Tom Mackey has been winemaker at St. Francis through nearly all of the '80s. A thick, muscular, but kindly sort, he's a fellow to whom you might pose the question, "Which football team did you used to be?" (He played offensive tackle in high school, then earned a degree in English from the University of San Francisco.)

"We've budded over all our Gewurztraminer, Riesling, and Pinot Noir to Merlot," says Mackey, who spent a couple of crushes in the chill of New York's Finger Lakes district at Gold Seal Winery after taking a master's in agricultural science from Fresno State. "We didn't feel we could make a top-ten Pinot Noir here, and Riesling just hasn't been selling.

Besides, Riesling grapes sell for $600 a ton and Merlot grapes go for three times that."

Mackey still makes a little Gewurztraminer, because St. Francis fans expect it, and some Muscat Canelli, Cabernet, and Zinfandel. But it's Merlot that makes St. Francis tick today. *RPH*

A gondola of Merlot, fresh from harvest in the vineyard that surrounds the winery, is dumped into a receiving hopper. You can see juice dripping from the gondola. That is from berries at the bottom, crushed by the weight of those on top.

SAUSAL WINERY

Sausal is a smallish winery, in the heart of the Alexander Valley. You might not hear about it directly. In fact the loudest praise you'll likely hear about a Sausal wine is that garnered by Grgich Hills' excellent Alexander Valley Zinfandels.

What Grgich doesn't widely publicize is that its Zinfandel comes from Sausal Winery. And Sausal is an excellent producer of that much-maligned varietal in its own right. Owner/winemaker David Demostene, a burly, curly-haired, and downright friendly fellow, credits his Zinfandelian success to vine maturity. "There are writers who say that Zinfandels don't age well," he mutters. "Well, that's true if they're made from younger vines, but Zinfandels made from more mature vines — those which are several decades old — do hold up in the bottle."

Sausal's Zinfandel is grown without irrigation on benchland, well above the fecund valley floor. "If you tried to grow Zinfandel down there, in the richer, more fertile soils, you'd get twice the tonnage and lose all the nose and flavor intensity," notes Demostene. "Our oldest vines yield from half a ton to a ton and a half an acre, and our younger vines only go up to, maybe, three tons an acre."

Sausal means "willow" in Spanish, but it's a massive limb of a giant California live oak that frames Sausal's modest little winery here. Today, Sausal means Zinfandel in California winedom.

If you get the impression that Demostene has been around the wine business much of his life, you're right. His grandfather, A. Ferrie, was owner/winemaker at Soda Rock for 25 years, with his partner, a Mr. Ferrero. It was David's dad, Leo Demostene — who had also been a winemaker at Soda Rock — who dreamed of building a small winery for his kids on the south side of Sausal Creek, which slithers through the property to the former quicksilver mine at Pine Flat. (Sausal means "willow" in Spanish, the creek naturally taking its name from the willow trees that line its banks.) "Dad bought the property in 1955, built a house up

on the hill, and ripped out apple and prune trees to plant vines," recalls David. "Then, in 1973, just as we were beginning to convert an old prune dehydrator into our winery, he died after having been ill a short time. So mom and I, and my brother and two sisters, went ahead with the winery.

"We were strictly a bulk winery at the beginning, making Napa Gamay and Petite Sirah. Now we're up to 15,000 cases a year, making some Chardonnay, which we ferment in oak puncheons. The French Colombard we grow goes into our Sausal Blanc. There's also some Cabernet Sauvignon and, of course, Zinfandel, some of which is still sold to Grgich Hills and Joseph Phelps. We have a little Pinot Noir, too, which goes to Kalin Cellars."

Sausal remains a family operation in the strictest and nicest sense. David makes the wines. Brother Edward, who also runs a heavy equipment business (Ed Demostene Bulldozing, if you're in the market), tends the 125 acres of vineyard on three family plots. Sister Roselee (better known as "Peachie") runs the tasting room and does some of the lab work — when she isn't working as a lab tech at Santa Rosa's Warrick Hospital. And sister Cindy Martin handles the bookkeeping chores.

"Don't forget mom, Rose," reminds Cindy. "She's cook and gardener. She brings us lunch and tends the flowers!" *RPH*

This neat little porch epitomizes the quiet, quaint hospitality offered at most Sonoma wineries. Nothing fancy, but you feel instantly at home, instantly comfortable. All that's missing are old slippers and a Golden Retriever. Some wineries even have those.

David Demostene knows his Zinfandel, and especially that older vines make better wines. "You get more varietal character from older vines because the bunches are smaller," he says, speaking a wisdom that's far older than he or his vines.

SEA RIDGE WINERY

It's well known that Pinot Noir, the red grape of Burgundy, grows best in cool climates where the grapes ripen slowly and stay on the vine for a long time. Moreover, based on the experiences of Burgundy, it's also known to be beneficial for Pinot Noir grapes to grow in lean soils that are chalky, or laced with limestone.

It was with those ideas firmly fixed in their minds that two couples, the Schmidts and the Wickhams, founded Sea Ridge Winery. The partners intended to specialize in Pinot Noir, knowing that the cool weather of far western Sonoma County favored it and gave them a shot to make wine similar to that of Burgundy.

"I had been a marine biologist in Bodega Bay, and I knew the coastal climate and the soils very well," says Dan Wickham, "and I had planted some grapes in Petaluma. Being a Burgundy nut, I realized this was an area that was not being looked at seriously in terms of Pinot Noir. So it interested me."

The western edge of Sonoma County has a soil that was essentially all marine deposits, "so there is a substantial amount of limestone here.

Sea Ridge started as a partnership between two couples. After an internal squabble, Dee and Dan Wickham gained control of the project and began to make wines reflecting their belief that it was possible to make great wines of the Burgundian varieties of Chardonnay and Pinot Noir from fruit grown on the Sonoma Coast.

And in France, it is the general feeling of the French that calcium carbonate makes great Burgundy."

Wickham started by planting eight acres of rootstock, but because of logistical and weather-related problems, it never got into production. Undaunted, with his wife, Dee, his mother, Tim and Susan Schmidt as partners, and a few limited partners, Wickham founded the Sea Ridge Winery in 1980. That first year a few cases of Pinot Noir were made. The wine received a gold medal at the 1983 Sonoma

The Sea Ridge project operates out of a building that looks more like a Midwestern barn with a hay loft than a winery. But, appearances aside, this is where Sea Ridge uses high quality, cool-climate fruit to make some sublime Pinot Noir.

County Harvest Fair wine competition, and the partners were off and running.

The first major vintage of Sea Ridge wines was 1981. The Bohan Vineyard Pinot Noir of that vintage "vindicated my feeling about what the area was capable of" says Wickham. The Bohan Vineyard was in a cool region where the grapes ripen slowly. The partners also were getting Pinot Noir from a vineyard owned by David Hirsch, the only vineyard that views the ocean.

Some of the early wines were shockingly good. Connoisseurs of Burgundy loved to toss in a Sea Ridge wine to a blind tasting of Burgundies and watch the unknowing squirm when the bottles were revealed.

By the mid-1980s, however, Sea Ridge hit more logistical problems. Some of the barrels were not cared for as they should have been and some wines that were released had more volatile acidity than they should have had. "As with a lot of partnerships, you get a little eager to market, and we bought more grapes than we really could handle. And that's where we got caught." Sales of the Sea Ridge wines, which had been brisk in the early years, slowed and finally the partnership ran out of steam.

No wine was made in 1987 and soon the partnership was dissolved. But Wickham retained the brand name and made some wine at the old site. In 1990, Sea Ridge came back on the market with wines reflecting what Dan and Dee hope will be the start of a long run. *DB*

SEBASTIANI VINEYARDS

The winery tasting room at Sebastiani Vineyards sits in an old stone cellar, a stone's throw from the first patch of vines cultivated north of San Francisco. Franciscan padres at the Sonoma Mission planted those vines in 1825.

Following the Act of Secularization, which ended the Church's reign over the mission system and replaced it with Mexican authority, the vineyard was acquired by General Mariano G. Vallejo. The mission itself still stands at the northeast corner of Sonoma's town plaza and park, the state's largest town square, laid out by Vallejo in 1835.

Samuele Sebastiani had been born into a peasant family who toiled in the vineyards of Tuscany. Short of formal education and impatient with a sharecropper's existence, he borrowed money for steerage to California in 1895. He worked the vegetable gardens of San Francisco, then moved north to Sonoma. Fond of physical exertion, he bought a stout cart and a team of horses, and began hauling cobblestones from local quarries. Sonoma's City Hall, a regional landmark, was built by the Italian immigrants whom he sponsored, and largely with cobblestones Sebastiani quarried and hauled.

In 1904 Sebastiani purchased an old

One of the most popular features of the tour at Sebastiani are hand-carved barrel heads, doors, and tanks executed by the late Earle Brown. The barrel heads on these redwood tanks represent the various varietal wines made at Sebastiani.

horse barn at the northeast corner of town, and later the Mission vineyard across the street. Visitors to the winery today are shown the hand crusher, small basket press, and 501-gallon redwood tank Samuele and his uncle used to make their first Zinfandel. Samuele sold it door-to-door from barrels on his horse-drawn wagon. During Prohibition he kept the winery alive by producing sacramental and medicinal wines. He also set up a fruit and vegetable cannery next door, to keep his employees at work and protect his investment.

The winery changed soon after Samuele's death in 1944. By the early '50s his son had

Samuel Sebastiani (left) came to the U.S. in 1895 and founded the winery less than a decade later. His son, August (right), started American traditions when he was at the helm. His oldest son, Sam (center), took charge from 1979-86, when management of the old mission winery was passed to brother Don.

begun to bottle wines under his own label. "One day my wife, Sylvia, returned from an afternoon of bridge," recalled August one summer's day at his hillside stone home, 100 yards from the winery. "She commented on the pale, dry cocktail sherry her hostess had served and asked why we could not make a wine like that. But it was my wine! Under someone else's label!! It really bothered me that I couldn't even get credit from my own wife."

August gained notoriety for the tailored, blue-and-white pin-striped bib overalls he habitually wore. It was no pose. "Gus" was farmer by inclination and businessman by necessity. And anyone taken in by his comfortable dress was liable to be taken for a fascinating but financially unrewarding ride.

Beaulieu Vineyard once suffered a cellar fire, and was ready to sell off tanks of wine. Most appraisers tasted the samples in the cellar, where smokey aromas lingered. August removed samples to his own lab for tasting. Discovering lots free of taint, he bought them for a song and sold them for a symphony.

Long before the rise of consumer sophistication in the early '70s, August had already begun vintage-dating his top varietal wines. When the demand came, he had the wines. And when prices got out of hand, he hit the market with varietals in half gallons at low prices, pre-dating by more than a decade the notion of "fighting varietals."

In 1972 he started an American tradition, albeit borrowed from France, with his Nouveau Gamay Beaujolais. The fruity, tantalizing red is meant to be drunk within months of its production. "In Beaujolais, a portion of each year's harvest is bottled without aging and sent off to bistros and cafes of Lyon, Marseille, and Paris, where it is announced with colorful banners lining the Champs Elysees," explained August. To this day, people make special trips to Sonoma around mid-November to witness the unveiling of this refreshing "new" wine, heralded in pomp and circumstance by an ermine-robed cadre of the Knights of the Vine.

When August's oldest son, Sam, returned from schooling and an Army stint, he was put in charge of marketing, and later production. Stainless-steel tanks replaced redwood fermenters, and white wines began to shine with distinctive varietal fruitiness.

In 1980, August died. Six years later, after a family disagreement, Sam left to start his own winery (Viansa), and Sebastiani Vineyards came under the management of August's youngest son, Don. A former two-term California State Assemblyman, Don had a more expansive image of what Sebastiani Vineyards should be, seeking like his father to be all things to all people.

Thus, Sebastiani competes in the fighting varietal categories with wines under the Vendange and August Sebastiani Country labels — mostly made in a San Joaquin Valley facility — as well as in the mid-range and premium categories.

Sebastiani's premium "estates" line features specific Sonoma Valley vineyard sites, and on each label the vineyard name itself boasts the largest block type. "In the Sonoma Valley, no one vineyard is like another," says Don. "The soils range from gray loam to red manzanita, and some get 60 inches of rain a

Here are another set of barrels whose heads have been rendered artwork by Earle Brown. The swan (center of row three) was done for the late August Sebastiani, who was a waterfowl expert and championed conservation.

year while others thrive on half of that. Each of these vineyards is unlike all of the others, and so too are the wines."

Sebastiani Vineyards has long been an easy winery to visit, with informational tours and educational tastings. Providing particular delight to tour-goers are the carvings of the late Earle Brown. Brown was a retired lettering artist when he came to Glen Ellen in 1965. Hired to paint a few signs and carve leafy arrows to guide the tours, he eventually took to carving the heads of oak ovals and anything else wooden that stood still long enough.

Brown used to tell of the wooden-legged man who came into the tasting room one warm afternoon, sat down and dozed off for a few moments — and left with an Earle Brown original! He was probably pulling our legs, but the fact is that he did leave more than 300 carvings before his death in 1984. Barrel ends depict the Sebastiani wines, an oval shows Father Junipero Serra (founder of the California mission system), a vintner's calendar serves to educate patrons about the seasons of winegrowing, and fanciful monks peer down over tasting-room counters. Look for the lower case "eb" — Earle was a modest fellow — that identifies all his work. *RPH*

These old redwood tanks represent historical Sonoma winemaking. Today they have largely given way to stainless steel and small oak barrels made from wood grown in French forests thousands of miles away.

Part of this stone cellar, at the main entrance to Sebastiani's tasting room, was built at the turn of the century. The seven flags out front represent those which have flown over Sonoma County throughout its history, from the Spanish to the American.

SEGHESIO WINERY

When you hear that Seghesio Winery first sold wine under its name in 1982, you figure the place is relatively new to Sonoma County. Yet Seghesio has been here since 1902, making wine for 80 years without a label. Economic conditions forced Seghesio to begin bottling wine under the family name, and the result is excellent wine at reasonable prices.

Edoardo and Angela Seghesio bought the family's original ranch at Chianti Station, a train stop between Asti and Geyserville, in 1894. The winery was built eight years later, but all their wine was sold in bulk to other wineries.

Before Prohibition, wine brands were not important. Back then wine was sold in bulk to major bottlers, or in shops straight from the barrel into a buyer's flask. Wine shops offered Sauterne, Chablis, Rhine (or Hock), Burgundy, Medoc. Vintner Lou Foppiano says his family winery sold white wine called Sauterne and Chablis. "We sold five times as much Chablis as we did Sauterne, even though it was from the same tank!"

Through 1974, Seghesio was one of the largest crushers in Sonoma County, handling 25 percent of the county's grapes. A huge amount went to E. & J. Gallo, the Modesto-

Seghesio Winery began life ostensibly making bulk wine that it sold to other wineries. Thus the facility had little need for small oak barrels — only large upright wooden vats for holding the wine. When the winery began to make wine under the family name, it brought in small French oak barrels.

based giant. But in 1974, Gallo built its Frei Bros. winery and stopped buying wine, leaving Seghesio with lots of unsold bulk wine.

"There was tremendous table wine competition," says Pete Seghesio Jr. "Some companies would ask themselves why they were blending in North Coast wine at $3.50 a gallon when you could use 80-cents-a-gallon stuff and make a bigger profit."

By 1977, it was clear that Seghesio needed a new way to sell wine. Ed Seghesio, a co-owner of the facility, and his son, Ted, favored bottling their wine under the Seghesio label. Eugene Seghesio (Pete Sr.), who was Ed's uncle and

Winemaker Ted Seghesio made some excellent wines in the late 1980s, yet in the tradition of many other Italian families (such as the Martinis, Foppianos, and Pedroncellis) the Seghesios always kept prices reasonable.

another co-owner, opposed the idea because of high start-up costs. (Pete Sr. and his late brother, Art, had been co-owners of the operation. Art's sons, Ed and Ray, inherited half the winery on the death of their father and today own it jointly with their uncle.) The debate in the family was hot. Finally, Pete Sr. was overruled.

Seghesio remains a family operation. Today, Ted Seghesio, Ed's son, is the winemaker; Ed is manager and president of Seghesio's farms; Ray is vice president of the winery; and Pete Sr. is president of the winery. Ted's younger brother, David, is vice president of operations and Pete Jr. is vice president of marketing. Jim Neumiller, who married Ted's sister, Julie, handles the vineyards.

The family owns about 400 acres here in Sonoma — 320 planted to vineyards in the Alexander Valley, Dry Creek Valley, and Russian River Valley. Production hit 100,000 cases in 1990. Seghesio also imports the Italian wines of Renzo Seghesio, a third cousin of Pete Sr. and the mayor of Monforte d'Alba. That line includes Barolo, Barbera, Dolcetto, and Nebbiolo.

One Seghesio house specialty, called Chianti Station, is 85 percent Sangiovese and the rest an old field blend of red grapes. It is similar to Italian Chianti and comes from a 90-year-old planting at the home ranch. *DB*

The home where Eugene (Pete) Seghesio and his wife, Rachael, live is set well off the main road and up a rise facing some of the old Sangiovese vines that the winery still uses to make a stylish, complex wine called Chianti Station.

SIMI WINERY

This plastic bung, hammered into the bung hole at the top of the barrel, protects the resting, aging wine from excessive oxidation. Every month or two, it must be removed so that additional wine may be poured into the barrel to replace that which has evaporated through the wood's semi-porous grain.

I t is the oldest joke in winedom: What's the easiest way to make a small fortune? Take a big fortune and start a winery. The curiosity is that most real winery histories begin in poverty and build their successes over decades, even centuries.

That is certainly the story at Simi Winery, which traces its origins to the Tuscan village of Montepulciano, "Hill of the Nobles." There, in 1848, young (they're never old, of course) Giuseppe Simi set out to discover a better life, carrying all he owned in a bandana.

Arriving in California, he tried the gold fields. But, victimized by claim jumpers, he turned to cabbages. At 50 cents a head to the fine restaurants of San Francisco they were a hot item, and Giuseppe's farming venture did well enough that he was soon able to send for

brother Pietro. Having worked Tuscan vines, and knowing something of winemaking, he dreamed of making his own wine one day.

As the United States was celebrating its centennial, the brothers Simi bought a three-story Victorian house on Green Street, still the heart of San Francisco's Italian district. They lived upstairs and made wine in the cellar, buying grapes from Healdsburg, shipping them by

wagon to Petaluma, and then by barge across the Bay.

Like many from their homeland, they were taken by the hills of Sonoma County. In 1881 they bought a winery on Front Street, on the south side of Healdsburg near the train depot, for $2,200. Two years later they added 126 acres on the north side of town, and began planting vines on what they called Colina de Florenza (The Little Hills of Florence).

In 1890, Chinese laborers, many of whom had worked on the Northwestern Pacific Railroad line whose track lay adjacent to the winery, were hired to construct a new Simi Winery. Capable of holding 200,000 gallons, its three-foot-thick basalt walls form the core of the present-day facility.

Then, as success-bred expansion was in full swing, tragedy struck. In August 1904 both Giuseppe and Pietro died. But the Simi clan had a backbone to match any Cabernet's. It fell to Giuseppe's daughter Isabelle, just 14, to take charge of things.

And she did. Neither the '06 earthquake nor the onset of Prohibition a decade later would tarnish her mettle. Having weighed grapes for the winery at age 12, and having taken business trips with her father, she had the full support of the whole staff when she set out to keep Simi well. In 1908 she married banker Fred Haigh. They were kindred souls, and their stubbornness allowed them to weather the 14 long years of Prohibition.

The Haighs refused to sell off any of their inventory for less than it was worth. "Once we arranged a big sale to Mexico," Isabelle recalled, "but President Hoover wouldn't let us ship it because we couldn't prove that it would be used only for sacramental or medicinal purposes."

Then, in December of 1933, Repeal came. This put Simi in the advantageous position of having a ready stock of fine, aged wines, while others were selling hastily fermented stuff. (Not all of Simi's cache was of high quality; lesser stock was sold off for vinegar and brandy.)

The flower garden at Simi, just outside the tasting room, is especially attractive during the spring, when most of the flowers are in bloom. But spring means frost protection in the vineyards, lest tender vine buds be damaged by ice-making temperatures.

The redwood grove that stands tall around the tasting room is testament to the renewed joy that Repeal brought, for those trees were planted by Isabelle in celebration of that long-awaited event. Isabelle also decided that having a tasting room and retail shop at the winery might help recapture some of the business lost during the Great Experiment. Built out of a 25,000-gallon Champagne tank, it was the first winery tasting room in California history.

During World War II, the winery gained attention for its fine old wines when Monterey's fashionable Hotel Del Monte selected Simi wines for its house label. Then Fred Haigh died, in 1954. And when their daughter died unexpectedly in 1969, Isabelle, then nearly 80 and hampered by arthritis, sold the winery to oilman/grape grower Russ Green.

New people, new ideas, and old wines came to the fore during Green's stewardship. Stocks of 1935 Cabernet Sauvignon were discovered. At the wine cellar's centennial in 1990, the '35 was still drinking beautifully: rich with oily licorice, tar, cedar, and mushroom fruit. So was the '34 Tawny Port, of which film director Alfred Hitchcock once wrote, "This port is far too good for most people."

Through the '70s and '80s, Simi went through ownership changes without missing a beat, largely due to then-president Michael

Stacked five rows high on these steel racks, each two-barrel cluster can be quickly moved by forklift. In most cellars, space is at a premium, and barrels must be stacked efficiently.

Dixon, the Buckinghamshire-born sportsman who lent a firm hand to the tiller.

Over the years Dixon has done much to give his people the best possible equipment to work with. And, in 1979, he matched that effort by luring one of the country's finest wine-makers, Zelma Long, to Simi. Having studied chemistry and microbiology at Oregon State University, Long pursued a career in nutrition before being attracted to wine. Long and lank, she is an active and engaging lady. She rides horses, swims, hikes, and plays tennis; she loves to read, take pictures, and cook.

"We've been lucky to have Moët-Hennessy as owners since 1981," notes Long, now

Zelma Long stands high among the world's vinous leadership. She brought innovation to Simi in viticulture (trellising reseach) and winemaking (investigating the softening effects of trickle pumpovers in Cabernet Sauvignon fermentations).

Simi's president. "They take the long view. They are interested in expanding and maximizing their assets. They want to build and they're not interested in short-term profits, which promote compromises that come back to haunt you ten or 15 years later."

At the turn of the century, Simi had owned some 700 acres of vineland, but sold them off during Prohibition to keep the winery open, quite an act of faith. In 1982, Simi bought and leased 175 acres in the Alexander Valley district, east of Healdsburg, a proven region for Cabernet Sauvignon.

Long, along with winemaker Paul Hobbs, has been especially busy trying to improve the Cabernet over the years. In the early '80s they tested two methods of pumping fermenting juice over its "cap" of skins and seeds. "We had assumed that using a powerful stream of juice to break up the cap was the best way to extract the most fruit and body," noted Long at the time. "But in examining a method called 'trickle down' [no relation to the political economic theory of the same name], which gently soaks the cap with a fine mist, we've gotten cleaner, more fragrant wines." *RPH*

This simple little sign marks the old train stop at Simi Winery. In the old days, the railroad was the main means of shipping wine to market. Today it remains as a peripheral method of transportation.

SONOMA-CUTRER VINEYARDS

Sonoma-Cutrer began life in 1972 not as the Chardonnay-oriented winery it is today, but as a Pinot Noir grape-growing limited partnership. The first venture was to be all Pinot Noir planted in the western Russian River Valley, but the vine supplier ran out of Pinot Noir, so "we planted the home ranch to half Pinot Noir, half Chardonnay, or else I wouldn't be here today," says Jones, the general partner of the operation.

Jones, a marketing-driven executive, was a fighter pilot in Vietnam. "I did two tours, and when they wouldn't send me back for a third tour, I left the Air Force."

"Frankly, I didn't know what a Chardonnay was," admits Jones, but he was frustrated trying to get the 145 acres planted on time. When told not enough Pinot Noir was available, "I said, hell, I'll take anything at this point."

But the serendipitous Chardonnay planting did not wield its influence right away. Sonoma-Cutrer first became known as a Pinot Noir grower, on wines made in the 1970s by Stonegate, Kistler, and Landmark.

The winery project started as an outgrowth of grape growing. Jones wanted to buy a property initially, but "all through the '70s I was looking at wineries that were going bust and making a bid on them. I'd get really close [to buying one] and someone would steal it right out from under me. These were guys for whom the return on investment didn't mean a thing. Finally I said, "We're never going to be able to buy a place, let's build our own." That was in 1981.

The winery became necessary because, even though he was getting top dollar for his grapes, "our soils are such that we were never getting more than three and a half tons an acre, and farming costs are the same." The cost of farming rose, however, and the tax shelters that had once lured investors to farming petered out. By '81, though Jones recapitalized the venture twice in the 1970s, he saw that to move ahead he needed a winery.

The Sonoma-Cutrer winery, located in the Russian River area, was designed by Roland/Miller/ Associates, which has won awards for its designs of numerous wineries. Adjacent to the winery is a professional croquet field on which major international tournaments are staged.

Sonoma-Cutrer winemaker Bill Bonetti tends new plantings of Chardonnay — a variety first grown there by chance, but now by very definite design.

So Sonoma-Cutrer Vineyards was formed, the second half of the name for his mother, Mary Eleanor Cutrer. More than $9 million later, 18 years after first planting the vineyards, in 1990 the venture made its first actual profit — "and the new federal excise tax will take 80% of my bottom line. Add that to the recession and the anti-alcohol forces and what's left?"

It is the three Chardonnays that Sonoma-Cutrer produces, under former Charles Krug and Souverain winemaker Bill Bonetti, that have brought it highest praise. The top-of-the-line wine, called Les Pierres, is made from a vineyard that Jones says is "the one piece of property I never wanted." He was offered the Sonoma Valley property in 1973 and said no, again in 1974 and said no again, and finally before the harvest in 1974 he bought it.

"Then five years later, I tried to sell it, and I almost got [Napa Valley grower] Andy Beckstoffer to buy it, but he wouldn't. The place is a mile southwest of Sonoma and it has so many rocks in it, it just tears up tractors and discs."

The Cutrer Vineyard is in the Russian River area. The third wine, called Russian River Ranches, is made from grapes grown in the Chalk Hill and Fulton areas as well as at the confluence of the Russian River and Mark West Creek, west of the winery. *DB*

The tasting room at Sonoma-Cutrer, with its large fireplace, is one of the most attractive in all of the wine country. It is where tours (Tuesdays through Saturdays, by appointment only) begin and end.

221

ROBERT STEMMLER WINERY

Sometimes the best success stories are those of pure serendipity. The story of Robert Stemmler is precisely that.

Stemmler attended the wine college in Bad Kreutznach in Germany, graduated in 1952, and worked in several wineries in the Mosel and in Baden. In 1961 he was hired by the Charles Krug Winery in the Napa Valley. Then operated by brothers Peter and Robert Mondavi, Krug was making a lot of Chenin Blanc with residual sugar, and the wine always threatened to referment in the bottle.

"I was hired by Bob Mondavi to develop a sterile filtration system for them. I came over to help solve a problem for them and then go home," says Stemmler. "The brothers were always feuding, and when there's bitterness at the top, it filters down. But I stayed for six and a half years."

He then was hired as winemaker at Inglenook, where he trained a young enologist by the name of Tom Ferrell, who later went on to become president of Sterling Vineyards. Stemmler stayed at Inglenook through early 1970 and then joined Russ Green, who had just bought Simi. He stayed through 1973, just before Simi was acquired by Scottish and Newcastle. After doing some consultation work in

In the late 1980s, Robert Stemmler signed an agreement with Buena Vista Winery to make his excellent Pinot Noir at Buena Vista, from his choice of grapes. He is prohibited, under terms of the contract, from making Pinot Noir for anyone other than the joint venture. His own Dry Creek winery still exists, but it's just a small project for Stemmler now.

Argentina and Chile, Stemmler became an important consultant for wineries such as Landmark, Mill Creek, Raymond, and Stonegate. But by 1977 he was restless to make wine again. "It seemed like everybody was doing a winery, so in 1977 I started my own."

The Robert Stemmler Winery was launched on his own small property on Lambert Bridge Road. His goal was to make Chardonnay and Sauvignon Blanc, nothing else.

In 1982, however, a critical decision was made down the road at Simi. Winemaker Zelma Long decided she would no longer make Pinot Noir, just weeks before the harvest.

Bob Stemmler's soaring success with Pinot Noir, totally unexpected, came more than 30 years after he graduated from a German wine academy and more than 20 years after he came to northern California.

"So the Pinot Noir idea was really thrown at me," says Stemmler. "At that time, a lot of people were getting out of the Pinot Noir business, and these grapes were contracted to Simi. And I was offered them, and I thought, 'Why should I start with Pinot Noir? Even people with money can't market it.' But I would make only 800 cases, so I figured I couldn't go wrong. Of course, that wine put me on the map."

That 1982 Pinot Noir showed depth of fruit and intense character. It won so many medals that Stemmler was vaulted into a pre-eminent position among the tiny coterie of top-notch Pinot Noir producers that existed then.

Stemmler grew bolder, acquiring fruit from the dramatic Bohan Ranch that had been used to some success by Sea Ridge Winery. Michael Bohan's ranch, 1,400 feet above sea level, produces only a small amount of fruit, but the non-irrigated vines have intensity, and the acidity of the grapes is always superb for the style of wine Stemmler wishes to make.

In 1988, Buena Vista, then looking to expand its portfolio, signed an agreement with Stemmler under which the parent company would market the wine and own the Stemmler Pinot Noir label. Stemmler still makes the wine from his choice of grapes, but at Buena Vista; and the Stemmler winery still exists, but it's just a small project for him now. *DB*

When Simi Winery nearby decided not to make Pinot Noir any longer, Stemmler was serendipitously presented with a crop of grapes in search of a home. He took them, made the wine, and soon joined the handful of cult wineries that connoisseurs praise for the variety.

RODNEY STRONG VINEYARDS

The Rodney Strong winery designed by the local architectural firm Roland/Miller/ Associates and the unique pyramid configuration won numerous design awards. Today it sits adjacent to the once-affiliated Piper Sonoma sparkling wine facility.

The fortunes of the Rodney Strong Vineyards have been like a roller coaster — once a struggling operation with no vines, then a soaring star in the stock market worth many millions, then a collapsing entity as the owners acquired too much land and were never able to produce and sell enough wine.

"There are a lot of emotional swings in the business of wine," said Strong shortly after the acquisition of his winery by Klein Foods of Stockton. The acquisition is the most recent chapter in the curious history of this winery, located at the northern end of the Russian River Valley appellation.

Strong had been a dancer/choreographer in New York and Paris, among other entertainment exploits, yet it was wine that brought him fame, happiness — and white hair.

Strong and his wife, Charlotte, got into the wine business in 1959 when they opened a tasting room in Tiburon in Marin County, an hour south of here. The idea was to buy wine made in Windsor and sell it at the tasting room, named Tiburon Vintners. In 1962, friend Pete Friedman joined the Strongs and the company moved to Windsor. A direct -mail division was set up to market some of the wine, called Wind-

sor. Soon the company expanded by issuing stock to private parties. In 1970, it went public with an initial stock offering at $5 per share. It was to prove a monumental decision, one of the rare times that a winery has offered shares to the public. That year, the company opened a new $2 million winery in Windsor.

Within a year, the growth of Windsor Vineyards was a *Wall Street Journal* item. The stock soared in 1972 to $41 a share, its all-time high. Later that year, a second stock offering, at $28.75 per share, raised $10 million. In 1973, Sonoma Vineyards became the name used for wine then marketed to stores and restaurants; Windsor remained the name of the mail-order wines. All looked rosy.

But one thing couldn't be predicted: an industry-wide slump. In 1974, Sonoma Vineyards' debt was listed as $11 million; by 1975, debt had risen to $20 million, yet the firm needed to grow to meet demand.

In 1976, the winery made major headlines. Its 1974 Cabernet Sauvignon, called Alexander's Crown, was rated highly by wine lovers and began to sell rapidly. The wine gave Sonoma Vineyards a shot in the arm. But times remained lean; Strong and Friedman, who had leveraged the company by acquiring land, found their assets not liquid enough to keep the company solvent. The success of the Alexander Crown Cabernet proved only a minor windfall.

In came more investors, including new executives John Andersen and Kenneth Kwit; Strong and Friedman took lesser roles. Another partner was Renfield Importers, with distilled spirits marketing experience.

Andersen and Kwit made changes in the structure of the firm, leaving no place for Friedman, who left. He later formed Belvedere Winery nearby with the aid of William Hambrecht, principal of the San Francisco investment house of Hambrecht and Quist.

Sonoma Vineyards, meanwhile, expanded under Renfield. The firm pumped $4 million into the winery and then began to buy up tool companies in a diversification move. But the

The spacious tasting room at Rodney Strong is located up a twin ramp and features tables at which guests can sit and sip in solitude, as well as windows that look down into the wine production facility.

TASTING ROOM

fit didn't work, and soon Sonoma Vineyards had higher debt than before and not enough capital to fund everything. Moreover, the brand had sunk in the public's estimation, so in 1982, the winery's name was changed to Rodney Strong Vineyards. With tool company sales added in, the revamped company announced revenues that year of a record $48 million, followed by $60.4 million in 1983. Yet profits in both years remained flat and debt rose — to $37 million in 1984.

The price of the company's stock, which had soared when it was only a wine business, tumbled. In 1985, with the stock trading at only $1.63 per share, Renfield decided to take the firm private in a $2 per share tender offer. Renfield then chose to sell pieces of the company to raise cash. Finally, in 1986, the Sonoma County winery and its vast vineyard holdings (nearly 1,600 acres) were sold to Schenley Industries of New York.

Schenley expressed hope that the Rodney Strong brand could be promoted, but in 1988 the owners changed yet again. Guinness, the huge British company with a greater interest in beer than wine, acquired Rodney Strong Vineyards as part of its acquisition of Schenley. Guinness wanted Schenley only for its spirits brands, not for wine, and began to sell off all of Schenley's non-spirits interests.

The lawn adjacent to the Rodney Strong winery is a broad expanse that in spring and summer is often used for concerts. Guests may sit on the lawn and sip wine and nibble foods while the performance goes on on a stage in the shadow or the winery.

Referring to the Renfield, Schenley, and Guinness eras, Strong says, "This place was unwanted and unloved for three regimes. No one wanted to put money into it because they weren't in it for the long haul." Proper equipment wasn't acquired, marketing suffered, and the place stagnated.

Still, some of those who worked here, including Forest Tancer (now at Iron Horse) and Dick Arrowood (Chateau St. Jean, Arrowood) praised the skill of Strong, who made excellent wine under financial stress — as wide-ranging as *méthode champenoise* sparkling wines to light, delicate Fumé Blancs, rich Cabernets, and even late-harvest wines.

Winemaker Rick Sayre, who heads up Rod Strong's winemaking team, made a number of award-winning wines after Strong assumed more and more of the marketing responsibilities of the property in the late 1980s. Sayre uses a wide variety of oak barrels for aging the wine, of both French and American production.

During the 1980s, Rick Sayre made the wine while Strong was on the road, hosting dozens of dinners for writers and the trade. With his satirical sense of humor, Strong gave speeches laced with biting allusions to Dryden and Donne, Lenin and Lennon, Dali, Bach, Milton, and Shakespeare. As an after-dinner speaker, he was in great demand. Thespians with his skill are paid thousands of dollars for such speeches; Strong was doing the same sort of oratory for the sale of bottles of his wine.

And though his efforts went unnoticed and unappreciated by the various entities for whom he toiled in that period, he grew more adept at handling the intricacies of the business world. When Guinness said it had no interest in wine, Strong rounded up a coterie of investors, promised cash of his own, and made an offer on the property. But Tom Klein of Klein Foods in Stockton won the bidding for the company and, in a deal valued at about $40 million, acquired the brand, inventory, vineyards, and winery. Strong stayed on when he was sure Klein would continue to make top-rate wine. Controversy arose later, when Klein angered neighbors by selling a lot of the acreage that had been vineyards for gravel mining.

But at last Strong's winery was in strong financial hands. *DB*

Various sizes and configurations of stainless-steel tanks are used in the Rodney Strong winery, which is one of the largest in the county, with a capacity of nearly 3.5 million gallons of wine.

JOSEPH SWAN VINEYARDS

The phrase "wine pioneer" may seem to apply only to those who made wine before 1900 or before Prohibition — makers of modest wine, wine without pretension.

The modern-day wine pioneer came to California's north coast hoping to make wine that could compete with the best in the world. Leading this second explosion was Joe Swan. His idea was to make great wine for his family, even if it meant making only a tiny amount of it. What he couldn't consume he'd sell.

Joe was attracted to wine as art, not wine as mammon. Once an artist, he had left that career to become a successful commercial airline pilot for Western Airlines. Always interested in wine, he tried to make it at home, but he was based in Salt Lake City, Utah — the wrong place. "My first home-made wine was supposed to be red, but the stuff never got any color," said Joe. "It sat in a crock on top of the refrigerator and my roommates called it José's Rosé."

Joe retired in 1973. But looking forward to that time he'd earlier bought some property in the cold Russian River Valley. On the 13-acre plot he planted Pinot Noir and Chardonnay. The Swan property had been planted to grapes in the 1800s, when the now-extinct town of Trenton still existed. But the area went into

The Russian River Valley, where Joseph Swan Vineyards is located, is a cool region surrounded by low lying hills and not far, as the crow flies, from the Pacific Ocean. The fog that blankets the valley on spring and summer mornings keeps the vines from maturing too quickly and makes the harvest season as much as a month longer than in warmer regions.

decline as a wine-growing place until Joe pioneered the classic Burgundian varieties.

Joe reasoned that Burgundy was cool, and so was the Russian River, maybe cooler. This would give him the ripening he'd need to make classic Pinot Noir, the hardest red wine to make. This was at a time when most California wineries were trying to solve the Pinot Noir conundrum with grapes from areas they thought were cool, but which actually weren't.

Joe also had faith that the region was warm enough to ripen the grapes of Bordeaux, so he planted a tiny amount of Cabernet Sauvignon, Cabernet Franc, and Merlot as well. Others

The "towers" so often seen in Napa and Sonoma counties are old pump houses. They were originally used to house the pumps that drew water from the wells, which were the main sources for both drinking and irrigating the vines in the days before reservoirs were constructed.

called him nuts; Joe just smiled.

Joe died of cancer in 1988, but in his last year he and son-in-law Rod Berglund spoke daily about the vineyard. "We talked about nearly every vine, where it came from, how it grew, what kind of fruit it gave," says Berglund, formerly the winemaker for La Crema Vinera. Many of Swan's winemaking procedures were adopted by Berglund, including *not* using sulphur dioxide during fermentation, and aging Chardonnay on the gross lees (in the French *sur lie* method).

One of Joe's "secrets" of great wine was tiny yield off the vines, less than two tons per acre. And he made wine with a minimum of handling. In Joe's last years, his complex Pinot Noirs were made by adding whole clusters to the fermentation tank. By 1988, the Pinot Noir was fermented using only whole clusters. Also, the time the juice spent in the vat in contact with the skins was lengthy — up to six weeks for the red wines — a technique Swan used long before it caught on widely.

Zinfandel was Swan's first and perhaps greatest wine, and today is prized by collectors. Joseph Swan Vineyards makes just 4,000 cases of wine; half of it is Zinfandel. Berglund makes some stylish Sonoma Mountain wines: a stunning Cabernet from David Steiner's Ranch, called Steiner; a Semillon called Berlin; and a Chardonnay called Wolfspierre. *DB*

The Joseph Swan winery was founded to make the highest quality wine, even if that meant making only a few gallons of it. Here a 10-gallon carboy of Zinfandel bubbles and ferments, either to be used in a blend or to be consumed by Rod and Lynn Berglund in front of the swimming pool some hot summer day.

TAFT STREET

I t is a delightful curiosity, in a winery so thoroughly grounded in practicality, that its name is utterly incongruous. The winery has never had an address on Taft Street, nor has any Taft Street ever been associated with the winery. What gives?

"Well, actually, my brothers and I got started making home wines in my brother Mike's garage on Taft Avenue, in Oakland," explains partner/winemaker John Tierney, who spends his spare time working with wood, building fences and furniture. "When we had to come up with a label, we came up with 'Taft Street Garage.' For some reason, Taft Avenue didn't quite sound right. And when we decided to start the winery, in 1982, we decided not to name it for ourselves, or for anything close by, in case we ever moved."

Which is exactly what happened during the crush of 1990, when Taft Street outgrew its original commercial quarters in Forestville, moving a few miles south to Barlow Lane in Sebastopol. "Where we were, we had room for one more barrel, and that was it," laughs Tierney, who

The Taft Street motto is consistency and simplicity. "We don't think that wines have to be made in a fancy place and we don't think that people have to pay $15 a bottle for a good Chardonnay," says winemaker John Tierney. Seems fair enough.

studied geography and climatology ("I can still tell if it's cloudy or not!") at U. C. Berkeley.

When Tierney finished school, he had no idea what he wanted to do. "I had made wine at home for a couple of years, so I headed for Sonoma County and took a job at Souverain, from 1976 to 1979. Then I thought I might enjoy trying the retail side of things, and moved back to Berkeley, selling grapes and winemaking equipment to home winemakers and professionals. It was a good experience, but I don't care much for sales."

Chardonnay is the essence of Taft Street. Pomace is the residue of Chardonnay. After the grapes have been pressed, what's left are these dried skins, seeds, and some pulp. Far from being waste, the pomace is disked back into the vineyard, to keep the soils loose and return nitrogen to the earth.

Fortunately, John's brother Mike — a schoolteacher by morning, a wine salesman by afternoon — likes selling. "My other brother, Marty, is a San Francisco tax attorney who sits on the California State Tax Board. Our other partners are Michael F. Martini and Andy Bartlett. Michael handles all our bookkeeping. Andy is an attorney who spent 25 years in the oil business in Indonesia. He's our president."

The first commercial vintage for the Tierneys and friends was 1982, when 2,200 cases of Chardonnay, Cabernet, Merlot, and Pinot Noir were made. Production today is more than ten times that, but the Pinot is no longer produced. "Pinot Noir proved to be somewhat variable to make," concedes John. "And even more variable to sell.

"We're not rich enough to have the luxury of educating people. Thus, Chardonnay makes up almost three-quarters of our production. For the insufferably studious wine drinkers we make two Chardonnays. We have a Sonoma County Chardonnay that's mostly tank fermented and has lots of fruit. Then we have a Russian River Chardonnay, more of which is barrel fermented, and taken through malolactic and barrel aging."

At the 1988 Sonoma County Harvest Fair, Taft Street's 1986 Russian River Chardonnay walked off with the white wine sweepstakes, prompting a Press Democrat headline, "CHALK ONE UP WITH THE LITTLE GUY." *RPH*

TOPOLOS AT RUSSIAN RIVER

Topolos at Russian River Vineyards — such a long name for such a small winery, but that's the way it goes for former author, longtime grape grower, and wine educator Michael Topolos, his brother Jerry, and Jerry's wife, Christine, the three owners.

Part of the reason for the lengthy name is, one suspects, to recognize the history of Russian River Vineyards while distinguishing its present owners from the winery's shaky and often uncertain past. The vineyards were originally planted in 1964 by Fred and Helene Riebli. In 1969 they added a winery, modeled on the hop kilns that once dotted the county.

In 1975 the Rieblis sold to Jack Lowe and Roy Giorgi Jr., who unloaded the property in December 1976 to San Francisco investor Norman Chan (who owned San Francisco's International Hotel and Santa Rosa's Flamingo Hotel). Chan hired wine merchant Don Baumhefner to run the winery, Don's wife, Kay, to open the restaurant, and winemaker Merry Edwards to create the wines. But things never got off the ground.

In 1978, Michael Topolos made his first wines in leased space at nearby Martini & Prati, then took on the lease at Russian River Vineyards the following year.

The hop kiln design is appropriate for the Russian River Valley, where hops were king in the '20s and '30s. Hops gave way to prunes, prunes gave way to grapes. Just as well, for neither hops nor prunes make particularly distinguished wines.

Even though Russian River Vineyards had an operating restaurant when they originally leased the winery, the Topolos family had no intention of running it. "We sublet the restaurant at first, but it wasn't being run very professionally so, on July 27, 1983, we took it over," recalls Michael. "Fortunately, we're Greek, we take to cooking, and there's no better place to showcase a wine than a meal. It really helps get people here to the winery, helps people get a better feeling for what we're up to. The restaurant is in an old manor house that was built in 1879, and it has stood up to weather and earthquakes."

The Topolos family didn't intend to run the winery's restaurant, but "there's no better place to showcase a wine than a meal," as Michael Topolos puts it.

Located on the west side of Gravenstein Highway, just south of Forestville, the winery restaurant features a "Vintner's Experience," where patrons can leave the wine selection entirely up to the sommelier. "Our menu selections are designed around the wines we produce," notes Michael. "We use the same wine in the reduction of our wine sauce as we'd serve with the dish. Our lamb on brochette is marinated in the same Zinfandel we suggest drinking with it. Executive chef Robert Engel loves to sauté chicken in our best Chardonnay, a real luxury."

Christine Topolos, who runs the restaurant with Engel, stresses that the cuisine is certainly not all Greek. "We're more traditional than trendy. We have duck, steak, chicken, pork, rack of lamb, and fresh seafood."

The winery itself, run by Michael and Jerry, produces under 10,000 cases a year, mostly leaning toward hearty, full-flavored red wines. Topolos' most distinctive wine is Alicante Bouschet, one of only a handful of the thousands of wine grape varieties that has naturally colored juice. A thick-skinned variety, Alicante was a favorite of growers who shipped grapes cross-country to home winemakers during Prohibition. At Topolos, it makes a heavily perfumed, inky-dark red wine that has flavor enough to satisfy the heartiest of palates. *RPH*

Vintners are a squirrelly lot who pray for rain in the spring and against it in the fall. Leave it to the Topolos clan to rate the distance to the Pool Hall as being just as important as the distance to San Francisco or Forestville.

TRENTADUE WINERY

Leo Trentadue — though for a time a jeweler by profession — is a farmer, first and foremost. His family had farmed the Santa Clara Valley since the early '30s. "We had apricots, prunes, cherries, and walnuts," remembers Leo, named Winemaker of the Year in 1981 by the Sonoma County Wine Growers Association.

"By the late '50s, it was becoming evident that we were going to be overrun by subdivisions," says Leo, "so Evelyn and I decided to move north, since she had relatives in and around Geyserville. It was the best move we ever made. We sold 60 acres down there and bought the Luchetti Ranch and the Wisecarver

Ranch — 200 acres — up here." "Up here" is really down there, in a sense, for the Trentadue estate sits well down and away from Old Redwood Highway, at the corner of Independence Lane on the floor of the Alexander Valley. "What we bought had 80 acres of grapes, 20 of apples, 30 of prunes, and 42 acres bare," Leo recalls. "We later added the ranch next door. Most of our vineyard was planted to Cabernet Sauvignon and Zinfandel. We also planted some Nebbiolo early on. Hey, it makes the best wines of Italy; why not here?"

If you know your Italian, you know that trentadue is the Italian for "thirty-two," a num-

This elaborate trellisway, shaded by grapevines, serves as picnic area, covered walkway, and the site for numerous weddings. Hospitality has long been a byword of the wine industry, worldwide.

ber that sat under the window sill on the old Trentadue label. The number appeared in Roman numerals, in gold, at their second apex of the label, introduced in 1983. The change came as the result of an informal wine label contest held one year at the Sonoma Harvest Fair. "When they hold a judging, and you come in dead last, you know the public is trying to tell you something," says Leo's son Victor, who started driving tractor on the ranch when he was eight ("for the prune shakers") and now manages the winery and vineyards.

So, the Trentadues hired Alder Fels' winemaker — and graphic artist (he created the

Works of art in one form inspire works of art in others. Wine has always drawn on the aesthetics of painting and sculpture — here the Venus de Milo — to complement the blend of artistry and science that creates fine wines.

Chateau St. Jean label) — David Coleman to come up with a new image for Trentadue wines. The design featured the gold-embossed Roman numerals on an ivory stock, surrounded by an intricate, lacy scroll tinged a soft, pinky beige. In 1991 the winery changed its label design again.

According to family legend, the Trentadue name came about many centuries ago, when a group of 32 Egyptians settled in the small Italian town of Bari (on the Adriatic coast, northeast of Brindisi). "Because they were newcomers, without a command of the local language and customs, they tended to stick to themselves," recounts Leo. "The townspeople, naturally enough, fell into the habit of referring to them as 'the thirty-two.' The name stuck, and their descendants became 'Trentadues,' part of the original clan of 32."

When the Trentadues first moved to Geyserville they were content to sell their entire grape crop to others, including Ridge Vineyards (whose "Geyserville Zinfandel" is still grown by the Trentadues). "In 1969, I was sitting and talking with Ridge Vineyards' winemaker, Paul Draper," laughs Leo, his olive-green eyes dancing. "He told me that I'd never make any money just selling my grapes, that I'd be better off making my own wine from my own grapes. So that's exactly what we did." *RPH*

In the old days, vines were head trained, which meant that each vine stood alone, close to the ground. Today, complex scientific trellising systems are employed to allow just so much sunlight in and support the vine so that it can mature the maximum amount of fruit.

VALLEY OF THE MOON WINERY

An old stemmer sits outside Valley of the Moon Winery. The bottom of a large redwood cask is set in stone, to round out this tableau of old-time winemaking. But things are changing here, as Colombard and Carignane make way for Chardonnay and Cabernet.

alley of the Moon Winery is operated by the Parduccis. Harry Sr. is the ostensible taskmaster ("He signs all the checks," chuckles Gerard) but, in truth, everybody chips in to do whatever is needed. Harry's wife, Rheda, used to be found in the tasting room, but now spends most of her time handling the financial and bookkeeping end of things.

Their two sons are integral parts of the winery's success. Harry Jr., balding a bit under his heavy responsibility as winemaker, studied viticulture at Santa Rosa Junior College. Gerard, who attended Santa Rosa, mostly handles sales. "I never actually got my degree," says Gerard. "When I was about 18, our Marin County salesman took me around to show me the ropes, and I loved it. Today I'm delivering wine to our San Francisco accounts. Tomorrow I may be repairing some mechanical

breakdown. You always have something break during crush. Fortunately, I have a knack for fixing things."

The Parduccis tend just over 100 acres of vineyard along Madrone Road, south of Glen Ellen. Half the acreage is planted to Zinfandel, which goes into the winery's premium Estate Reserve Zinfandel.

The first grapes were probably planted in the Madrone Road area by Joseph Hooker in the early 1850s. Hooker was part of the county road works in those days, and during the War Between the States became famous as "Fighting Joe Hooker" of the Union Army. (He was also known for his camp followers — dubbed, as you may have guessed by now, "hookers.")

Subsequent owner George Whitman, who probably made the first commercial wines on the property, produced 50,000 gallons of wine

A full moon rises
above the
Mayacamas Range
to the east of the
land local Indians
dubbed "Valley of
the Moons." Plural.
For them, the moon
seemed to rise
several times as it
darted behind one
peak, then another.

and 2,000 gallons of brandy in 1876. Seven years later, the land went to Eli T. Sheppard, who used the name Madrone Vineyards and imported French grape varieties.

Mining millionaire and newspaper publisher George Hearst, once a U.S. Senator and the father of newspaper mogul William Randolph Hearst, bought the property from Sheppard and built a pair of stone cellars capable of storing nearly a quarter of a million gallons of wine. Louis Engelberg owned Madrone Vineyards through Prohibition and the Depression, selling grapes to wineries that produced sacramental and medicinal wines.

Enrico Parducci entered the picture in 1941, when he purchased the property as a weekend retreat. Parducci had previously founded the San Francisco Sausage Company. In 1942, the Parduccis began making wine. Three years later they hired as winemaker Otto Toshi, whose parents had previously been caretakers of the property. Toshi would remain as winemaker for nearly four decades before Harry Jr. took over in 1981.

Much has changed since that time. Concrete fermenters have given way to stainless steel, and giant redwood vats are being pushed over by tiny French oak barrels. And the old label, long splashed across gallon jugs, has been replaced by a pastel watercolor featuring the multi-trunked laurel tree that stands outside the tasting room . . . and has been there for more than four centuries. *RPH*

Wine grapes were planted and a winery built on this site in the late 1900s. The Parducci family has had Valley of the Moon since 1941. Senator George Hearst, father of William Randolph, once owned the property.

VIANSA WINERY

Sam and Vicki Sebastiani quickly confirm the age-old premise that man does not live by bread alone. You need a little olive oil. The occasional glass of wine. Perhaps a piece of sausage. Some Reggiano Parmesan cheese, the real thing, from northern Italy — one of the charmed places on the third planet.

Sam Sebastiani's namesake grandfather came to California from Tuscany nearly a hundred years ago. Today, Sam has set out to create a full slice of northern Italian country life on a spectacular bluff, south of Sonoma, that overlooks Carneros vineyards and the lower Sonoma Valley.

"I think that there is a great deal of satisfaction to be derived from growing grapes and grain and olives, harvesting them, and turning them into finished products," says Sam, sitting at a picnic table outside the tasting room at the newly finished Viansa winery, on Highway 121 just north of Sears Point Raceway.

The first phase of the project was completed in 1990. It includes a marvelous tasting room, reminiscent of an Italian market, with food and wine tasting. The initial phase's winemaking capacity was sufficient to handle the Italian varieties planted immediately around the building.

Seven million dollars and all of Sam Sebastiani's heart and soul have been put into the execution of this Tuscan/ Californian estate. Sam calls the style "Cal-Ital." It certainly would not look out of place planted in the brown hills around Siena.

The ensuing phases, however, are yet more intriguing. Caves and fermentation facilities are to be constructed at the base of the hill when Viansa sales near 20,000 cases; up to 50 acres will be planted to vines; grain will be grown for pasta; 85 olive trees will provide Viansa's own cold-press olive oil; another 35 fig, pomegranate, persimmon, and almond trees, along with a flower (edible) and vegetable garden, will yield Italian delicacies for creations by Vicki; and a piggery will provide meat for Italian sausages!

"If we can push the concept all the way out to the pigs, well, we'll have created the

Sam and Vicki Sebastiani pose amid some of the bounty food and wine — that they offer daily in their festive, instructive tasting room, a veritable marketplace of smells and flavors.

style of life like the one my grandfather left in Italy because it no longer provided an economic return," muses Sam. "If we can flip that around — do what brings us satisfaction, and have an economic return — well, nothing could be better."

It might be best to step back a moment, to put this into historical perspective. Samuel Joseph Sebastiani was raised to the wine life, driving a tractor along long vine rows and hauling hose ("for 50 cents an hour!") in the winery grandfather Samuele founded in 1904. If Sam's dad, August, gave the world varietal wine in jugs, it was Sam's destiny to elevate the Sebastiani wines and name to world-class status.

After a stint in the Army, Sam went back to the University of Santa Clara to earn an MBA. He came home in 1966 and, in the early '70s, installed a stainless-steel fermentation cellar that brought instant life to Sebastiani white wines. In 1979 he took over operations from his ailing father and set a course toward the utmost in quality levels. "Quality is the only means of survival today," he told anyone who would listen as he toured the country, pouring wines and preaching the gospel of wine and food with his new wife, Vicki.

Then, in January of 1986, the bottom fell out. Sam's siblings and mother decided that too much money was being spent in lowering

Italianate columns mark the entry to Viansa as you come over the last hill before entering the Sonoma Valley from the south. Here, the Italian influence of Sam Sebastiani's ancestry is conjoined with the California sway of his birthplace.

production and improving quality and in extensive promotional efforts, and that it might be best for all if Sam would leave.

It was a devastating blow to the pride. But Sam's talisman is the eagle. "The eagle stands for independence and endurance," says Sam quietly. "It took me a while to see it all clearly, but my family did me a favor by kicking me out, unintentionally forcing me to go out and do it my way, on my own."

What is fully evident is that Viansa is not just Sam doing his wine gig. The operation, from its name up, is the joint venture of VIcki ANd SAm Sebastiani. Vicki's side is the creative use of a wondrous array of fine foods to help bridge the gap from wine ignorance to wine knowledge.

"We don't mind if people come in just for the food," notes Vicki. "Our tasting room is just that, a place where visitors can taste food and wine and, hopefully, make the connection between the two. If they aren't interested in wine, we offer espresso, fruit juices, and Italian mineral water, too.

"One thing, I think, that sets us apart is that we offer our wine and food tasting on a daily basis to the general public at no charge. We need to make food and wine a daily part of everybody's lives. I mean, we're pretty basic people: we wear jeans and drive pickup trucks, although I guess even that's gotten to be a bit chic these days. But I tend the vegetable and flower garden, I like to wiggle my toes in the dirt."

The main entry to the winery itself blends the old and the new. In the foreground are stainless-steel tanks with concrete facings adorned with frescoes — "technology dressed in an historical vein," explains Sam.

With the wines, Sam has drifted slightly from the Sonoma-Valley-only stance he had while running Sebastiani Vineyards. "I don't think America needs another winery," he says, weighing his words carefully, "but I do think there's room for another style, a style based on the strengths of different vineyards working in concert with one another. We're buying grapes from parts of top vineyards in both Sonoma and Napa counties, trying to blend the best aspects of each individual place. We find that we're blending the strength and backbone of Napa Valley fruit with the softer, rounder, more fleshy Sonoma County fruit."

Sam's Italian heritage is the keystone of the whole operation, from the ground up. Sam hired Alessio Carli away from Italy's justly

Left is the crest of Viansa: the Indian arrowhead for California, the rust color for Lucca, Italy, the ram's head for the Carneros district, the grape leaves and wheat stalks to symbolize food and wine. The fresco at the right symbolizes Sam's Italian heritage.

famed Badia a Coltibuono. Carli not only has a background in viticulture and enology, but helped make olive oil there as well.

"Alessio's first job was to plant different clones on a variety of rootstocks of Italian grape varieties — Sangiovese, Nebbiolo, Vernaccia, Primitivo, and Malvasia. Out of these we hope to settle on one good red and one good white. But I'll settle for one good red if I have to!"

From the Renaissance music piped throughout the winery, through frescoes painted on concrete facings of fermentation tanks, to a stairwell copied from the Farneta church where his grandfather was baptized, Sam has given an authentic small-town-Italy feel to Viansa. Everything, down to the last detail, is symbolic of the quest to display his Italian roots coupled with his Californian upbringing. In a sense, it is the flip side of how grapevines are grown here: the European scion grafted onto American rootstock. *RPH*

The delicatessen is the heart of Viansa's tasting room area. Vicki Sebastiani is intent upon showing visitors that wine and food are and should be everyday companions, and there's no better way to do it than offering samples of both together.

WILLIAM WHEELER WINERY

The estate vineyards of William Wheeler are draped across gentle slopes of the hills west of Healdsburg. From the lobed leaf pattern of these framing vines one might hazard a guess: Cabernet Sauvignon.

Bill and Ingrid Wheeler have joined a movement that one might call The Rhone Gambit. Sounds rather like a chess opening. Ruy Lopez. King's Knight's Gambit.

The Rhone Gambit clings closely to further chess analogies, since all of marketing and sales is an intricate chess game, on a dramatic scale and with high stakes.

"Bill's always liked Rhone wines, so we had been talking about doing a Rhone-styled wine for quite some time," says winemaker Julia Iantosca, a coverall-clad pixie with short, curly hair. "We make a Cabernet Sauvignon that needs cellaring, so we thought a counterpoint would be nice — a red wine that was more accessible, that didn't need all that aging but was still interesting."

The wines of France's Rhone Valley are interesting and complex, in part because they are blends of several grape varieties, including white varieties Marsanne, Rousanne, and Viognier. But it's the reds that have lured ever-growing numbers of California winegrowers to experiment seriously with the Rhone Gambit. Bonny Doon's Randall Grahm has led the charge of the "Rhone Rangers," donning a Lone Ranger outfit and saying things like, "Certain vintages of Chateau Beaucastel are the most erotic wines I've ever consumed."

Eroticism aside — well, not entirely aside — Rhone reds are alluring for the challenge of getting the blend right. "Blending used to be a pejorative term, but now people are beginning to respect the complexity you can create by doing it right," assesses Iantosca, whose husband Bob is chief Champagne maker at Gloria Ferrer. "We don't have all the Rhone varietals available to us yet, but we're doing what we can with their closest equivalents."

A bottle of William Wheeler Chardonnay sits in a handsome glass ice bucket. The quickest way to chill a white is to fill the bucket with ice, then add water to the top. Twenty minutes should be quite sufficient.

"But the main thing about the Rhone Style is that it's been a fun project. I've been able to work with varieties that I had never worked with before. I mean, I love Cabernet Sauvignon, but boy, it's a tough, tannic wine that's just not going to come around quickly. That's the biggest advantage of this project. It's nice to have a red that can be drinkable almost immediately after it's been bottled."

Iantosca is also excited about the new opportunities that have come to the winery since its joint venture with French financier Paribas in 1989. "Well, obviously, it brings new capital to the winery," she begins. "Paribas is a French merchant bank, and they have holdings in French vineyards and wineries. They recognize that the United States is almost the only country in the world where wine consumption still has growth potential. They also know that their forte is not active participation, but rather in financial support. What that means in the short term is new French oak barrels for me. Then, when we get through all the planning procedures, we can expand our facilities, another great need."

Paribas' American entity is also looking to acquire other wineries. "We'll probably avoid Sonoma County, and try to diversify our appellation coverage," says Wheeler, a former foreign-aid officer for the U. S. government. "We are, fortunately, not driven to be hasty. The Paribas people are patient people, so we'll go slowly and try to do it right." *RPH*

This seven-by-ten-feet tapestry hangs in the winery's downtown Healdsburg tasting room. Designed by New York City artist Dinah Shore, the tapestry was woven in wool and silk by Romanian weavers.

WHITE OAK VINEYARDS

Gaining an appreciation for fine wine can be accomplished anywhere, even on a fishing trawler in the waters off Anchorage. That's where Bill Myers gained his love for wine. One thing led to another and today Myers is the founder and general partner of White Oak Vineyards in Healdsburg.

Myers, who also operated a successful business as a building contractor while living in Alaska, had relatives who were residents of Sonoma County. When he desired a change from the cold winters of the north, he contacted them and in·1981 decided to settle on a small property in Healdsburg in northern Sonoma County. There he designed a winery and began to make wine under the name White Oak.

"The winery was going to be on a residential street in Healdsburg, so he wanted it to look as much like the other buildings here as possible," says Paul Brasset, who came on board in 1983 and began to make the wines. Myers designed his winery to look like one of the neighboring homes.

For the first few years, White Oak's wines were well made but unspectacular and not as consistent as Myers would have liked. One reason was the limited supply of grapes from his own vines. Myers owned just six acres,

Winemaker Paul Brasset drizzles wine out of a "thief," a glass device that takes wine through the small bung hole in the barrel. After a string of excellent white wines, Brasset's recent reds have gained wide praise.

planted to Chardonnay and Cabernet Sauvignon, which meant he had to buy the grapes from various growers around the county. Since the source of grapes changed from year to year, so did the wines.

In the late 1980s, however, Myers changed that. He recapitalized the winery as a limited partnership, bringing in new partners. And most of the new partners were local grapegrowers who owned vineyards in such diverse locales as the cold Russian River area, the warmer Dry Creek Valley, and the warmer-still Alexander Valley.

"That restructuring gave us a more consistent supply of grapes, and they were from

White Oak has made some excellent, multidimensional Chardonnays. Here a sample is drawn during fermentation, showing that before grape juice turns into wine it is cloudy and not particularly attractive. Wine is always clarified before final bottling and release.

three complementary areas of the county," says Brasset.

By 1991, White Oak was making about 12,000 cases of wine a year. The wines were not only more consistent, but showing some real style as Brasset became familiar with the fruit he was getting.

Brasset had come to White Oak from nearby Fritz Cellars, and before that had made wine as an assistant at Clos du Bois, Louis Martini, and Charles Krug. At White Oak he fashioned an exceptional wine called Myers Limited Reserve Chardonnay, which won broad plaudits for its persistent fruitiness, concentration, and excellent balance. His delicate touch showed with an attractive off-dry Chenin Blanc and a light and crisp Sauvignon Blanc.

One of the winery's best wines is the Cabernet Sauvignon from Alexander Valley fruit, grown on a ranch on Red Winery Road. The vineyard is located within sight of the famed Robert Young Vineyard, which for years produced great Chardonnays at Chateau St. Jean and, later, Cabernets at Belvedere Winery. White Oak's Cabernet, which also uses about 15 percent Cabernet Franc, has wonderfully rich flavors with just a trace of herbal complexity.

The winery also makes a limited amount of Zinfandel from old vines growing in Dry Creek Valley. *DB*

White Oak founder Bill Myers was a contractor and commercial fisherman in Alaska when he was bitten by the wine bug. He moved to the Alexander Valley, where he built his winery to look like a private residence. But inside are tanks, hoses, barrels, and all the fittings needed to make world-class wines.

WILLIAMS-SELYEM WINERY

Reflections of a range of reddish hues offer but a poor preview of pleasures to come. Pinot Noir is a wine of texture rather than flavor, best described by words like "supple," "juicy," "meaty," "succulent."

Burt Williams and Ed Selyem have weathered some of the usual wine industry "rags to riches" handicaps. Their early wines were fermented in salvaged milk tanks in a rented garage; their original name, Hacienda Del Rio ("ranch on the river"), drew ire and threats from Sonoma's previously established Hacienda Wine Cellars.

"We still use the milk tanks," laughs Ed (who continues to work his former full-time job a few hours a week as wine buyer for Speer's Market in Forestville). "They're perfect for fermenting Pinot Noir. They're shallow enough so that we can get in and step on the grapes, which is the only way to fully break open the whole berries we add for fruitiness. The steel is better quality than you get in most wine tanks these days, and it was half the price."

"We changed our name in 1984," reflects the burly Burt Williams, who also keeps his old job ("once a week into San Francisco, I'm a typesetter") to secure hard-earned medical and retirement benefits. "We went to a lawyer when Hacienda said they'd sue us. He told us that we could win, but that it'd cost us 50 thousand bucks and it wouldn't improve the wines any. Then we talked to the owners of Quail

Run, in Washington State. They had been sued by Quail Ridge [a Napa Valley winery], and they had spent 50 thousand . . . and lost! That's why they're now Covey Run and we're Williams-Selyem."

The pair figured they'd rather put money and effort into the Holy Grail quest for The Great Pinot Noir. So they sought out great grapes, the foundation of all great wines, and put Old-World-tested techniques to bear on the problem. And came up with winners, their 1985 Pinot Noir taking top prize at the California State Fair two years later.

They made their first commercial wine in 1981, and from 1983 through 1989 operated out of a small garage on River Road in Fulton. In 1990 they moved to a new winery building, built for them by vineyardist Howard Allen on his Westside Road vineyard property, a half mile south of Rochioli. Rochioli is one of several vineyards Ed and Burt buy Pinot Noir from. Others include Howard Allen, Olivet Lane, and Summa Vineyard out near Bodega Bay.

"Summa sits on a 1,200-foot ridge, just two miles from the Pacific," explains Burt. "You can see the ocean from the vineyard and, as you'd expect, it has a pretty cool climate.

"Pinot Noir is the most complex of red wines. There are so many clones, and each vineyard plot is a completely different animal. Pinot Noir really expresses its place of origin, and is capable of showing more complexity than any other wine."

Burt sees wisdom in Burgundian practices, to the point of using the same barrels as Domaine de la Romanée-Conti. "We put in whole clusters, unbroken berries, to extend the fermentation and add another dimension of complexity. We use about 25 percent of the fruit, sometimes as much as 40 percent, but never more than that. I mean, we're not making Beaujolais. We crush very gently.

"We still use an old basket press, supposedly made in 1906, but it's not enough to break the whole clusters. We have to get in and step on the fruit eventually." *RPH*

Burt Williams, in suspenders, works part-time as a typesetter for a San Francisco newspaper, while Ed Selyem is a wine buyer for a local market. It is common for owners of small wineries to have other jobs to support their vinous habits.

Z MOORE WINERY

Daniel Moore loved the Chardonnay grapes growing in the cool Russian River Valley, where his winery is located, but the style of wine he felt they made best was lean and austere, a style hard to sell. Eventually, he quit making Chardonnay and concentrated instead on a stylish, complex

The demand for Chardonnay in the 1980s was so high that Daniel Moore made it for a few years. But Moore was irked that the Chardonnay he made was misunderstood by people. And he wasn't about to compromise on that style just to sell a little wine.

The point, he felt, was to make a style of wine that fit the Chardonnay grapes he had access to from the cool Russian River Valley. At their best, they would lead to a lean, flinty, austere, almost Chablis-like type of wine; to make wine from these grapes that was richer and laden with oak would have been unnatural. The Chardonnay Z Moore Winery made at the start was in that steely, crisp style. The result: those who favored lean qualities as well as a wine that would improve in the bottle got excited over what Moore was doing.

Z Moore is a prototype do-it-yourself winery. Moore, a food science graduate of Michigan State University ("we called it moo U"), worked part time for his father, an accountant, while in college. One client was a wine shop that owed the firm money. Moore took it out in trade: wine.

In 1981, hoping to find a way to ski while living near the ocean, Moore hooked on as a cellar worker at Milano winery in Mendocino for the harvest. By 1985, he was hooked on making wine, so he leased space at Whaler Winery in Mendocino and created Z Moore. His name was preceded by the initial of Natalie Zuccarelli; they married later that year.

Moore liked Gewurztraminer best because of the exceptional fruit of the Russian River area. He made it dry, to marry with spicy foods. But he also needed cash flow, and dry Gewurztraminer isn't cash-flow wine. So to get started on his project, he created a wine called Quaff — an off-dry Gewurztraminer to be a picnic wine or to go with sweeter foods.

In 1987, Moore moved into the former facility of Lee Martinelli, whose orchard across the road still produces some of the finest apples in the county. A "tour" of the Z Moore winery is literally a one-minute look at a room filled with stainless-steel wine tanks and some former milk tanks, and a one-minute look at the barrel room next door, where French oak barrels are stacked. That's it.

The Chardonnay still made here is a handsome wine for those who understand the high acidity and complex though delicate finish. But the best wine remains dry Gewurztraminer, with its wonderful floweriness showing apple-spice, cinnamon, and clove components.

Unfortunately, there weren't enough of those people around who understood the wine. "Every time we'd go to sell it, we'd get bloody," says Moore. "The wine was just too lean for a lot of people. They didn't understand what we were doing."

So Moore cut his production of Chardonnay to a few hundred cases and decided to make Gewurztraminer for a living.

Moore also makes a lovely Zinfandel and he has made some Pinot Noir. But he says, "If there's going to be a Z Moore Pinot Noir, it's going to be the Holy Grail." His early attempts were not good enough to release under the Z Moore label, so were "declassified" and sold as Quaff Gamay Beaujolais. *DB*

Operating out of a leased former apple plant along River Road, Daniel Moore is virtually the entire employment force at his small winery. But the early wines, including an intriguing Zinfandel, were strikingly good. Moore also produces a lighter-styled Gewurztraminer under the designation Quaff.

SAVORING SONOMA

Much the way the yellow-flowered mustard weed intertwines with the grapevine in the springtime, food is intertwined with the lifestyle of Sonoma County.

Food is at the heart of this verdant region's image, and not just the abundance of it. Sonoma produce is exceptional and at the forefront of a growing trend in the United States toward more excitement in dining, experimentation with unusual combinations of foods and the wines that go with them.

For instance, for decades mustard weed flowers were little more than ornamentation. Now they're popping up atop "field salads," composed of myriad wild greens such as arrugula, raddicchio, and chicory. Here that salad might have a base of greens from Ya-Ka-Ama or Lucky Duck, some Laura Chenel goat cheese, a sprinkle of edible flowers, a garnish of Timber Crest Farms' dried tomatoes, blackberries from Kozlowski's Berry Farm, herbs from a local garden, and a hunk of Cousteaux sourdough bread from a pull-apart loaf. This may set you back 15 bucks in a chichi New York boîte. Here you can get it at a dozen local diners for a fifth the price. Not even the famed Napa Valley offers the diversity of foods found here. That's because the agricultural roots of Sonoma County are longer and deeper than just about any region in the state. Dairy ranked N° 1 in revenue here until 1987, when grapes and wine passed it. But dairy's strength remains, in Clover-Stornetta dairy products as well as fine cheese from smaller dairies, including Rouge et Noir with soft-ripened cheeses; Chenel, whose standard chevre is widely available but whose specialty cheeses are sold only locally; Ig Vella with its dried Sonoma Jack; and Joe Matos' Portuguese-style cheese, sold out of a garage.

Kozlowski berries and jams are legend, but there are a dozen other berry growers, many located in the Sebastopol area, where some of the finest apples in the nation grow. Sonomans devour oodles of Gravensteins during the short

Wild greens such as arrugula as well as edible flowers adorn the typical "field salad" so often found in northern California's wine country region. Often included is a wedge of goat cheese from a local dairy.

*Restaurants are not
the only ones who
thrive on the
sumptuous produce
available in Sonoma
County. Outdoor
markets allow
shoppers of all kinds
to sample the new,
the fresh, and the
different, and provide
plentiful picnic fare.*

mid-summer season. The locally famed Crane
melon is seen nowhere else. Also appetizing
are oysters from Hog Island and Bay Bottom
Beds, both in Tomales Bay, as well as the area's
prunes and walnuts.

Sonoma also supplies main dishes. The
county boasts the West Coast's second largest
salmon fleet, based in Bodega Bay, and some of
the nation's best baby lamb. There're Rocky the
Range Chicken, ducks from Reichardt Farms,
and Joe Piotrkowski's smoked fowl, all from
Petaluma, as well as fresh turkeys from both
Willie Bird and Nicholas, and sausages from the
Sonoma Sausage Factory.

The Sonoma County Farmers' Market pops
up twice a week at the Veterans Building park-
ing lot to make some produce available to the
public. It is such a matter of local pride that in
1988 the city of Santa Rosa decided to close the
downtown main street to traffic and open it as a
street fair. Local restaurants thrive on the local
ingredients. One noteworthy restaurateur notes
that half of his ingredients are local.

Perhaps the greatest achievement of the
produce here is its wide acceptance. A Sonoma
winery might be hard-pressed to get one of its
wines onto a wine list in the Napa Valley, but
one of Napa's top restaurants proudly points to
the fact that it serves Sonoma baby lamb.

*Sonoma County
apples are a bountiful
crop in late August.
Many varieties are
grown commercially
here, but it is the
local Gravenstein --
yellow with a reddish
blush or striping --
which commands the
greatest attention,
including a special
Apple Fair in its
honor. Gravensteins
are hard, both tart
and sweet, and
superb for baking into
pies and tarts or
eating on a picnic.*

GLOSSARY

BENCH: A slightly elevated plateau above a valley floor, which supposedly yields a better quality of fruit and thus better wine.

BOTRYTISED: Describes wine made from grapes that were infected with the beneficial mold Botrytis cinerea, or the condition affecting the grapes.

BRIX: The percentage of sugar by weight in grapes still on the vine, or, less often, the percentage of sugar remaining in wine.

BUNG: The wooden (or more recently neoprene) stopper for a cask.

CARBONIC MACERATION: A technique for fermenting wine. Whole grapes are put into a tank, the tank is sealed, and the fermentation is begun without air, until a small amount of alcohol is created inside the grapes.

CHAI: A barrel-aging cellar.

COOPERAGE: Barrels.

CRUSH: Used as a noun, the term refers to the harvest.

CUVÉE: The blend of various wines into a single wine.

EGG-WHITE FINED: The whites of eggs are commonly used to remove tiny matter from wine. The egg whites are removed before bottling.

EN TIRAGE: Bottles (usually of sparkling wine) left to age on the side, so the wine is in contact with the yeast.

ENOLOGY: The science of winemaking.

FINING: Removing tiny particles from wine.

GONDOLA: Large bin used for hauling grapes from the field to the winery.

IMPERIAL: A large bottle, holding six liters.

LACTIC ACID: An acid found in wines, said to cause a milky or buttery aroma.

LEES CONTACT: Leaving the wine in contact with the lees, the spent yeast cells.

LUGBOX: A small box for hauling grapes, usually from the vines to gondolas.

MAGNUM: A double-size bottle, holding 1.5 liters.

MALIC ACID: An acid found in grapes, supposedly yielding an aroma like apples.

MALOLACTIC FERMENTATION: The process of converting the stronger malic acid into the weaker lactic acid, using malolactic yeast.

MÉTHODE CHAMPENOISE: The fermentation process, used after the primary fermentation, that gives sparkling wine its bubbles.

MUST: Unfermented or partially fermented grape juice.

NÉGOCIANT: A person who buys wines in bulk, bottles them, and sells them under a proprietary or company name.

NON-VINTAGE: In California, a wine that does not carry a vintage date.

PHYLLOXERA: The root louse Phylloxera vastatrix, which devastated the vineyards of California and France in the late 1800s and which reappeared in California in the late 1980s. The problem is controlled by replanting vines onto resistant rootstocks.

PIERCE'S DISEASE: A systemic disease that can rapidly destroy a vine.

POT STILL: A small copper device used to distill liquids slowly, usually wine into brandy.

PUNCHEON: A barrel about 2.5 times bigger than the standard 55-gallon wine barrels.

REPEAL: The 21st Amendment to the U.S. Constitution, which went into effect on Dec. 5, 1933, repealing the 13-year Prohibition on the manufacture, transportation, or sale of alcoholic beverages.

ROOTSTOCK: Vine roots that may be "budded" with a specific variety of grape after planting.

SUR LIE: The process in which wine is left in contact with the spent yeast cells, usually in a barrel.

U.C. DAVIS: The University of California campus at Davis, which has one of the world's finest schools of viticulture and enology.

UCLA: University of California at Los Angeles.

VITICULTURE: The science of grape growing.

TANNIN: The polyphenols that give wine its roughness and astringency; also found in tea.

VINIFY: To ferment.

WINE TRAIN: A controversial tourist attraction that began operating in the Napa Valley in the late 1980s in spite of very strong, unified opposition by most residents of the valley.

INDEX

PHOTO CREDITS

All photographs in this book are by Jean-Paul Paireault, except for those listed below.

(T = top, B = bottom, R = right, L = left)

p.	18-9		Cindi Kinney	p.	107		Gamma
p.	21	T	Cindi Kinney	p.	108		Gamma
p.	23	T	M. J. Wickham	p.	109	R	Pat Sherman
p.	25	L	Bellerose Vineyard	p.	111	T	Gamma
p.	28		Buena Vista Winery	p.	114		Gundlach-Bundschu Winery
p.	43	R	Gamma	p.	115	B	Gundlach-Bundschu Winery
p.	45		Chateau Souverain	p.	131		Jordan Vineyard and Winery
p.	49	T, R	Faith Echtermeyer	p.	154		Faith Echtermeyer
p.	61	B	De Loach Vineyards	p.	171	T	Faith Echtermeyer
p.	66	T	William Miller	p.	185	T	J. Pedroncelli Winery
p.	67	T	Domaine Michel	p.	187		Piper Sonoma Cellars
p.	67	R	William Miller	p.	189	T	Piper Sonoma Cellars
p.	69	R	Faith Echtermeyer	p.	191	B	Gamma
p.	70		Dry Creek Vineyard	p.	197	T	Ravenswood
p.	71		Dry Creek Vineyard	p.	203	T	Gamma
p.	72	R	Dry Creek Vineyard	p.	208-9		Faith Echtermeyer
p.	77	L	Gary Farrell	p.	211	T	Sebastiani Vineyards
p.	78		Ferrari-Carano Winery	p.	219	T	Simi Winery
p.	80-1		Ferrari-Carano Winery	p.	223	T	Robert Stemmler Winery
p.	82		Andrée Abecassis	p.	238		Viansa Winery
p.	83		Philip Wallich	p.	239	T	Viansa Winery
p.	84		Field Stone Winery	p.	240		Viansa Winery
p.	85		Field Stone Winery	p.	241		Viansa Winery
p.	86		Fisher Vineyards	p.	250		Faith Echtermeyer
p.	96	B	John Harding	p.	251	B	Faith Echtermeyer
p.	97	T	E. & J. Gallo Winery	p.	251		Cindi Kinney
p.	101	B	Faith Echtermeyer	p.	252		Faith Echtermeyer
p.	106		Glen Ellen Vineyards and Winery				

ACKNOWLEDGMENTS

The publisher acknowledges with gratitude the cooperation and support given by the companies listed below during the preparation of this book:

Beltane Ranch, Glen Ellen, California
California Visitors Review, El Verano, California
Faith Echtermeyer, St. Helena, California
Meadowood Resort, St. Helena, California
The New Lab, San Francisco, California
Sonoma Mission Inn & Spa, Sonoma, California